GRAMMAR
EXPRESS
BASIC

GRAMMAR EXPRESS BASIC

Marjorie Fuchs | **Margaret Bonner**

with Answer Key

Longman

To Rick.—MF

To Aline and Luke.—MB

Grammar Express Basic: For Self-Study and Classroom Use
With Answer Key

Pearson Education, 10 Bank Street, White Plains, NY 10606

Executive editor: Laura Le Dréan
Senior development editor: Françoise Leffler
Senior production editor: Robert Ruvo
Marketing manager: Oliva Fernandez
Director of manufacturing: Patrice Fraccio
Senior manufacturing buyer: Edie Pullman
Photo research: Dana Klinek
Cover design: Pat Wosczyk
Text composition: Preface, Inc.
Text font: 9/10 New Century Schoolbook
Cover image: © David Barnes/Image State/Panoramic Images, Chicago
Illustrations: **Ron Chironna:** pp. 44, 86, 106, 186 (bottom), 207, 209; **Chris Gash:** pp. 66, 84, 100, 110 (bottom), 111, 114, 117 (bottom), 130 (bottom), 140 (top), 145, 158, 174, 182 (bottom), 204, 214, 220, 222; **Peter Grau:** pp. 110 (top), 154, 190; **Jock MacRae:** pp. 73, 82, 87, 117 (top), 122 (bottom), 138, 141, 168, 208; **Paul McCusker:** pp. 5, 30 (bottom), 38 (bottom), 72, 102, 120, 123, 124, 130 (top), 132, 134, 135, 140 (bottom), 142, 156, 186 (top), 205, 206, 210, 218; **Andy Myer:** pp. 6, 8, 13, 16, 20, 32, 39, 42, 60, 62, 74, 88 (bottom), 92, 112, 122 (top), 133, 144 (bottom), 146, 150, 162, 164, 180, 212, 221; **Dusan Petricic:** pp. 2, 9, 14, 28, 34, 36, 38 (top), 54, 63, 64, 88 (top), 90, 104, 118, 136, 144 (top), 148, 172, 182 (top), 184, 197, 216
Photo credits: **page 4** © RubberBall Productions; **page 9** © Jon Feingersh/CORBIS; **page 10** © The New Yorker Collection 2000 Sidney Harris from cartoonbank.com. All Rights Reserved; **page 12** © Tom & Dee Ann McCarthy/CORBIS; **page 24** © Chuck Savage/CORBIS; **page 26** © www.laughteryoga.org; **page 30** © CORBIS; **page 34** Mark Hill, CNN International; **page 35** AP/Wide World Photos; **page 38** Comstock Images; **page 46** © The New Yorker Collection 1987 Lee Lorenz from cartoonbank.com. All Rights Reserved; **page 48** © Bettmann/CORBIS; **page 49** © Christie's Images/CORBIS; **page 50** © Bettmann/CORBIS; **page 52** TM and Copyright © 20th Century Fox Film Corp. All rights reserved; Courtesy: Everett Collection; **page 53** © Bettmann/CORBIS; **page 54** © Ann Hawthorne/CORBIS; **page 56** yourexpedition.com; **page 57** yourexpedition.com; **page 67** © Image 100/Royalty-Free/CORBIS; **page 70** © Rune Hellestad/Corbis; **page 73** © TOUHIG SION/CORBIS SYGMA; **page 76** © Sony Pictures. All Rights Reserved; **page 77** top: © Royalty-Free/CORBIS; bottom: © Liu Liqun/CORBIS; **page 80** © Jack Hollingsworth/CORBIS; **page 94** Courtesy of Wu Bai; **page 96** © Royalty-Free/CORBIS; **page 99** © AMET JEAN PIERRE/CORBIS SYGMA; **page 121** top left: © Roger Wood/CORBIS; top right: AP/Wide World Photos; bottom left: © Richard Hamilton Smith/CORBIS; bottom right: © Joseph Sohm; ChromoSohm Inc./CORBIS; **page 128** Comstock Images; **page 131** © Royalty-Free/Corbis; **page 134** left: © Ron Watts/CORBIS; right: © Royalty-Free/CORBIS; **page 138** AP/Wide World Photos; **page 142** top left: © Richard Kelly Photography. All Rights Reserved; top right: www.ladybwear.com; center left: © Mary Kate Denny/PhotoEdit; center right: PhotoSpin, Inc. © 2003; bottom left: archives levi strauss museum Buttenheim; bottom right: AP/Wide World Photos; **page 146** Courtesy of MINI USA; **page 148** © Duomo/CORBIS; **page 156** Courtesy of Juan Martin Baratti; **page 166** © Robert W. Ginn/PhotoEdit; **page 169** © Royalty-Free/CORBIS; **page 176** © Aaron Horowitz/CORBIS; **page 192** top: Parker McKenzie © Liane Enkelis from *On Being 100*; center right: www.TheLivingCentury.com; center left: Photograph from Westsidelifemagazine.com, © 2000; bottom: Courtesy of Severo Ornstein; **page 194** Photodisc/Getty Images; **page 197** AP/Wide World Photos; **page 200** © Philip Wallick/CORBIS; **page 208** © Yann Arthus-Bertrand/CORBIS; **page 211** top: © Wolfgang Kaehler/CORBIS; center: © Rose Hartman/CORBIS; bottom: © Francesco Venturi/CORBIS; **page 223** Photograph from www.mangaroms.com

ISBN: 0-13-049669-3 (International Version with Answer Key)
ISBN: 0-13-049671-5 (International Version without Answer Key)

Printed in the United States of America
3 4 5 6 7 8 9 10–V011–14 13 12 11 10

Contents

About the Authors

Marjorie **Fuchs** has taught ESL at New York City Technical College and LaGuardia Community College of the City University of New York and EFL at the Sprach Studio Lingua Nova in Munich, Germany. She holds a Master's Degree in Applied English Linguistics and a Certificate in TESOL from the University of Wisconsin–Madison. She has authored or co-authored many widely used books and multi-media material, notably *Crossroads, Top Twenty ESL Word Games: Beginning Vocabulary Development, Around the World: Pictures for Practice, Families: Ten Card Games for Language Learners, Focus on Grammar: An Intermediate Course for Reference and Practice, Focus on Grammar: A High-Intermediate Course for Reference and Practice, Focus on Grammar Intermediate CD-ROM, Focus on Grammar High-Intermediate CD-ROM, Longman English Interactive Levels 3 and 4, Grammar Express* (Intermediate), and the workbooks to the *Longman Dictionary of American English,* the *Longman Photo Dictionary, The Oxford Picture Dictionary,* and *Focus on Grammar: Intermediate* and *High-Intermediate.*

Margaret **Bonner** has taught ESL at Hunter College and the Borough of Manhattan Community College of the City University of New York, at Taiwan National University in Taipei, and at Virginia Commonwealth University in Richmond. She holds a Master's Degree in Library Science from Columbia University, and she has done work towards a Ph.D. in English Literature at the Graduate Center of the City University of New York. She has authored and co-authored numerous ESL and EFL print materials, including textbooks for the national school system of Oman, *Step Into Writing: A Basic Writing Text, Focus on Grammar* (*Intermediate* and *High-Intermediate* Student Books, and *High-Intermediate* Workbook), *Grammar Express* (Intermediate), and *The Oxford Picture Dictionary Intermediate Workbook.* Her non-print materials include co-authorship of the *Focus on Grammar CD-ROM* (*Intermediate* and *High-Intermediate*) and contributions to *Longman English Interactive Level 3.*

About the Book

Welcome to *Grammar Express Basic*—the fast way to study and learn English grammar.

Grammar Express Basic features

- Short, easy-to-use **four-page units**
- **Grammar points** presented and **contextualized** through cartoons, photos, and other illustrations
- Clear **Grammar Charts** showing the forms of the grammar point
- **Chart Checks** to help you use the grammar charts
- Clear **Grammar Explanations** and **Examples**
- **Usage Notes** telling you how English speakers use the grammar point
- **Be careful! Notes** showing typical mistakes students make
- A **variety of exercise types** to practice the grammar points
- **SelfTests** to check your progress
- **Appendices** with helpful lists and information
- A **Glossary** of grammar terms
- An **Index** to help you quickly find grammar points
- An **Answer Key** so you can check your answers.

UNITS

Grammar Express Basic has 50 units. Each unit has four pages—two pages of grammar presentation and two pages of practice. Here's how a typical unit looks:

Presentation

The grammar point is presented in three steps.

1. Illustration

Each unit begins with an **illustration**—a cartoon, comic strip, photo with speech bubbles, newspaper headline—which introduces the grammar point in a real-life, real-language context. It also introduces the topic of the unit. *(For example, in Unit 25 the cartoon introduces the grammar point—subject and object pronouns. It also introduces the unit topic—gift-giving.)*

A **Check Point** helps you think about the meaning of the grammar point in the illustration.

2. Charts

Grammar Charts show the forms of the grammar point. *(In Unit 25 you can see two charts: one with subject pronouns, the other with object pronouns.)*

Chart Checks ask questions about the grammar charts. They help you notice important information about the forms and uses of the grammar point you are studying.

An **Express Check** follows the Grammar Charts. This is a quick and easy way for you to try out the forms in the charts.

3. Notes

Grammar Notes present **Grammar Explanations** on the left and **Examples** on the right. Timelines show the meaning of verb forms. *(For example, in Unit 5 the timeline for the simple present shows that you can use it for something that happened in the past, that is happening now, and that will continue in the future.)*

Usage Notes tell you how English speakers use the grammar point. *(In Unit 25 the Usage Note explains that object pronouns are more common than subject pronouns after* be.*)*

Be careful! Notes point out typical mistakes that English students make. *(The Be careful! Note in Unit 25 tells you not to use a noun and a pronoun together.)*

Check it out! tells you where to look in the book (appendices or other units) to find more information about the grammar point.

Practice

Two pages of exercises give you practice in understanding and using the grammar point. A typical unit has four exercises.

Exercise 1

The first exercise is always a "**for recognition only**" exercise. This means that you will have to find or understand the grammar point, but you will not have to use it yet. *(For example, in Unit 25 you will read a short article about gift-giving, and find and circle all the examples of subject and object pronouns. Then you will draw arrows from the pronouns to the nouns.)*

Exercises 2 and 3

In these exercises you actively practice the grammar point. There are a **variety of exercise types**, including multiple choice, fill-in-the-blanks, describing pictures, sentence combining, and asking and answering questions. The exercises always show the grammar point in a context that is related to the unit topic. *(In Unit 25, Exercise 2, you will complete sentences about customs around the world while you describe pictures. In Exercise 3, you will complete short paragraphs about gift-giving.)*

Exercise 4

This is always an **editing** exercise. In this exercise, you will have to find and correct typical mistakes that students make when they use the grammar point.

TESTS

The 50 units of *Grammar Express Basic* are divided into 12 parts. After each part you will find a **SelfTest**. These tests will help you review and see how well you have learned the material in the part. The **SelfTests** have multiple-choice questions similar to questions found on the TOEFL®.

APPENDICES AND GLOSSARY

In the back of the book, you will find 27 **Appendices** with useful information, such as lists of common irregular verbs, verbs followed by the gerund, verbs followed by the infinitive, and spelling and pronunciation rules. You will also find a **Glossary** with an alphabetical list of all the grammar terms used in the book. Each grammar term has a definition and one or more examples.

ANSWER KEY

The **Answer Key** provides answers to the Check Points, Chart Checks, Express Checks, all the practice exercises, and the SelfTests.

CD-ROM

A **CD-ROM** is included with the book. On it you will find additional practice in listening, speaking, reading, and writing.

WORKBOOK

A separate **Workbook** with more practice for each unit and tests for each part is available.

Grammar Express Basic can be used for self-study or in the classroom. Start with Unit 1 and work through the entire book, or choose the units you want to focus on. *Grammar Express Basic* can help you reach your language goals quickly.

Your journey through English grammar can be an adventure of discovery. We hope you will enjoy traveling with *Grammar Express Basic*.

All Aboard!!! . . .

Acknowledgments

Writing *Grammar Express Basic* has been the continuation of a wonderful adventure for us, the authors. The company of the following editors and colleagues have made the journey even more enjoyable. We are grateful to:

Françoise Leffler, our editor *extraordinaire*, whose creativity and wit are evident throughout, for her untiring effort to make every page perfect. As always, working with her has been a true pleasure.

Laura Le Dréan, for her total dedication and commitment to the project, and for always being there for us. She jumped on board with enthusiasm and energy, guiding the book from start to finish.

Robert Ruvo, for taking the book through all the steps of production with efficiency, speed, and good humor.

Dana Klinek, for her attentive and conscientious work on many of the details of the project, especially for her efforts in finding just the right photos.

Irene Schoenberg, for her enthusiastic support, her helpful feedback, and for her valuable contributions during the early stages of *Grammar Express Basic*.

We would also like to acknowledge the following reviewers for their careful reading of the manuscript and their thoughtful suggestions, many of which we incorporated into the book:

■ **Haydée Alvarado Santos**, University of Puerto Rico—Río Piedras Campus, Río Piedras, Puerto Rico ■ **Richard Atkinson**, Le Collège de Limoilou (Cégep), Charlesbourg, Québec, Canada ■ **Shannon Bailey**, Austin Community College, Austin, TX ■ **Joan Barnet**, Douglas College, Coquitlam, British Columbia, Canada ■ **Yoon-Q Cho**, Oe Dae Language Institute, Koyang City, South Korea ■ **Linda Davis**, Oakton College, Skokie, IL ■ **William Landry**, Collège Montmorency, Laval, Québec, Canada ■ **Elena Lattarulo**, Cuesta College, Pismo Beach, CA ■ **Hun-Yong Park**, Kyonggi-Do, South Korea ■ **Margery Toll**, California State University, Fresno, CA ■ **Alexandre Trigo Veiga**, Seven Idiomas, São Paulo, Brazil.

Thanks to the following teachers for pointing us in the right direction with their valuable feedback during the developmental stages of this project:

■ **Belgún Akgeúk**, Private ATA High School, Turkey ■ **Marlene Almeida**, Escola de Linguas, Belo Horizonte, Brazil ■ **Fatima Badry**, American University of Sharjah, Dubai, United Arab Emirates ■ **Ellen Balleisen**, CUNY Language Immersion Program, Bronx Community College, Bronx, New York ■ **Sheila Barbosa Fialho**, English Proficiency Institute, SJ Campos, SP, Brazil ■ **Matthew Bellman**, TCLC Language Academy, Nagoya, Japan ■ **Patricia Brenner**, University of Washington, Seattle, Washington ■ **Heloisa Burrowes Raposo Dias**, English Proficiency Institute, SJ Campos, SP, Brazil ■ **Elton Carvalho**, Centro de Linguas #2, Brasília,

Brazil ■ **Sergio J. Chiri**, Universidad Del Pacifico, Lima, Peru ■ **Judy A. Cleek**, Intensive English Program, Martin, Tennessee ■ **Jill Cook**, Zayed University, Dubai, United Arab Emirates ■ **Jason H. Davis**, CUNY Language Immersion Program, Bronx Community College, Bronx, New York ■ **Ricardo Delgado**, Florida School, Umarizal, Brazil ■ **Beatriz B. Diaz**, Robert Morgan Voc. Tech., Miami, Florida ■ **Luiz Alberto Ferrari**, College Uni ABC/SCS, São Paulo, Brazil ■ **Patty Heiser**, University of Washington, Seattle, Washington ■ **Jung-Sinn Hyon**, Hunter College, New York, New York ■ **Amy Lewis**, Keio University, Tokyo, Japan ■ **Chao-Hung Lin**, Hunter College, New York, New York ■ **Maria Esther Linares de Pedemonte**, International Exams, Lima, Peru ■ **Joan McAuley**, CUNY Language Immersion Program, Bronx Community College, Bronx, New York ■ **Sandra M. Moreno Walter**, Private Language School, Sorocaba, Brazil ■ **Angelita Moreno**, Instituto Cultural Brasil-Estados Unidos, Belo Horizonte, Brazil ■ **Gabriella Morvay**, CUNY Language Immersion Program, Bronx Community College, Bronx, New York ■ **Marisa Nickle**, University of Washington, Seattle, Washington ■ **Martha Oval**, Orel Bilim Koleg, Ankara, Turkey ■ **Hyangmi Pae**, Hannam University, Segu Daegon, Korea ■ **Rosemary Palmer**, Bloomfield College, Bloomfield, New Jersey ■ **Stephen Russell**, Tokyo University of Foreign Studies, Tokyo, Japan ■ **John Ryder**, Kyoto Gakuen High School, Kyoto, Japan ■ **Cleide da Silva**, Encino da Lingua Inglesa, Santos, SP, Brazil ■ **Maria Benedita da Silva Santos**, Private Language School, Brazil ■ **Sávio Síqueira**, Instituto Cultural Brasil-Estados Unidos, School of English, Salvador, Bahia, Brazil ■ **Ricardo A. de Souza**, Escola de Linguas, Belo Horizonte, Brazil ■ **Lee Spencer**, CUNY Language Immersion Program, Bronx Community College, Bronx, New York ■ **Ann Streeter**, Seattle Central Institute of English, Seattle, Washington ■ **Cláudia Suzano de Almeida**, Private Language School, Brazil ■ **Gerald Talandis, Jr.**, Toyama College of Foreign Languages, Toyama, Japan ■ **Lorena Trejo**, AU. Los Samanes, I. E. Henry Clay, Caracas, Venezuela ■ **Diane Triester**, University of Washington, Seattle, Washington ■ **Elkin Urrea**, Hunter College, New York, New York ■ **Fábio Delano Vidal Carneiro**, Applied Linguistics – VECE, Fortaleza, Ceará, Brazil ■ **Dr. Wilma B. Wilcox**, Southern Illinois University at Carbondale in Niigata, Japan ■ **Belkis Yanes**, AU. Los Samanes, I.E. Henry Clay, Caracas, Venezuela ■ **Shari Zisman**, CUNY Language Immersion Program, Bronx Community College, Bronx, New York

In addition we are grateful to the following institutions for helping us organize Focus Groups for teachers and students:

■ **Bronx Community College**, Bronx, New York
■ **Hunter College**, New York, New York
■ **University of Washington**, Seattle, Washington

Finally, we would like to thank **Rick Smith** and **Luke Frances**, as always, for their help and support along the way. They made the journey and the stops, few and far between as they were, a lot more fun.

MF and MB

The Present of *Be*:
Statements

I am tall. I am not a good dancer.

CHECK POINT

Check all the correct information.

- ☐ The man is a prince.
- ☐ He isn't tall.
- ☐ The woman is a princess.
- ☐ She is a good dancer.

CHART CHECK 1

Circle T (True) or F (False).

T F The present of ***be*** has three forms.

T F ***Not*** goes before ***am***, ***is***, or ***are***.

AFFIRMATIVE			NEGATIVE			
SUBJECT	***BE***		**SUBJECT**	***BE***	***NOT***	
I	**am**		I	**am**		
You	**are**		You	**are**		
He She It	**is**	tall.	He She It	**is**	**not**	tall.
We You They	**are**		We You They	**are**		

CHART CHECK 2

*Circle T (True) or
F (False).*

T   F   All contractions
with ***not*** have
two forms.

CONTRACTIONS			
AFFIRMATIVE		**NEGATIVE**	
I	'm	I	'm not
He She It	's	He She It	's not isn't
We You* They	're	We You They	're not aren't

*You = one person or several people.

EXPRESS CHECK

Check all the sentences with the present of **be**.

☐ They're tall.   ☐ We're not in the same class.   ☐ Please e-mail me!

☐ They don't dance.   ☐ I'm 20 years old.   ☐ He's not a student.

Grammar Explanations

Examples

1. The **present of be** has three forms:
am, ***is***, and ***are***.

- I **am** a student.
- He **is** a student.
- We **are** students.

2. Use **contractions** in conversation,
notes, and e-mail.

Is not and ***are not*** have two contractions.

▶ **BE CAREFUL!** *Am not* has only one contraction.

A: Hi! I'**m** Tina. This is Ali. We'**re** students.
B: Hi. I'**m** a student too.

- He'**s not** tall.   OR   He **isn't** tall.
- We'**re not** rich.   OR   We **aren't** rich.

- I'**m not** a prince.
  NOT ~~I amn't~~ a prince.

3. We often use ***there is*** or ***there are*** to talk about
something for the first time.

Use ***there is*** or ***there's*** for one person or thing.

Use ***there are*** for two or more people or things.

Don't use a contraction with ***there are***.

- **There is *one computer*** in the library.
  OR
- **There's *one computer*** in the library.

- **There are *two computers*** here.

NOT ~~There're~~ a lot of people . . .

Check it out!

There is, There are ▶▶▶ **UNIT 24, page 104.**

1 **FIND** • *Read this Web page. Underline the present forms of* **be**.

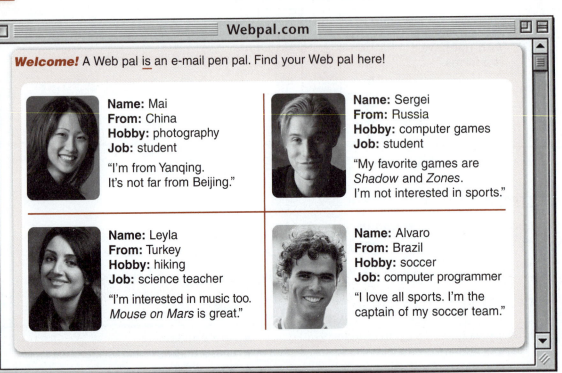

Webpal.com

Welcome! A Web pal <u>is</u> an e-mail pen pal. Find your Web pal here!

Name: Mai
From: China
Hobby: photography
Job: student

"I'm from Yanqing.
It's not far from Beijing."

Name: Sergei
From: Russia
Hobby: computer games
Job: student

"My favorite games are
Shadow and *Zones*.
I'm not interested in sports."

Name: Leyla
From: Turkey
Hobby: hiking
Job: science teacher

"I'm interested in music too.
Mouse on Mars is great."

Name: Alvaro
From: Brazil
Hobby: soccer
Job: computer programmer

"I love all sports. I'm the
captain of my soccer team."

2 **WRITE** • *Write sentences with the words in parentheses. Use the present of* **be**.
Use contractions when possible.

1. (You / my first Web pal) <u>You're my first Web pal.</u>

2. (We / the same age) _____

3. (I / from Izmir) _____

4. (It / in Turkey) _____

5. (I / not / a student) _____

6. (My family / not / large) _____

7. (My parents / from Istanbul) _____

8. (There / two children) _____

9. (My sister / in high school) _____

10. (She / 16) _____

11. (Her hobby / music) _____

12. (We / not / rich) _____

13. (But we / very happy) _____

3 **COMPLETE •** *Look at these pictures. Complete the sentences with the present of* **be**. *Use contractions when possible.*

My house

1. My house ___isn't___ big, but it _____ comfortable.

2. I _____ in the living room. There _____ a computer in that box. It _____ for me.

3. There _____ four people in my family. I _____ in this picture. I _____ the photographer.

4. I _____ with my team here. We _____ happy! But we _____ good friends.

Me at home

My family

Me and my team

4 **EDIT •** *Read this e-mail message. Find and correct eight mistakes in the use of* **be**. *The first mistake is already corrected.*

Webpal.com

Hi Sergei,

    You're
    ~~You's~~ interested in computer games! I'm interested in them too. My favorite game are

Polar Ice, but I amn't very good at it. My other hobby is baseball. You no are interested in

sports. Why? Baseball is a great game. It very popular here. My friends and I are always

in the ballpark after work. They is good hitters. I'm a pretty good catcher.

    We is both students. Computer class are your favorite, right? My favorite class is history.

    Well, it's time for class now. Write soon.

Your Web pal,

Mike

The Present of *Be*:
Questions

Are you OK? Yes, I am.

Man with Fish Phobia

CHART CHECK 1

Circle T (True) or F (False).

T F In *yes/no* questions, **am, are,** or **is** goes first.

T F We don't use contractions in short answers.

YES/NO QUESTIONS

Be	Subject	
Am	I	
Are	you	
Is	he she it	afraid?
Are	we you they	

SHORT ANSWERS

AFFIRMATIVE			NEGATIVE		
	you	**are.**		you	**'re not. aren't.**
	I	**am.**		I	**'m not.**
Yes,	he she it	**is.**	**No,**	he she it	**'s not. isn't.**
	you we they	**are.**		you we they	**'re not. aren't.**

6

CHART CHECK 2

Check the correct answer.

Which word can begin
a *wh-* question?

☐ *Am*

☐ *Why*

WH- QUESTIONS			
QUESTION WORD	**BE**	**SUBJECT**	
	am	I	
What **Who**	**is**	he she it	afraid of?
	are	we you* they	

*You = one person or several people.

CONTRACTIONS

What is = **What's**
Who is = **Who's**

EXPRESS CHECK

Check the questions and answers with forms of **be**.

☐ Who's afraid?   ☐ Is it a fish?   ☐ Yes, it does.   ☐ No, it isn't.

Grammar Explanations

Examples

1. Begin *yes/no questions* with *am, is,* or *are.*

- ■ **Am** I late?
- ■ **Is** he afraid of dogs?
- ■ **Are** cats good pets?

2. Use **short answers** to answer *yes/no* questions.

A: Am I late?
B: **Yes, you are.** OR **Yes**.

Use contractions in short answers with *No.*

A: Is he afraid?
B: No, he**'s not**. OR No, he **isn't**.

REMEMBER: *Am not* has only one contraction.

- ■ No, I**'m not**.
  NOT No, I ~~amn't.~~

Don't use contractions in short answers with *Yes.*

A: Are they afraid?
B: Yes, **they are**.
NOT Yes, ~~they're.~~

▶ **BE CAREFUL!** Use pronouns (*I, she, they, . . .*) in short answers.

A: Is Scott afraid?
B: Yes, **he** is.
NOT Yes, ~~Scott~~ is.

3. Begin *wh-* questions with a **question word** (*what, who, why, where, when, how, . . .*). Then use the same word order as in *yes/no* questions.

- ■ *What* **is** that?
- ■ *Who* **is** your doctor?
- ■ *Why* **are** you afraid?

Use contractions in conversation, notes, and e-mail.

A: **Where's** the newspaper?
B: On the table.

1 **MATCH** • *Each question has an answer. Match the questions and answers.*

Questions	Answers
_f_ **1.** What's a phobia?	**a.** No, you're not.
_____ **2.** What are you afraid of?	**b.** Yes, I am.
_____ **3.** Is your phobia a problem?	**c.** Yes, he is.
_____ **4.** Why is it a problem?	**d.** Cats.
_____ **5.** Are you a new patient?	**e.** Yes, it is.
_____ **6.** When is your appointment?	**f.** It's a very strong fear.
_____ **7.** Am I late?	**g.** Three o'clock.
_____ **8.** Is he Dr. Scared?	**h.** My girlfriend has a cat.

2 **ASK & ANSWER** • *Look at the pictures. Complete the questions and write short answers.*

3 **COMPLETE** • *Read this newspaper column about phobias. Complete the questions. Use the words in parentheses. Write the short answers.*

Fear or Phobia? by I. M. Scared, M.D.

Q: <u>What is a phobia?</u>
            1. (What / a phobia / is)

A: It's a very strong fear of an everyday thing, for example, cats or high places.

Q: I'm confused about fears and phobias. _____
                                      2. (the same / they / Are)

A: _____, _____. They're very different.
              3.

Q: _____
          4. (is / the difference / What)

A: People with phobias often fear common things. These

things usually aren't really dangerous.

Q: My sister says I have a phobia about cars. I say she drives

much too fast. _____
                            5. (right / is / Who)

hypnosis

A: You are. You have a healthy fear, not a phobia.

Q: I'm in love with a woman who has a goldfish. I have a phobia of fish.

_____ for phobias?
                 6. (hypnosis / helpful / Is)

A: _____, _____. Hypnosis helps many people. Ask your doctor about it.
              7.

4 **EDIT** • *Read this quiz about phobias. Find and correct six mistakes in the use of questions and short answers with* **be***. The first mistake is already corrected. When you are finished, you can take the quiz!*

Do you have phobias?

            are you
What ~~you are~~ afraid of? Are you afraid of long words? *Yes*? Then, you have *hippopotomonstrosesquippedaliophobia!* Phobias have strange names, but they are very common.

Do you know these phobia facts?

1. What is *triskadekaphobia*?
   a. Fear of the number 13.
   b. Fear of school.

2. Are *octophobia* the fear of the
   number 8?
   a. No, it's not. It's the fear of clocks.
   b. Yes, it's!

3. *Cyberphobia* is a new phobia.
   What it is?
   a. It's the fear of motorcycles.
   b. It's the fear of computers.

4. Am hypnosis helpful for phobias?
   a. Yes. If you don't have *hypnophobia*!
   b. No, they're not.

Answers: 1a, 2b, 3b, 4a

U N I T 3

The Present Progressive:
Statements

She is talking. She is not sleeping.

CHECK *POINT*

Finish the woman's sentence. Check the correct word.

"I'm getting off the train _____."

☐ yesterday

☐ now

CHART CHECK 1 →

Circle T (True) or F (False).

T F For the present progressive, add **verb + -ing** to *am, are,* or *is.*

T F The word **not** goes before *am, are,* or *is.*

PRESENT PROGRESSIVE

SUBJECT	BE	(NOT)	VERB + -ING	
I	**am**			
You	**are**			
He She It	**is**	**(not)**	**working** **coming** **leaving**	now.
We You They	**are**			

CHART CHECK 2 →

Circle T (True) or F (False).

T F All contractions with **not** have two forms.

CONTRACTIONS

AFFIRMATIVE		NEGATIVE	
I**'m**		I**'m not**	
You**'re**	**working**.	You**'re not** You **aren't**	**working**.
She**'s**		She**'s not** She **isn't**	

EXPRESS CHECK

Check all the present progressive sentences.

☐ They're calling.

☐ Call!

☐ He calls.

☐ She isn't calling.

Grammar Explanations	Examples
1. Use the **present progressive** for something happening <u>now</u>. Now *She's talking.* Past ·················x···············➤ Future	■ She**'s talking** on the phone *now*. ■ I**'m calling** my sister. ■ Paul's cell phone **isn't working**. ■ We**'re not studying** *right now*.
2. Form the present progressive with: the present of **be + verb + -ing**	■ I **am talking** to my mother. ■ She **is leaving** for the train station. ■ Tom **is sleeping**. ■ The children **are playing**.
3. Use **not** for negative statements.	■ I**'m** *not* **talking** to my father. ■ He**'s** *not* **working**. ■ My friends **aren't studying**.
4. Use **contractions** in conversation, notes, and e-mail. **REMEMBER!** There is only one contraction for *am not*.	**A:** Hi, Jana. I**'m sitting** on the train. Is Dan home? **B:** Yes, but he**'s taking** a shower. ■ We**'re not working** at home tonight. OR ■ We **aren't working** at home tonight. ■ I**'m not** working right now. NOT I ~~amn't~~ working . . .

Check it out!

Spelling Rules for Base Form of Verb + *ing* ➤➤➤ APPENDIX 17, page 239.

Contractions of *be* ➤➤➤ UNIT 1, page 3.

1 **FIND** • *Read this newspaper column. Underline the present progressive verbs.*

Section 5/TECHNOLOGY   4A

Always in Touch *By Howie Call*

I'm sitting on the train. All around me people are using their cell phones. They're making calls. They're getting calls. They're speaking to their boyfriends and girlfriends, their parents, and their bosses! Phones are ringing everywhere! I'm getting a headache! Cell phones are very useful, but they are also a big problem. There is no "quiet" or "alone" time. Oh, er, . . . excuse me. I have to go. My phone is ringing.

2 **COMPLETE** • *Carla is on the train. Complete her conversations. Use the present progressive form of the verbs in the boxes.*

| ~~call~~ | use | look | take | go |

CARLA: Hi, Dave. It's me. I __'m calling__ from the train. I _____
              1.   2.
              to Detroit to visit Miguel. Where are you?

 DAVE: At home. I _____ a bath!
                            3.

CARLA: Really?

 DAVE: Yes. I _____ my cell phone.
                      4.

CARLA: Well, don't get it wet! Er, one moment, Dave. The man in the seat

              next to me _____ at me. I think he wants to say something.
                                  5.

| talk | listen | try | try |

 MAN: Excuse me, miss, but I _____ to sleep, and you _____
                                              6.   7.
              on the phone!

CARLA: Well, excuse *me*! I _____ to have a private conversation,
                                        8.
              and *you* _____!
                              9.

3 **DESCRIBE** • *Look at these pictures of people on the train. Write sentences about what they* **are doing** *or* **are not doing.** *Use the words in parentheses.*

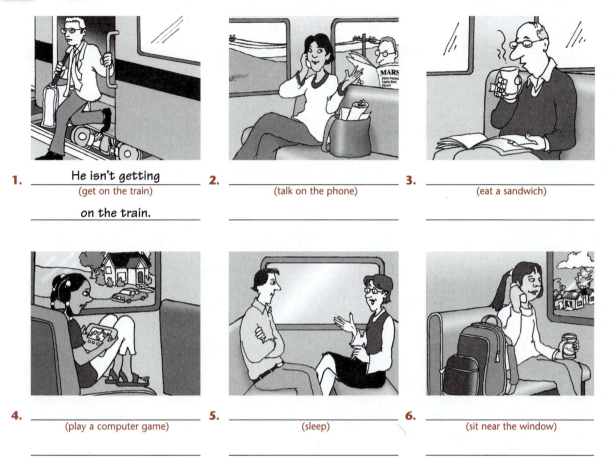

1. _He isn't getting_
   (get on the train)

   on the train.

2. _____
   (talk on the phone)
   _____

3. _____
   (eat a sandwich)
   _____

4. _____
   (play a computer game)
   _____

5. _____
   (sleep)
   _____

6. _____
   (sit near the window)
   _____

4 **EDIT** • *Read this e-mail message. Find and correct ten mistakes in the use of the present progressive. The first mistake is already corrected.*

---

messenger.com

writing

Hi. I'm ~~write~~ to you from the train. I are traveling with my brother Dan. We go to Miami to visit

our aunt. I can't make calls because Dan sleeps. He no feeling well. That's why I send this

e-mail. There's a problem with this train. It moving really slowly. Wait a minute—the conductor

makes an announcement. Uh-oh. Now it *isn't* moving. We're have engine problems!

Oh, good, Dan wakes up. Now I can CALL you!

The Present Progressive:
Questions

Are you sleeping? No, I'm not.

Are you sleeping?

No, I'm not.

CHECK POINT

Circle T (True) or F (False).

T F The man is sleeping.

CHART CHECK 1

Check the correct answer.

In questions, a form of **be** goes _____ the subject.

❑ before
❑ after

YES/NO QUESTIONS		
BE	**SUBJECT**	**VERB + -ING**
Am	I	
Are	you	
Is	he she it	**dreaming?**
Are	we you they	

SHORT ANSWERS					
AFFIRMATIVE			**NEGATIVE**		
	you	**are.**		you	**'re not. aren't.**
	I	**am.**		I	**'m not.**
Yes,	he she it	**is.**	**No,**	he she it	**'s not. isn't.**
	you we they	**are.**		you we they	**'re not. aren't.**

CHART CHECK 2

Circle T (True) or F (False).

T F In *wh-* questions, the subject goes before **am, are,** or **is.**

WH- QUESTIONS	
Why	**is** she **sleeping?**
Where	

EXPRESS CHECK

Complete the chart with these words.

| they | they | sleeping | are | Are | Yes |

Be	Subject	Verb + -ing		SHORT ANSWER		
			?		**,**			**.**

Grammar Explanations

1. Use the **present progressive** to ask **questions** about something that is happening <u>now</u>.

Now
Are you sleeping?
Past ·········**x**·········► Future

2. Begin *yes/no questions* with *am*, *is*, or *are*.

Use **short answers** to answer *yes/no* questions.

REMEMBER! Do not use contractions in short answers with *Yes*.

3. Begin *wh- questions* with a **question word** (*what, who, why, where, when, how, . . .*). Then use the same word order as in *yes/no* questions.

Examples

- **Are** you **sleeping**?
- What **are** you **doing**?
- Why **is** your TV **making** that noise?

- *Am* I **making** too much noise?
- *Is* she **working**?
- *Are* you **reading**?

A: Is it raining?
B: **No, it isn't**. OR **No**.

- Yes, **it is**.
  NOT Yes, ~~it's~~.

- *What* **are** you **doing**?
- *How* **is** he **feeling**?

1   **MATCH •** *Each question has an answer. Match the questions and answers.*

Questions	Answers
<u> h </u> **1.** Hi, honey. Are you sleeping?	**a.** Yes, it is.
_____ **2.** What are you doing?	**b.** No, she's not.
_____ **3.** Are the neighbors making noise?	**c.** A movie.
_____ **4.** What are they doing?	**d.** No, you're not.
_____ **5.** Is Cindi sleeping?	**e.** Yes, they are.
_____ **6.** What is she doing?	**f.** I'm talking to you!
_____ **7.** What is she watching?	**g.** She's watching TV.
_____ **8.** How are you feeling?	**h.** No, I'm not.
_____ **9.** Am I keeping you awake?	**i.** No, we're not.
_____ **10.** Is it still raining there?	**j.** Tired!
_____ **11.** Are we talking too much?	**k.** They're dancing!

2   **ASK & ANSWER •** *Look at the picture. Write questions using the words in parentheses. Then answer the questions.*

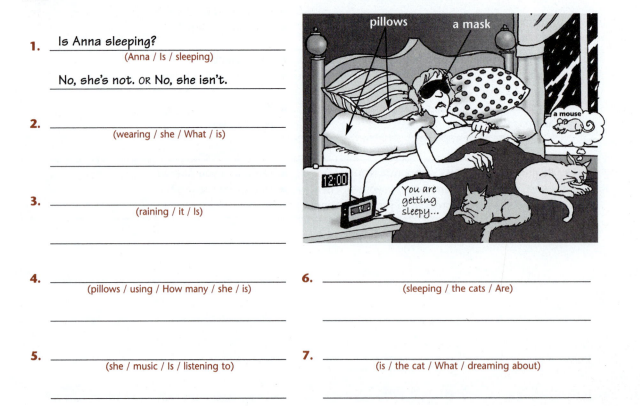

1. <u>Is Anna sleeping?</u>
        (Anna / Is / sleeping)

<u>No, she's not. OR No, she isn't.</u>

2. _____
        (wearing / she / What / is)

_____

3. _____
        (raining / it / Is)

_____

4. _____
      (pillows / using / How many / she / is)

_____

5. _____
      (she / music / Is / listening to)

_____

6. _____
      (sleeping / the cats / Are)

_____

7. _____
      (is / the cat / What / dreaming about)

_____

3 **COMPLETE •** *Anna's sister is calling. Complete their conversation. Use the present progressive form of the verbs in parentheses in the questions. Write short answers.*

LOLA: Hi, Anna. It's me, Lola. _____Are_____ you _____sleeping_____?
1. (sleep)

ANNA: _____No_____, I _____'m not_____.
2.

LOLA: What _____are_____ you _____doing_____?
3. (do)

ANNA: I'm trying to sleep. It's 3:00 A.M.! Why _____ you _____ so
4. (call)
late? Are you OK?

LOLA: I'm fine. And I have some news. _____ you _____?
5. (sit)

ANNA: _____, _____. I'm lying in bed! You sound funny. Where
6.
_____ you _____ from?
7. (call)

LOLA: Well, right now I'm flying to Seattle. I'll be at your door before 5:00 A.M.

ANNA: _____ you _____ from the plane?
8. (call)

LOLA: _____, _____. There's a phone in the seat.
9.

ANNA: Why _____ you _____ to Seattle?
10. (come)

LOLA: It's a very exciting story! _____ you _____?
11. (listen)

ANNA: _____, _____. I want to hear the whole story. That's what
12.
sisters are for.

4 **EDIT •** *Read this ad. Find and correct six mistakes in the use of present progressive questions and short answers. The first mistake is already corrected.*

SelfTest

Circle the letter of the correct answer to complete each sentence.

> **EXAMPLE:**
> Alicia and Paulo _____ students.   A Ⓑ C D
> (A) am   (C) be
> (B) are   (D) is

1. My teacher _____ from Canada.   **A B C D**
   (A) am   (C) be
   (B) are   (D) is

2. Josh is a basketball player, but he _____ tall.   **A B C D**
   (A) is no   (C) no is
   (B) isn't   (D) not

3. There _____ two books on the kitchen table.   **A B C D**
   (A) are   (C) 're
   (B) is   (D) be

4. —Are you OK?   **A B C D**
   —Yes, _____.
   (A) I am   (C) you are
   (B) I'm   (D) you're

5. —Where's Sara?   **A B C D**
   —She's _____ lunch now.
   (A) are eating   (C) eating
   (B) eat   (D) eats

6. _____ I late?   **A B C D**
   (A) Am   (C) Do
   (B) Are   (D) When

7. —Is Doug a teacher?   **A B C D**
   —No, he _____.
   (A) is   (C) 's
   (B) not   (D) 's not

8. We _____ working today.   **A B C D**
   (A) are no   (C) no
   (B) aren't   (D) not

9. _____ the baby sleeping?   **A B C D**
   (A) Am   (C) Be
   (B) Are   (D) Is

18

10. Where _____ studying?   A B C D
    (A) are   (C) they
    (B) are they   (D) they are

11. There _____ a new student in our class.   A B C D
    (A) are   (C) 're
    (B) be   (D) 's

12. Are they happy _____?   A B C D
    (A) at 5:00   (C) tomorrow
    (B) now   (D) yesterday

13. —Is Anna your sister?   A B C D
    —Yes, _____ is.
    (A) Anna   (C) it
    (B) he   (D) she

SECTION TWO

Each sentence has four underlined parts. The four underlined parts of the sentence are marked A, B, C, and D. Circle the letter of the one underlined part that is NOT CORRECT.

EXAMPLE:

My friends <u>is</u> here, but we <u>are</u> <u>not</u> <u>studying</u>.   (A) B C D
         A   B   C   D

---

14. <u>What</u> <u>does</u> he <u>reading</u> right <u>now</u>?   A B C D
      A   B   C   D

15. <u>Who</u> <u>is</u> she <u>talks</u> <u>to</u>?   A B C D
      A   B   C   D

16. <u>Why</u> <u>cats</u> <u>are</u> good <u>pets</u> <u>?</u>   A B C D
      A   B   C D

17. Marta <u>is</u> home, but her friends <u>are</u> <u>study</u> at the <u>library</u>.   A B C D
           A   B   C   D

18. Diego <u>is</u> <u>studying</u> English also, but we <u>are</u> <u>no</u> in the same class.   A B C D
          A   B   C D

19. The children <u>is</u> <u>talking</u> to their <u>mother</u> <u>now</u>.   A B C D
                A   B   C   D

20. I <u>amn't</u> <u>working</u> <u>now</u>, but I <u>am</u> busy.   A B C D
       A   B   C   D

21. Who <u>are</u> <u>you</u> <u>calling</u> <u>now</u>.   A B C D
        A   B   C   D

22. <u>There</u> <u>is</u> fifteen students in my class, and <u>they</u> <u>are</u> all very nice.   A B C D
    A   B   C   D

23. <u>They's</u> good friends, but <u>they're</u> <u>not</u> <u>living</u> together.   A B C D
    A   B   C   D

24. <u>There're</u> two bottles of apple juice in the kitchen, but <u>they</u> <u>are</u> <u>not</u> cold.   A B C D
    A   B   C D

25. Lila <u>is</u> <u>talk</u> on the phone, and the children <u>are</u> <u>playing</u> in the living room.   A B C D
       A   B   C   D

The Simple Present:
Statements

She usually drinks tea.

What's wrong with Sara?

*She usually **drinks** tea.*

CHECK POINT

Circle T (True) or F (False).

T F Sara is drinking tea now.

CHART CHECK 1

Check the correct sentence.

☐ The verb for **he**, **she**, or **it** ends in **-s**.

☐ The word **always** goes after the verb.

AFFIRMATIVE STATEMENTS		
SUBJECT		**VERB**
I / We / You* / They	always	**work**.
He / She / It		**works**.

*You = one person or several people.

CHART CHECK 2

Circle T (True) or F (False).

T F Negative statements have the word **no**.

NEGATIVE STATEMENTS			
SUBJECT	**DON'T DOESN'T**		**BASE FORM OF VERB**
I / We / You / They	**don't**	always	**work**.
He / She / It	**doesn't**		

CONTRACTIONS
don't = do not
doesn't = does not

EXPRESS CHECK

Circle the correct words.

Sara never <u>drink / drinks</u> coffee. She <u>doesn't / don't</u> like it.

Grammar Explanations	Examples

1. Use the **simple present** for things that <u>always</u>, <u>often</u>, <u>sometimes</u>, or <u>never</u> happen.

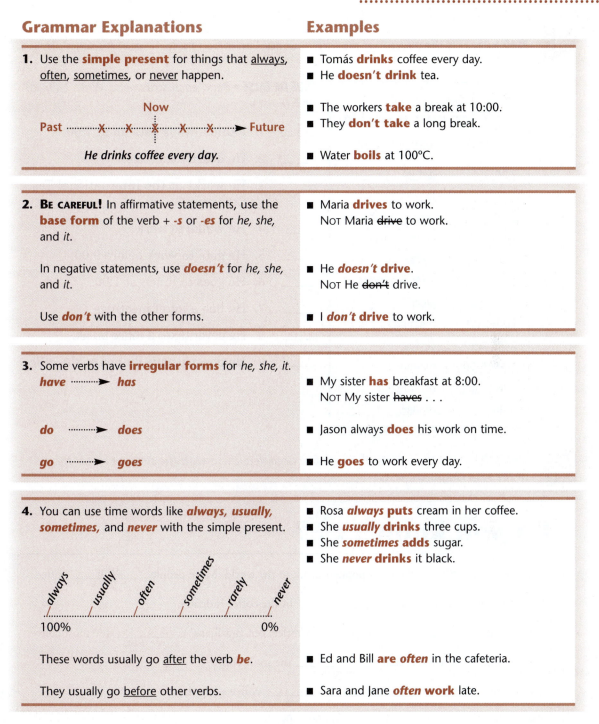

■ Tomás **drinks** coffee every day.
■ He **doesn't drink** tea.

■ The workers **take** a break at 10:00.
■ They **don't take** a long break.

■ Water **boils** at 100ºC.

2. **BE CAREFUL!** In affirmative statements, use the **base form** of the verb + **-s** or **-es** for *he, she,* and *it.*

In negative statements, use **doesn't** for *he, she,* and *it.*

Use **don't** with the other forms.

■ Maria **drives** to work.
  NOT Maria ~~drive~~ to work.

■ He **doesn't drive**.
  NOT He ~~don't~~ drive.

■ I **don't drive** to work.

3. Some verbs have **irregular forms** for *he, she, it.*
have ·········▶ **has**

do ·········▶ **does**

go ·········▶ **goes**

■ My sister **has** breakfast at 8:00.
  NOT My sister ~~haves~~ . . .

■ Jason always **does** his work on time.

■ He **goes** to work every day.

4. You can use time words like **always, usually, sometimes,** and **never** with the simple present.

These words usually go <u>after</u> the verb **be**.

They usually go <u>before</u> other verbs.

■ Rosa **always puts** cream in her coffee.
■ She **usually drinks** three cups.
■ She **sometimes adds** sugar.
■ She **never drinks** it black.

■ Ed and Bill **are often** in the cafeteria.

■ Sara and Jane **often work** late.

Check it out!

Spelling Rules for the Third-Person Singular *(he, she, it)* ▶▶▶ **APPENDIX 18, page 240.**
Pronunciation Rules for the Third-Person Singular *(he, she, it)* ▶▶▶ **APPENDIX 25, page 243.**

1 **READ** • *Paulo is the director of the International Coffee Company. Look at his schedule.*

International Coffee Company, Ltd.

Monday–Friday Schedule

7:00	get up
7:30	jog
8:05	drive to office
8:30–9:30	check e-mail
9:30–10:00	coffee
10:00–12:00	work on reports
12:00–1:00	lunch
1:00–2:00	meetings
2:00–2:30	coffee
2:30–5:00	meetings
5:15	drive home
8:00	dinner

TRUE OR FALSE • *Read each statement. Write T (True) or F (False).*

__T__ **1.** Paulo always gets up at 7:00.

_____ **2.** He doesn't exercise.

_____ **3.** He works at the International Tea Company.

_____ **4.** He walks to work.

_____ **5.** He gets to work before 9:00.

_____ **6.** He goes to lunch at 1:00.

_____ **7.** He has a lot of meetings.

_____ **8.** He never takes a coffee break.

_____ **9.** He doesn't have dinner at the office.

2 **COMPLETE** • *Read these facts about coffee. Complete them with the simple present form of the verbs in parentheses.*

Do you know . . . ?

- Tea ___is not___ the most popular drink in the world. More people ___drink___ coffee.
  1. (not be)   **2.** (drink)

- Twenty-five million people _____ in the coffee industry.
  3. (work)

- Brazil _____ 30% of the world's coffee, but Brazilians _____ the most coffee.
  4. (grow)   **5.** (not drink)

- People in the United States _____ the most coffee.
  6. (drink)

- In the United States, most adults _____ coffee every day.
  7. (have)

- Italy _____ more than 200,000 coffee bars.
  8. (have)

- In Turkey and Greece, the oldest person always _____ his or her coffee first.
  9. (get)

- In the United States, most coffee drinkers _____ their coffee black.
  10. (not take)

  They _____ sugar, milk, or cream.
  11. (add)

3   **DESCRIBE •** *Johan is Paulo's office assistant. He has the same schedule every day. Look at his schedule and write sentences about his day. Choose between affirmative and negative statements. Use the correct form of the verb.*

1. Johan / have / a long day
   <u>Johan has a long day.</u>

2. He / work / eight hours
   <u>He doesn't work eight hours.</u>

3. His workday / begin / at 9:00
   _____

4. He / leave the office / at 7:15
   _____

5. He / have / a half hour for lunch
   _____

6. He / take / breaks
   _____

7. He / always / have / a meeting in the morning
   _____

8. He / have / meetings in the afternoon
   _____

Schedule	
8:00–9:00	meet with Paulo
9:00–11:00	answer e-mail
11:00–2:00	do paperwork
2:00–2:30	lunch
2:30–4:00	return phone calls
4:00–7:00	write reports
7:15	lock the office!

4 **EDIT •** *Read Johan's journal entry. Find and correct nine mistakes in the use of the simple present. The first mistake is already corrected.*

1:00 A.M.

I'm so tired. I work too much. I ~~take never~~ ^{never take} a break. My boss always

want me to stay late. HE doesn't stays late! I gets up every day at

6:00, and I no stop work until 7:00. I rarely having time to see my

friends. I also drink too much coffee! I usually have more than five

cups a day. Some people say that coffee relax them, but not me! It

help me stay awake at the office, but the caffeine makes me usually

nervous. Then, I can't sleep at night. Like now! Maybe I should try tea.

UNIT 6

The Simple Present:
Questions

Do you laugh a lot? Yes, we do.

Do you **smile** a lot?

Do you **laugh** every day?

West Park Laughing Club members say,

"Yes, we do!"

CHECK *POINT*

Circle (T) True or F (False).

T F   People in the club often laugh.

CHART CHECK 1

Circle T (True) or F (False).

T F   After **does**, the verb always ends in **-s**.

T F   The contraction of **do + not** is **doesn't**.

YES/NO QUESTIONS

Do/Does	Subject	Base Form of Verb	
Do	I / we / you* / they	**laugh**	every day?
Does	he / she / it	**meet**	

*You = one person or several people.

SHORT ANSWERS

Yes,	you / we / I / they	**do.**	No,	you / we / I / they	**don't.**
	he / she / it	**does.**		he / she / it	**doesn't.**

CHART CHECK 2

Check the correct answer.

The question word goes _____ *do* or *does*.

❏ after

❏ before

WH- QUESTIONS			
WH- WORD	**DO/DOES**	**SUBJECT**	**BASE FORM OF VERB**
When **Where**	**does**	it	**meet?**
	do	they	

EXPRESS CHECK

Check the simple present questions.

❏ Why are they laughing?

❏ Do you laugh a lot?

❏ Don't laugh now!

❏ When do you laugh?

❏ They laugh at his jokes.

Grammar Explanations

Examples

1. Use **simple present questions** to ask about things that <u>always</u>, <u>often</u>, <u>sometimes</u>, or <u>never</u> happen.

■ **Do** you **tell** jokes?
■ When **does** your club **meet**?

---

2. Begin *yes/no questions* with *do* or *does*. Use the base form of the verb (*go, have, speak, . . .*).

■ **Do** you **laugh** a lot?
■ **Does** Marti **tell** jokes?

Use **short answers** with *yes/no* questions.

A: **Do** you speak English?
B: **Yes, I do.** OR **Yes.**

Use <u>contractions</u> in short answers with *No*.

A: **Does** your sister like jokes?
B: No, she **doesn't**.

REMEMBER! Don't use *do* with questions that have *am, are,* or *is*.

■ **Is** it funny?
■ **Are** you sure?

---

3. Begin *wh- questions* with a **question word** (*what, who, why, where, when, how, . . .*). Then use the same word order as in *yes/no* questions.

■ **When does** your club **meet**?
■ **Why do** you **go** there?

1 **MATCH** • *Every question has an answer. Match each question with the correct answer.*

Questions

___e___ **1.** Where do you go every Thursday?

_____ **2.** Where do you meet?

_____ **3.** Why do you go to a laughing club?

_____ **4.** Do you enjoy it?

_____ **5.** Do they tell jokes there?

_____ **6.** Does it cost a lot?

Answers

a. Because it's fun.

b. No, they don't.

c. In the park.

d. No, it doesn't.

e. To my laughing club.

f. Yes, I do.

2 **ASK & ANSWER** • *Use the words in parentheses to form questions. Write the short answers.*

Laughs.org

Q: _Where does your laughing club meet?_
1. (does / meet / Where / your laughing club)

A: In West Park.

Q: _____
2. (meet / How often / you / do)

A: Once a week. We meet Thursday mornings at 7:00 A.M.

Q: _____
3. (a leader / have / Do / you)

A: _____, _____. Her name is Misha Jensen.
4.

Q: _____
5. (she / a degree in laughing / have / Does)

A: Ha ha! _____, _____. But she has training.
6.

Q: _____
7. (cost /does / How much / your club)

A: Nothing. It's free. Come join us!

3 **CHOOSE & COMPLETE** • *Complete this conversation. Use the correct form of the verbs in the box.*

mean	~~come~~	do	wear	wear	meet

KIM: Where _____*do*_____ laughing clubs ___*come*___ from?
1.

MISHA: From India. Dr. Mudan Kataria started the first club in 1995.

KIM: What are classes like? What _____ you _____ first?
2.

MISHA: First we chant, "Ha, ha, ho, ho." Then we look at each other and laugh.

KIM: What _____ people _____? _____ they _____
3. 4.
special clothes?

MISHA: No. Just something comfortable. So are you interested?

KIM: Maybe. What time _____ you _____?
5.

MISHA: 6:00 A.M.

KIM: 6:00 A.M.? Ha, ha, ho, ho, hee, hee!

MISHA: _____ that _____ "No"?
6.

KIM: Yes, it does. Sorry!

4 **EDIT** • *Read this letter to Dr. Kataria. Find and correct six mistakes in the use of simple present questions. The first one is already corrected.*

Dear Dr. Kataria,

    I am very interested in your laughing clubs. They sound wonderful! I'd like to become a trainer. I have just a few questions:

1. Where ~~train you~~ *do you train* people?
2. When the training begins?
3. How long does it takes to become a trainer?
4. How much costs the training?
5. Do trainers make a good salary?
6. Do you gets part of the money?

Sincerely yours,

Hee Hee Jones

P.S. Has you an e-mail address?

UNIT 7

Non-Action Verbs

I see the moon.

CHECK *POINT*

Check the correct answer.

The children are talking about things they see _____.

☐ sometimes   ☐ now

CHART CHECK

Circle T (True) or F (False).

T F Non-action verbs end in *-ing*.

STATEMENTS

I **see** the moon.
It **looks** like a man.
It**'s** beautiful.
I **want** to take a picture of it.
I **don't have** my camera.

YES/NO QUESTIONS

Do you **see** the moon?
Does it **look** like a man?
Is it clear?

WH- QUESTIONS

What do you **see**?
How does it **look**?
Where is it?

EXPRESS CHECK

Check the sentences with non-action verbs.

❏ We're looking at the moon.

❏ I see the stars.

❏ My sister has a rabbit.

❏ They're taking a walk.

Grammar Explanations

Examples

1. **Action verbs** describe <u>actions</u>.	■ I**'m walking** in the park. ■ He**'s looking** up at the sky.
Non-action verbs do not describe actions. They describe:	
a. **thoughts** *know, remember, think, understand, mean*	■ I **know** Klaus. ■ I **think** you're wrong. ■ He **doesn't understand**. ■ What **do** you **mean**?
b. **feelings** *hate, like, love, want, need*	**A:** **Do** you **like** this photograph? **B:** I **love** it!
c. **senses** and **appearance** *see, hear, smell, taste, feel,* *look, sound, seem*	■ **Do** you **see** the man in the moon? ■ It **looks** like a rabbit.
d. **possession** *have, own*	■ Listen. I **have** an idea.
The verb **be** is also a non-action verb.	■ Alicia **is** happy today.

2. We usually do not use the present progressive (**be** + verb + **-ing**) with non-action verbs. We use the **simple present**.	■ I **want** to go for a walk *now*. Not I'm wanting to go . . .

3. **Be careful!** Some verbs have an action and a non-action meaning.	**Action** ■ I**'m looking** at the moon. **Non-action** ■ It **looks** beautiful.

Check it out!

Common Non-Action Verbs ►►► APPENDIX 2, page 230.

1 **FIND** • *Read this part of a magazine article. Underline the non-action verbs.*

What <u>do</u> you <u>see</u>?

It<u>'s</u> a beautiful night. Todd, Kim, and Omar are looking up at the sky.

TODD: Do you see the man in the moon?

KIM: What do you mean? It looks like a rabbit to me.

OMAR: I don't understand you guys! I think it's a woman. And she's reading a book!

Three people are looking at the same moon, but they see three different things. What about *you*? Look at the moon. What do *you* see?

2 **CHOOSE** • *Read these conversations. Circle the correct words to complete them.*

A: We're going to the Space Museum. <u>Are / (Do)</u> you <u>wanting / want</u> to go?
1.   **2.**

B: Sure. What <u>are / do</u> they <u>showing / show</u> now?
3.   **4.**

A: I <u>'m not knowing / don't know</u> exactly. Something new about the planet Mars.
5.

B: It <u>'s sounding / sounds</u> good. <u>Are / Do</u> we <u>needing / need</u> tickets?
6.   **7.**   **8.**

A: Yes. I <u>remember / 'm remembering</u> the moon show. It was really crowded.
9.

★   ★   ★

A: Look at this photo of Mars.

B: That's Saturn. Mars <u>isn't having / doesn't have</u> rings.
10.

A: You're right. Wow! It really <u>is looking / looks</u> beautiful.
11.

★   ★   ★

The Planet Saturn

A: What <u>is / does</u> *constellation* <u>meaning / mean</u>?
12.   **13.**

B: A group of stars. What <u>is / does</u> this one <u>looking / look</u>
14.   **15.**

like to you?

A: A dog.

B: A dog? Oh, now I <u>'m seeing / see</u> it. That's the head
16.

and there's the tail.

The Constellation Canis Major

3 **COMPLETE** • *Read this conversation. Complete it with the correct form of the verbs in parentheses. Use the present progressive or the simple present.*

A: You _____*look*_____ tired. Are you OK?
1. (look)

B: I'm fine. Just hungry. I _____ something to eat.
2. (need)

A: _____ the Space Museum _____ a cafeteria?
3. (have)

B: Sure, but I _____ where it is. Hey, where _____ you _____?
4. (not know)   **5.** (go)

A: Well, I _____ food, so I _____ my nose!
6. (smell)   **7.** (follow)

[A little later.]

A: This cake _____ great. Try some.
8. (taste)

B: No, thanks. I _____ sweets. What's wrong with your tea?
9. (not like)
You _____ it.
10. (not drink)

A: It _____ funny. I _____ the milk is bad. I'll get another cup.
11. (smell)   **12.** (think)

B: Good idea. You know, I really _____ the postcards we bought.
13. (like)

A: Me too. I _____ to send one to Klaus. _____ you _____
14. (want)   **15.** (have)
a pen?

4 **EDIT** • *Read this postcard. Find and correct seven mistakes in the use of action and non-action verbs. The first mistake is already corrected.*

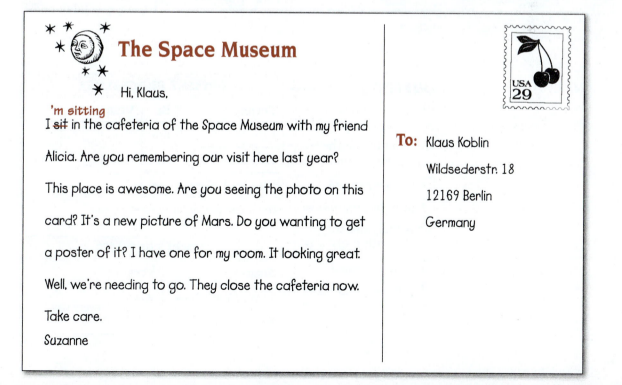

The Space Museum

Hi, Klaus,

 'm sitting
I ~~sit~~ in the cafeteria of the Space Museum with my friend

Alicia. Are you remembering our visit here last year?

This place is awesome. Are you seeing the photo on this

card? It's a new picture of Mars. Do you wanting to get

a poster of it? I have one for my room. It looking great.

Well, we're needing to go. They close the cafeteria now.

Take care.

Suzanne

To: Klaus Koblin
Wildsederstr. 18
12169 Berlin
Germany

Present Progressive and Simple Present

They're watching TV. / They watch TV every day.

Today I'm **reporting** from the Himalayas. I'm **talking** to the Abominable Snowman . . .

She always **interviews** interesting people!

They **think** that's a man?!

PRESENT PROGRESSIVE

SUBJECT	BE	VERB + -ING	
I	am		
He / She / It	is	working	now.
We / You* / They	are		

You = one person or several people.

SIMPLE PRESENT

SUBJECT	VERB	
I / We / You / They	work	every day.
He / She / It	works	

EXPRESS CHECK

Check the correct box.

	Now	Every day
We're watching TV.	❑	❑
Do you watch the news?	❑	❑
She isn't reporting the news.	❑	❑
What does she do?	❑	❑
The TV isn't working.	❑	❑

Grammar Explanations

Examples

1. Use the **present progressive** for things that are happening <u>now</u>.

Now
We're watching the news.
Past ·················· X ···········► Future

- What **are** you **doing** *now*?
- We**'re watching** the news.
- *Right now* she**'s reporting** from Paris.

2. Use the **simple present** for things that <u>always</u>, <u>often</u>, <u>sometimes</u>, or <u>never</u> happen.

Now
We watch the news.
Past ·········· X····X····X····X····X ··········► Future

- What **do** you **do** after dinner?
- We *always* **watch** the news.
- She **reports** the news *every day*.

3. **REMEMBER!** We usually don't use the present progressive with non-action verbs. We use the simple present.

- I **want** to watch the news *now*.
  NOT ~~I'm wanting~~ to watch . . .

1 **FIND** • *Read about Daljit Dhaliwal. Underline all the present progressive verbs. Circle all the simple present verbs.*

 It's 11:00 P.M. and Daljit Dhaliwal is reporting the news. All around the world people are watching her. Who is she? Why do millions of people watch her every weekday night?

Dhaliwal is a newscaster. Her family comes from India, but Dhaliwal was born in London. Now she is living in the United States. She works for CNN International, the 24-hour international news channel. Dhaliwal is very serious about the news. "News is serious business," she often says. And when Dhaliwal reports the news, people listen.

2 **CHOOSE** • *Look at the pictures. Circle the correct words to complete the sentences.*

Usually

Now

1. It's 11:00 P.M. Jennifer Robbins sits / is sitting at home.

2. She usually reports / is reporting the news on television, but now she watches / is watching it.

3. At work she wears / is wearing a suit.

4. Now she wears / is wearing jeans and a T-shirt.

5. She drinks / is drinking a cup of tea.

6. At work she drinks / is drinking bottled water.

7. Jennifer is a newscaster. She thinks / is thinking the news is very important.

8. She loves / is loving her job, but at the moment she enjoys / is enjoying her day off.

3 **COMPLETE** • *Read this news report. Complete it with the present progressive or simple present form of the verbs in parentheses.*

REPORTER: Good morning. It's Sunday, July 7, 7:55 A.M.

I _____'m standing_____ in the streets of
    1. (stand)

Pamplona, Spain. Every year hundreds of

people _____ with the bulls, and
           2. (run)

thousands of other people _____.
                              3. (watch)

I _____ to one of the runners.
     4. (talk)

Sir, why are you here?

RUNNER: I _____ ready to run with the bulls!
              5. (get)

I _____ every year. I _____ it!
     6. (run)   **7. (love)**

REPORTER: I _____ that you _____ a white shirt, white pants,
              8. (see)   **9. (wear)**

and a red belt.

RUNNER: Yes. The runners usually _____ these colors.
                                      10. (wear)

REPORTER: This is a very exciting event. But it's dangerous too.

Every year people _____ hurt, and sometimes people
                      11. (get)

_____ too. It's 8:00 A.M.! The race _____!
  12. (die)   **13. (start)**

Reporting live, so far, from Pamplona, this is Roberto Cruz for CWBS.

4 **EDIT** • *Read this journal entry. Find and correct seven mistakes in the use of the present progressive and the simple present. The first mistake is already corrected.*

>   'm sitting
> I ~~sit~~ in my new home in Atlanta, Georgia, and I'm looking out my living room window.
>
> It's looking very different from my street in London. The sun shines! In London, it rains
>
> a lot. Also, only one person walks on the street right now. In London, people usually walk
>
> everywhere. I REALLY need a driver's license! My friend Rina is driving me to work every
>
> day. My schedule is different too. I'm reporting the news at 5:00 every afternoon, not
>
> 11:00 at night. It's time to go now. Rina drives into my driveway.

The Imperative

Open the door! Don't touch the plate!

*Dave, your dinner is ready. Please **open** the door.*

***Take** it out now. **Don't touch** the plate! It's very hot.*

Thanks, Hal.

No problem, Dave

CHECK POINT

Check the correct answer.

The microwave is _____.

☐ asking the man questions

☐ telling the man to do things

CHART CHECK

Circle T (True) or F (False).

T F The affirmative begins with **You**.

T F The negative begins with **Don't**.

AFFIRMATIVE	
BASE FORM OF VERB	
Open	the door.
Take	it out.

NEGATIVE	
***DON'T* + BASE FORM OF VERB**	
Don't open	the door.
Don't take	it out.

CONTRACTION
Don't = Do not

EXPRESS CHECK

Check all the imperative sentences.

☐ Open the door.

☐ She opens the door.

☐ Don't open the door.

☐ He's not opening the door.

Grammar Explanations	Examples
1. The **imperative** tells someone to do something. Use it for one person or for two or more people.	■ **Listen** to the instructions. ■ **Open** the door. ■ **Come** in, Paulo. ■ **Come** in, Paulo and Emi.
2. Use the **base form** of the verb *(open, read, go, use, . . .)* for the imperative.	■ **Read** the instructions. ■ **Look** at page 35.
3. Use *don't* + **base form** of the verb for the negative.	■ *Don't* **be** nervous. ■ *Don't* **use** it now. ■ *Don't* **touch** it.
4. **BE CAREFUL!** Do not use *you* in the imperative.	■ **Open** the door. NOT ~~You~~ open the door. ■ **Don't** touch that. NOT ~~You~~ don't touch that.
5. Use *please* to be more <u>polite</u>.	■ *Please* **help** me. ■ *Please* **don't be** late.
6. Use the imperative to: • give **instructions** • give **directions** • give **commands** • make **requests** • give **advice**	 TEACHER: **Don't use** a pen. **Use** your computer. OFFICER: **Turn** left at the corner. **Don't turn** right. MOTHER: **Be** quiet! **Don't make** so much noise! FRIEND: *Please* **help** me with my homework. DOCTOR: **Don't eat** too much bread.

1 **MATCH** • *Read the sentences on the left. Match each one with a picture on the right.*

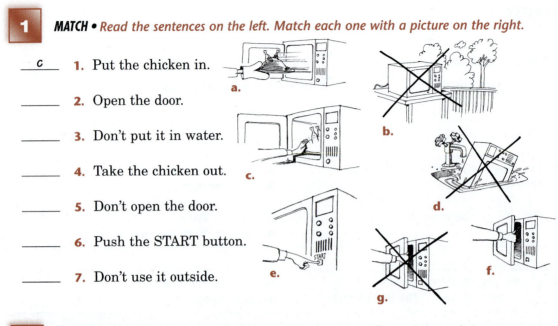

_c_ **1.** Put the chicken in.

_____ **2.** Open the door.

_____ **3.** Don't put it in water.

_____ **4.** Take the chicken out.

_____ **5.** Don't open the door.

_____ **6.** Push the START button.

_____ **7.** Don't use it outside.

2 **COMPLETE** • *Read this recipe. Complete it with the correct form of the verb in parentheses.*

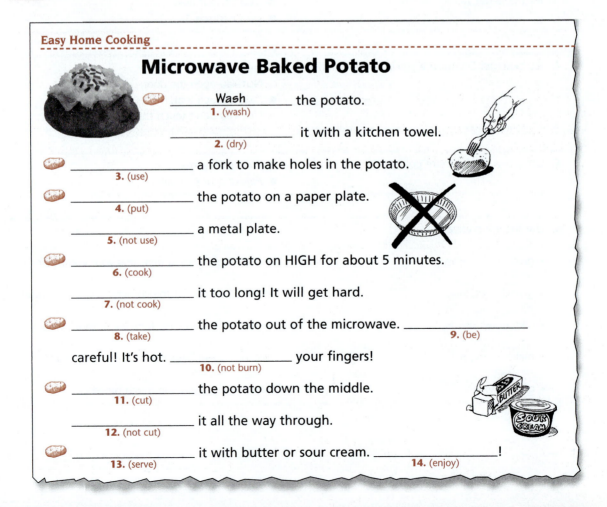

Easy Home Cooking

Microwave Baked Potato

_____Wash_____ the potato.
1. (wash)

_____ it with a kitchen towel.
2. (dry)

_____ a fork to make holes in the potato.
3. (use)

_____ the potato on a paper plate.
4. (put)

_____ a metal plate.
5. (not use)

_____ the potato on HIGH for about 5 minutes.
6. (cook)

_____ it too long! It will get hard.
7. (not cook)

_____ the potato out of the microwave. _____
8. (take)   **9. (be)**

careful! It's hot. _____ your fingers!
                  10. (not burn)

_____ the potato down the middle.
11. (cut)

_____ it all the way through.
12. (not cut)

_____ it with butter or sour cream. _____!
13. (serve)   **14. (enjoy)**

3 **CHOOSE & COMPLETE •** Look at the pictures. Complete the sentences with the correct verb from the box. Use affirmative or negative imperatives.

be   come   eat   forget
park   touch   ~~turn~~   sit

1. Don't turn right. Turn left.

2. Please _____ down.

3. Please _____ quiet!

4. _____ the oven! It's hot!

5. _____ your chicken!

6. Please _____ in.

7. _____ your umbrella!

8. _____ here!

4 **COMPLETE •** Read this note to a roommate. There are six mistakes in the use of the imperative. Find and correct them. The first mistake is already corrected.

> call
> Jana—Your Mom is home this evening. Please ~~calls~~ her at 6:00. There are some samosas from the Indian restaurant in the refrigerator. You try them. They're delicious. Heats them for one minute in the microwave. But no use HIGH. Joan and Ana are coming tonight. Buy please some more soda. You not forget, OK? I don't have time to go to the store. Thanks. R. ☺

SelfTest

SECTION ONE

Circle the letter of the correct answer to complete each sentence.

> **EXAMPLE:**
> Alicia and Paulo _____ students.   A Ⓑ C D
> (A) am   (C) be
> (B) are   (D) is

1. Martin _____ every day.   A B C D
   (A) are working   (C) working
   (B) work   (D) works

2. They _____ at home.   A B C D
   (A) don't work   (C) not work
   (B) no work   (D) not working

3. Ian _____ like coffee.   A B C D
   (A) doesn't   (C) isn't
   (B) don't   (D) not

4. When _____ breakfast?   A B C D
   (A) eat you   (C) do you eat
   (B) you eat   (D) you do eat

5. —Do you laugh a lot?   A B C D
   —Yes, I _____.
   (A) laugh   (C) do
   (B) do laugh   (D) don't

6. Why _____ you take the train?   A B C D
   (A) are   (C) do
   (B) is   (D) does

7. Tania _____ the problem now.   A B C D
   (A) is understanding   (C) understand
   (B) am understanding   (D) understands

8. I want to leave _____.   A B C D
   (A) always   (C) yesterday
   (B) never   (D) now

9. It's cold in here. Please _____ the window.   A B C D
   (A) close   (C) closing
   (B) closes   (D) you close

10. _____ call me after 10:00.   A B C D
    (A) No   (C) Don't
    (B) Not   (D) Doesn't

40

11. Please _____ quiet. My roommate is sleeping.   **A B C D**
   (A) be   (C) to be
   (B) being   (D) you are

12. Water _____ at 0°C.   **A B C D**
   (A) freeze   (C) is freezing
   (B) freezes   (D) don't freeze

13. Brian always _____ e-mail in the morning.   **A B C D**
   (A) is answering   (C) answers
   (B) are answering   (D) answer

14. —Does Natalie speak Spanish?   **A B C D**
   —No, she _____.
   (A) don't   (C) isn't
   (B) doesn't   (D) speaks

15. Jana _____ out the window now.   **A B C D**
   (A) look   (C) is looking
   (B) looks   (D) looking

SECTION TWO

Each sentence has four underlined parts. The four underlined parts of the sentence are marked A, B, C, and D. Circle the letter of the one underlined part that is NOT CORRECT.

> **EXAMPLE:**
>
> My friends <u>is</u> here, but we <u>are</u> <u>not</u> <u>studying</u>.   Ⓐ **B C D**
>   A   B   C   D

16. Gretchen <u>usually</u> <u>drinks</u> tea, but <u>now</u> she <u>drinks</u> coffee.   **A B C D**
            A   B   C   D

17. He<u>'s</u> <u>speaking</u> English <u>now</u>, but he <u>speaks usually</u> French.   **A B C D**
      A   B   C   D

18. <u>Wear</u> your raincoat, and <u>you</u> <u>don't</u> <u>forget</u> your umbrella!   **A B C D**
     A   B   C   D

19. The phone <u>rings</u>—<u>please</u> <u>answer</u> it <u>now</u>.   **A B C D**
           A   B   C   D

20. <u>I'm</u> <u>read</u> a book, but I <u>don't</u> <u>understand</u> it.   **A B C D**
     A   B   C   D

21. <u>Please</u> <u>come</u> in, <u>sit</u> down, and <u>tells</u> us all about your trip.   **A B C D**
     A   B   C   D

22. He <u>always</u> <u>drives</u> expensive cars, but he <u>never</u> <u>is having</u> any money.   **A B C D**
      A   B   C   D

23. Olga <u>usually</u> <u>arrives</u> early, but she <u>is</u> <u>being</u> late now.   **A B C D**
       A   B   C D

24. I <u>never</u> <u>get</u> home before 6:00, so <u>not</u> <u>call</u> me before then.   **A B C D**
     A   B   C D

25. Enrique <u>is</u> <u>watching</u> TV, but he <u>don't</u> <u>like</u> the program.   **A B C D**
       A   B   C D

The Past of *Be*

Were you there yesterday? Yes, I was.

How old **were** you then, Mommy?

CHECK *POINT*

*Circle T (True) or
F (False).*

T F The boy thinks
his mother is
very old.

CHART CHECK 1 →

*Circle T (True) or
F (False).*

T F The past of
be has two
forms.

T F There are no
affirmative
contractions
with ***was***
or ***were***.

STATEMENTS

SUBJECT	WAS/WERE	(NOT)	
I	**was**		
He / She / It		**(not)**	there yesterday.
We / You* / They	**were**		

*You = one person or several people.

CONTRACTIONS

was not = **wasn't**
were not = **weren't**

YES/NO QUESTIONS

WAS/WERE	SUBJECT	
Was	I	there yesterday?
	he / she / it	
Were	we / you / they	

SHORT ANSWERS

	AFFIRMATIVE				NEGATIVE	
Yes,	you	**were.**	**No,**	you	**weren't.**
	he / she / it	**was.**		he / she / it	**wasn't.**
	you / we / they	**were.**		you / we / they	**weren't.**

CHART CHECK 2 →

Check the correct answer.

In questions, *was* or *were* goes _____ the subject.

❏ before ❏ after

WH- QUESTIONS			
QUESTION WORD	**WAS/WERE**	**SUBJECT**	
When	was	he	there?
Why	were	you	

EXPRESS CHECK

Circle the correct words.

I <u>were / was</u> at the museum yesterday. My friends <u>were / was</u> there too.

Grammar Explanations

Examples

1. The **past of *be*** has two forms: ***was*** and ***were***.

- ■ I **was** at the museum yesterday.
- ■ Some dinosaurs **were** very big.

2. We often use **contractions** in negative statements.

- ■ The museum **wasn't** open yesterday.
- ■ Some dinosaurs **weren't** big.

3. Begin *yes/no questions* with *was* or *were*.

Use **short answers** to answer *yes/no* questions.

We almost always use <u>contractions</u> in short answers with *No*.

- ■ ***Was*** Tyrannosaurus rex the largest dinosaur?
- ■ ***Were*** dinosaurs very dangerous?

A: **Was** it very big?
B: **Yes**, **it was**. OR **Yes**.

A: **Were** they alive a million years ago?
B: No, they **weren't**.

4. Begin *wh- questions* with a **question word** (*what, who, why, where, when, how, . . .*). Then use the same word order as in *yes/no* questions.

- ■ ***Where*** **were** you yesterday?
- ■ ***How long*** **were** you there?

5. We often use ***there was*** and ***there were*** to talk about something for the first time. Use ***there was*** for one person or thing. Use ***there were*** for two or more people or things.

- ■ **There was** a dinosaur exhibit at the museum.
- ■ **There were** a lot of people there.

Check it out!

There is, There are ▶▶▶ **UNIT 24, page 104.**

1 **FIND** • *Read these facts. Underline all the past forms of* **be***.*

Dinosaur Facts and Figures

They <u>were</u> on Earth for about 160 million years.

They were everywhere on Earth.

There were many different kinds.

Tyrannosaurus rex was 20 feet (6 meters) tall.

Compsognathus wasn't big. It was only 3.3 feet (1 meter) long.

Some of the big dinosaurs weren't meat-eaters.

2 **READ & COMPLETE** • *Read these facts about three famous dinosaurs. Look at the pictures. Complete each sentence with* **was, wasn't, were,** *or* **weren't***.*

	Stegosaurus	Compsognathus	Tyrannosaurus rex
Size	30 feet long (9 meters)	3.3 feet long (1 meter)	39.4 feet long (12 meters)
Weight	6,800 pounds (3,100 kilograms)	7.9 pounds (3.6 kilograms)	15,400 pounds (7,000 kilograms)
Food	plants	meat	meat

1. Stegosaurus _____was_____ very big, but its head _____ very small.

2. It _____ a plant-eater.

3. Its back _____ very unusual. There were two rows of sharp plates on it.

4. Compsognathus and Tyrannosaurus _____ plant-eaters.

   They _____ meat-eaters.

5. Compsognathus _____ big. It _____ small and light.

6. Tyrannosaurus' head _____ very large, but its front legs _____ very short.

3 **COMPLETE** • *Read this interview between* **Discovery Magazine (DM)** *and Professor Bones. Complete it with* **was, wasn't, were,** *or* **weren't,** *and short answers.*

DM: _____Were_____ all dinosaurs very large?
1.

BONES: __No__ , __they weren't__ . Some dinosaurs _____
2.   3.

very small. Compsognathus _____ the size of a chicken.
4.

DM: _____ dinosaurs intelligent?
5.

BONES: Tyrannosaurus _____ probably smart. Its head _____
6.   7.

very large. Remember—dinosaurs _____ all the same.
8.

There _____ many different kinds.
9.

DM: _____ the Earth different in the time of the dinosaurs?
10.

BONES: _____, _____. It _____ probably warmer at that time.
11.   12.

DM: How long _____ dinosaurs on Earth?
13.

BONES: For millions and millions of years.

DM: When _____ the last dinosaurs on Earth?
14.

BONES: About 65 million years ago. But many scientists believe that birds

are living dinosaurs!

4 **EDIT** • *Read these Instant Messages. Find and correct nine mistakes in the use of the past of* **be.** *The first mistake is already corrected.*

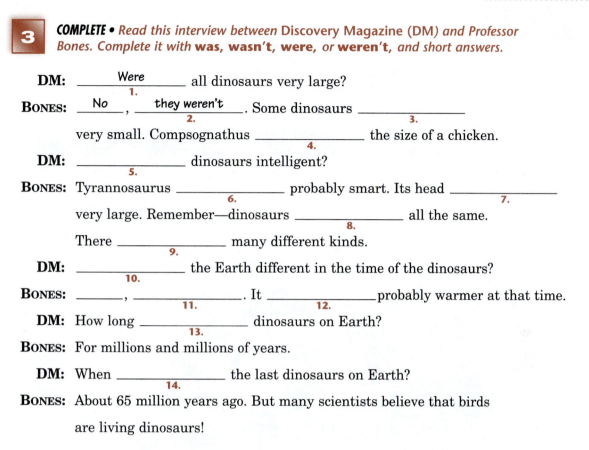

| Instant Message | _ □ ✕ |

weren't OR were not
Dino1: Hi. You ~~were no~~ at the party last night. Where was you?

Rex223: I was at the movies with my sister. We saw Jurassic Park 4.

Dino1: How it was?

Rex223: Great! The dinosaurs was fantastic.

Dino1: Was the movie scary?

Rex223: No, it was. I no was scared, but my sister was a little scared. How the party was?

Dino1: OK. There was a lot of people.

But I was disappointed that you wasn't there. :-(

| □ Done | ● Internet |

UNIT 11

The Simple Past of Regular Verbs:
Statements

He painted a picture yesterday.

"You moved."

CHECK *POINT*

Circle T (True) or F (False).

T F The son painted a picture of his father.

CHART CHECK 1

Check the correct answer.

The past of regular verbs ends in _____.

☐ *-e*

☐ *-ed*

☐ *-t*

AFFIRMATIVE STATEMENTS		
SUBJECT	**VERB**	
I You He She It We You They	**worked** **arrived** **stopped**	yesterday.

CHART CHECK 2

Circle T (True) or F (False).

T   F   Use *didn't* with all sub-jects.

NEGATIVE STATEMENTS			
SUBJECT	***DIDN'T***	**BASE FORM OF VERB**	
I You He She It We You They	didn't	**work arrive stop**	yesterday.

CONTRACTION
didn't = did not

EXPRESS CHECK

Check all the sentences in the simple past.

☐ The boy paints pictures.

☐ He painted a picture of his father.

☐ His father moved.

☐ His father didn't like the painting.

☐ The boy is painting a new picture.

Grammar Explanations

Examples

1. Use the **simple past** for things that are now <u>finished</u>.

He painted.   Now

Past ········x·····················➤ Future

- He **painted** a picture yesterday.
- It **looked** great.
- I **liked** it a lot.

2. Form the simple past of **regular verbs** with: **base form** of verb + **-d** or **-ed**.

▶ **BE CAREFUL!** There are often **spelling changes** when you add **-ed** to the verb.

Base Form		Simple Past
move	➔	mov**ed**
paint	➔	paint**ed**
study	➔	stud**ied**
stop	➔	stop**ped**

3. For the **negative**, use *didn't (did not)* before the base form of the verb.

- They *didn't* **like** the painting.
- She *didn't* **want** to buy it.
- It *didn't* **look** like her father.

Check it out!

Spelling Rules for the Simple Past of Regular Verbs ➤➤➤ APPENDIX 19, page 240.

Pronunciation Rules for the Simple Past of Regular Verbs ➤➤➤ APPENDIX 26, page 243.

1 ***TRUE OR FALSE*** • *Look at the poster. Read the sentences. Circle T (True) or F (False).*

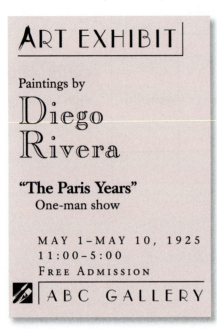

A RT EXHIBIT

Paintings by

Diego
Rivera

"The Paris Years"
One-man show

MAY 1–MAY 10, 1925
11:00–5:00
FREE ADMISSION

A B C G A L L E R Y

(T) F **1.** The exhibit started May 1.

T F **2.** The doors opened at 5:00.

T F **3.** The gallery charged $5.00 admission.

T F **4.** Rivera didn't paint all the paintings.

T F **5.** Rivera lived in Paris.

T F **6.** The exhibit closed after ten days.

T F **7.** It ended May 10.

2 ***CORRECT THE FACTS*** • *Look at the timeline of Diego Rivera's life. Correct the statements. Write two sentences for each item.*

Born in Mexico	Starts art classes	Travels to Spain	Lives in Paris	Returns to Mexico	Marries Frida Kahlo	Dies
1886	1896	1907	1912–1921	1921	1929	1957

1. Diego Rivera started art classes at age six.

　　He didn't start art classes at age six. He started art classes at age ten.

2. He traveled to Russia in 1907.

_____

3. He lived in Paris for twenty years.

_____

4. He returned to Spain in 1921.

_____

5. He married Frida Kahlo in 1939.

_____

6. He died at age eighty.

_____

3 **COMPLETE** • *Read about Diego Rivera's art. Complete the paragraph with the simple past form of the verbs in parentheses.*

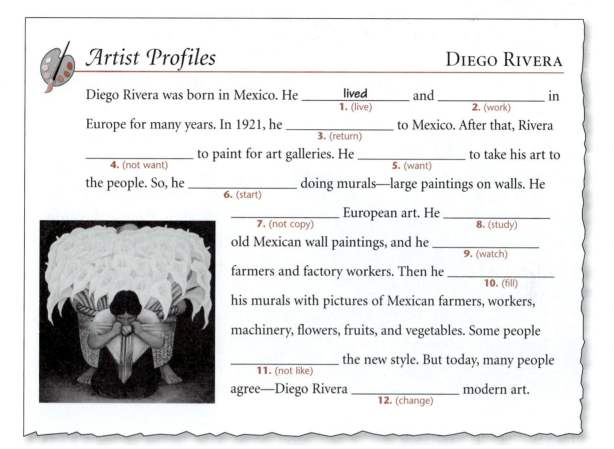

🎨 *Artist Profiles*   Diego Rivera

Diego Rivera was born in Mexico. He _____lived_____ and _____ in
              1. (live)   **2.** (work)

Europe for many years. In 1921, he _____ to Mexico. After that, Rivera
                        3. (return)

_____ to paint for art galleries. He _____ to take his art to
4. (not want)   **5.** (want)

the people. So, he _____ doing murals—large paintings on walls. He
              6. (start)

_____ European art. He _____
7. (not copy)   **8.** (study)

old Mexican wall paintings, and he _____
                  9. (watch)

farmers and factory workers. Then he _____
                  10. (fill)

his murals with pictures of Mexican farmers, workers,

machinery, flowers, fruits, and vegetables. Some people

_____ the new style. But today, many people
11. (not like)

agree—Diego Rivera _____ modern art.
                  12. (change)

4 **EDIT** • *Read this student's essay. Find and correct six mistakes in the use of the simple past. The first mistake is already corrected.*

              started
At fifteen, I ~~starting~~ art classes. After that, I hated school. I did not do

homework. I carryed art books with me all the time. In math class, I look

at pictures. In English class, I copied them. In history class, I colored them.

I save all my money for paints and brushes. Then my report card arrived.

My mother looked at it, and she said, "You not learn a thing!" "I learned a

lot about art," I said. The next week we visited the High School for the Arts.

I did walk in the door, and I smelled paint. I liked school again.

UNIT 12

The Simple Past of Irregular Verbs:
Statements

We saw the movie last night.

The year **was** 1912. The *Titanic* **was** a new, very large ship. People **thought** it **was** safe. But, on April 15, 1912, the *Titanic* **hit** an iceberg and **sank**. More than 1,500 people **lost** their lives.

CHECK *POINT*

Check the correct answer.

❏ The *Titanic* was safe.

❏ It was in an accident with another ship.

❏ Many people died.

CHART CHECK 1

Circle T (True) or F (False).

T F The past form of irregular verbs always ends in **-d** or **-ed**.

T F The past form of irregular verbs is the same for all subjects.

AFFIRMATIVE STATEMENTS		
SUBJECT	**VERB**	
I You He She It We You They	**left** **began** **came** **went**	last night.

CHART CHECK 2

Check the correct answer.

❏ The base form of the verb goes after *didn't*.

❏ *Did not* has two contractions.

NEGATIVE STATEMENTS			
SUBJECT	**DIDN'T**	**BASE FORM OF VERB**	
I You He She It We You They	didn't	leave begin come go	yesterday.

CONTRACTION
didn't = did not

EXPRESS CHECK

Check the sentences with irregular past verbs.

❏ I saw the movie last night.

❏ I loved it.

❏ I want to see it again.

❏ It had a sad ending.

Grammar Explanations

Examples

1. Many verbs are **irregular** (not regular). They do not end in *-ed* in the simple past.

The simple past form of an irregular verb often looks very different from its base form.

Base Form	Simple Past
have	**had**
get	**got**
go	**went**
do	**did**
leave	**left**
be	**was/were**

2. Use irregular simple past forms in **affirmative statements**.

▶ **BE CAREFUL!** The irregular simple past form does not change. Do not add *-s* for *he, she,* or *it*.

■ The *Titanic* **left** from Southampton, England.
■ It **had** more than 2,000 passengers on board.

■ It **left** yesterday.
  NOT It ~~lefts~~ yesterday.

3. In **negative statements** use *didn't* + the **base form** of the verb (*have, know, leave,* . . .).

▶ **BE CAREFUL!** Don't use the simple past form after *didn't*.

■ It *didn't* **have** enough lifeboats.
■ People *didn't* **know** about the icebergs.

■ They *didn't* **leave** at 3:00.
  NOT They didn't ~~left~~ at 3:00.

Check it out!

Irregular Verbs ▶▶▶ APPENDIX 1, page 229.
The Past of *Be* ▶▶▶ UNIT 10, page 42.

1 **FIND** • *Read about the love story in the movie* Titanic. *Circle all the irregular past verbs.*

Jack (was) very happy, but he had no money. He met Rose on the *Titanic*. Rose had pretty clothes and rich friends, but she was very unhappy. She wanted to end her life. Jack stopped her, and the two fell in love. They were happy together, but Rose's mother didn't like Jack. She wanted a rich husband for Rose. At the end, Rose found Jack on the sinking ship. They held hands and jumped into the water. Rose lived. She lost Jack, but she never forgot him.

COMPLETE • *Now complete this chart with the simple past forms of the verbs.*

	Base Form	Simple Past		Base Form	Simple Past
1.	be	was, were	**5.**	have	_____
2.	fall	_____	**6.**	hold	_____
3.	find	_____	**7.**	lose	_____
4.	forget	_____	**8.**	meet	_____

2 **COMPLETE** • *Read this story about the* Titanic. *Complete it with the simple past form of the verbs in parentheses. Go to Appendix 1 on page 229 for help.*

On April 14, 1912, the *Titanic* _____got_____ six iceberg warnings. The captain
                                    1. (get)

_____ them. Finally, some sailors _____ the icebergs,
2. (not hear)   **3.** (see)

but it _____ too late. The *Titanic* _____ an iceberg. At first,
       4. (be)   **5.** (hit)

people _____ the holes in the ship. But very soon, water _____
       6. (not see)   **7.** (begin)

to enter the ship.

The ship _____ enough lifeboats—only 22 boats for more than 2,000
        8. (not have)

people! Women and children _____ into the boats first. Men _____
                           9. (get)   **10.** (go)

next. Another ship, the *Carpathia*, _____ to help the *Titanic*. Only people in
                                     11. (come)

the lifeboats _____ a chance. Only 705 lived.
              12. (have)

3 **READ** • *Newspaper headlines often use the simple present for past events. Read these headlines about the* **Titanic.**

SHIP SINKS!

TITANIC LEAVES SOUTHAMPTON

Captain Goes Down with Ship

Titanic Hits Iceberg!

"I see a light!"
Carpathia Comes to Save Them

1,571 PEOPLE LOSE THEIR LIVES

WHITE STAR BEGINS
WORK ON TITANIC

Scientists Find Titanic at
Bottom of the Atlantic Ocean

CHOOSE & COMPLETE • *Complete the sentences with the simple past forms of the verbs in the headlines. Go to Appendix 1 on page 229 for help.*

1. In 1908, the White Star Line _____began_____ work on the *Titanic.*

2. On April 10, 1912, the *Titanic* _____ Southampton, England, on its first trip.

3. Four days later, at 11:40 P.M., it _____ an iceberg.

4. About two and a half hours after that, the ship _____ .

5. The captain of the *Titanic* _____ down with his ship.

6. People in lifeboats _____ a bright light. It was another ship, the *Carpathia.*

7. The *Carpathia* _____ to save them.

8. But 1,571 people _____ their lives in the disaster.

9. In 1985, scientists _____ the *Titanic* at the bottom of the Atlantic.

4 **EDIT** • *Read about a passenger on the* **Titanic.** *Find and correct seven mistakes in the use of irregular simple past verbs. The first mistake is already corrected.*

Molly Brown ~~comes~~ *came* from a poor family. She didn't went to high school. She left home and gots married. In 1894, her husband finded gold and they became rich. Soon after, her husband left her, but Molly didn't feel sad. She maked friends with rich and famous people in New York and Europe. She were with many of them on the *Titanic.* On that terrible day in 1912, Molly was a hero. She helped save many other passengers. Because of this, she become famous as "the unsinkable Molly Brown."

UNIT 13

The Simple Past:
Questions

Did they come alone? Yes, they did.

SOUTH POLE →

Why **did** they **come** here?

Where **did** they **come** from?

Where **did** they **go**?

Did they **come** alone?

CHECK *POINT*

Check the correct answer.

The questions are about something that is _____.

❏ finished

❏ happening now

CHART CHECK 1

Check the correct answer.

Yes/No questions about the past _____.

❏ start with **did**

❏ use the simple past form of the verb

YES/NO QUESTIONS			
DID	**SUBJECT**	**BASE FORM OF VERB**	
Did	I / you / he / she / it we / you / they	**get**	there first?
		arrive	on time?

CHART CHECK 2

Circle T (True) or F (False).

T F Short answers use the base form of the verb.

T F We use contractions in short answers with *No*.

SHORT ANSWERS					
AFFIRMATIVE			**NEGATIVE**		
Yes,	you / I / he / she / it you / we / they	**did**.	**No**,	you / I / he / she / it you / we / they	**didn't**.

CONTRACTION
didn't = did not

CHART CHECK 3

Check the words that can begin a wh- question.

☐ **What**   ☐ **We**
☐ **Did**   ☐ **How**

WH- QUESTIONS			
QUESTION WORD	DID	SUBJECT	BASE FORM OF VERB
Where	did	I / you / he / she / it we / you / they	**go**?
How			**travel**?

EXPRESS CHECK

Complete the charts with these words.

they	they	Did	did	go	Yes

DID	SUBJECT	BASE FORM OF VERB	
			?

SHORT ANSWER		
	,	

.

Grammar Explanations

Examples

1. Use **simple past questions** to ask about something that is <u>finished</u>.

- **Did** they **travel** last summer?
- **Did** you **go** alone?
- How **did** he **travel**?
- Where **did** she **go**?

2. Begin *yes/no questions* with *did*.

Use **short answers** with *yes/no* questions.

Use <u>contractions</u> in short answers with *No*.

- **Did** you **have** fun?

A: **Did** he fly there?
B: **Yes**, **he did**. OR **Yes**.

A: **Did** they send postcards?
B: No, they **didn't**.

3. Begin **wh- questions** with a **question word** (*what, who, why, where, when, how, . . .*). Then use the same word order as in *yes/no* questions.

- *What* **did** you **wear**?
- *When* **did** she **leave**?
- *Why* **did** they **go**?

4. **REMEMBER!** Don't use *did* with questions that have *was* or *were*.

- **Was** it cold?
- When **were** you there?

1 **READ** • *Liv Arnesen (from Norway) and Ann Bancroft (from the United States) crossed Antarctica in 2000–2001. Read these facts about their trip.*

Trip Facts

Liv Arnesen and Ann Bancroft

- **Plan:** cross Antarctica
- **How:** on skis
- **Started:** November 13, 2000
- **Finished:** February 13, 2001
- **Traveled:** 92 days, 2,300 miles (3,850 km)
- **Temperature:** around –30°F (–34°C)

MATCH • *Each question has an answer. Match each question with the correct answer.*

Questions	Answers
1. __c__ Where did they go?	**a.** Yes, they did.
2. _____ Did they walk across Antarctica?	**b.** 2,300.
3. _____ When did they start?	**c.** To Antarctica.
4. _____ Did they complete their trip in February?	**d.** No, it wasn't.
5. _____ How many miles did they travel?	**e.** November 13, 2000.
6. _____ Was the weather warm?	**f.** No, they didn't.

2 **COMPLETE** • *Will Frees (WF) went to Antarctica. Complete his interview with Geo Magazine (GM). Use the simple past of the verbs in the box and short answers.*

GM: Why ___did___ you ___go___ to Antarctica?
        1.
WF: I'm a teacher. I wanted to teach about this beautiful place.

GM: How _____ you _____ that?
                        2.
WF: A lot of people followed the trip on my Web site.

GM: _____ you _____ messages to the Web site?
                        3.
WF: _____, _____. Every day.
                4.
GM: _____ you _____ a computer?
                        5.
WF: _____, _____. I had a special telephone.
                6.
GM: How long _____ your trip?
                    7.
WF: Four months. But I stopped for two weeks. I hurt my foot.

be

~~go~~

send

do

use

3 ASK & ANSWER • *Look at the pictures of the Arnesen-Bancroft trip. Write questions about the trip. Use the words in parentheses. Then answer the questions.*

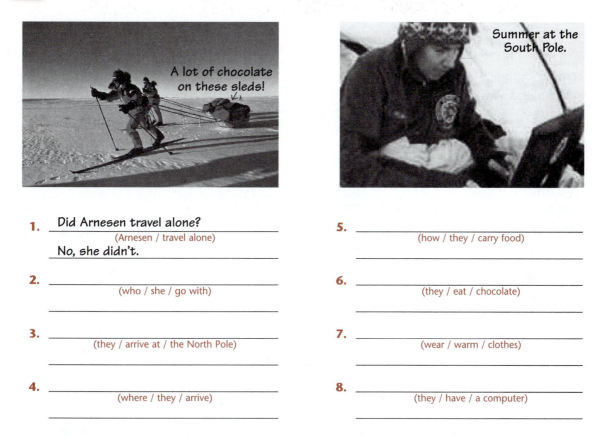

A lot of chocolate on these sleds!

Summer at the South Pole.

1. Did Arnesen travel alone?
   (Arnesen / travel alone)
   No, she didn't.

2. _____
   (who / she / go with)
   _____

3. _____
   (they / arrive at / the North Pole)
   _____

4. _____
   (where / they / arrive)
   _____

5. _____
   (how / they / carry food)
   _____

6. _____
   (they / eat / chocolate)
   _____

7. _____
   (wear / warm / clothes)
   _____

8. _____
   (they / have / a computer)
   _____

4 EDIT • *Read this e-mail message from a student. Find and correct seven mistakes in the use of simple past questions. The first mistake is already corrected.*

SPEEDY MAIL _ □ ✕

Dear Mr. Frees,

I am writing a report about your trip, and I have some questions.

How did you ~~went~~ go to Antarctica? Does you leave from South America?

How many miles you traveled every day? Did it snows?

What did you ate? What your favorite food on the trip?

Where did you sleeping at night?

Why did you stop your trip for two weeks?

Thank you.

Eddy Rose

RE: Antarctica   ● Internet

SelfTest

Circle the letter of the correct answer to complete each sentence.

> **EXAMPLE:**
> Alicia and Paulo _____ students.   A Ⓑ C D
> (A) am   (C) be
> (B) are   (D) is

1. We _____ at school yesterday.   A B C D
   (A) are   (C) was
   (B) be   (D) were

2. The movie was _____ very good.   A B C D
   (A) don't   (C) doesn't
   (B) not   (D) no

3. My friends _____ at home last night.   A B C D
   (A) aren't   (C) wasn't
   (B) isn't   (D) weren't

4. —Were you on time for the meeting?   A B C D
   —Yes, I _____.
   (A) was   (C) wasn't
   (B) were   (D) weren't

5. Where _____ at 5:00 yesterday?   A B C D
   (A) you are   (C) you were
   (B) are you   (D) were you

6. There _____ a lot of interesting people at the party last night.   A B C D
   (A) was   (C) is
   (B) were   (D) are

7. I studied Portuguese _____.   A B C D
   (A) now   (C) tomorrow
   (B) last year   (D) never

8. Sara _____ to Mexico City last month.   A B C D
   (A) move   (C) moved
   (B) moves   (D) 's moving

9. They _____ like the movie yesterday. It wasn't interesting.   A B C D
   (A) don't   (C) did
   (B) doesn't   (D) didn't

10. —Did your brother paint that?   A B C D
    —Yes, _____.
    (A) did he   (C) he did
    (B) he didn't   (D) he was

11. The Michaud family _____ Paris in 1999.   **A B C D**
    (A) leave   (C) leaves
    (B) left   (D) are leaving

12. Diana didn't _____ home before midnight.   **A B C D**
    (A) gets   (C) got
    (B) get   (D) getting

13. _____ you see Tomás yesterday?   **A B C D**
    (A) Did   (C) Was
    (B) Do   (D) Were

14. —Did Emilia send you an e-mail message?   **A B C D**
    —No, she _____.
    (A) did   (C) didn't send
    (B) didn't   (D) doesn't

15. Why _____?   **A B C D**
    (A) they go   (C) they did go
    (B) they went   (D) did they go

SECTION TWO

Each sentence has four underlined parts. The four underlined parts of the sentence are marked A, B, C, and D. Circle the letter of the one underlined part that is NOT CORRECT.

> **EXAMPLE:**
>
> My friends <u>is</u> here, but we <u>are</u> <u>not</u> <u>studying</u>.   (**A**) **B C D**
>   A   B   C   D

16. We <u>left</u> home at 8:00 <u>yesterday</u>, but because of the traffic we <u>didn't</u> **A B C D**
         A   B   C
    <u>arrived</u> at school on time.
      D

17. <u>Where</u> <u>you did</u> <u>have</u> dinner <u>last night</u>?   **A B C D**
       A   B   C   D

18. Tim <u>were</u> at the party <u>last week</u>, but we <u>didn't</u> <u>see</u> his sister there. **A B C D**
          A   B   C   D

19. The museum <u>wasn't</u> open <u>yesterday</u>, so <u>we</u> <u>go</u> to the movies. **A B C D**
               A   B   C D

20. Why <u>he was</u> unhappy before <u>he</u> <u>moved</u> to England <u>last year</u>? **A B C D**
         A   B   C   D

21. I <u>didn't</u> <u>paint</u> pictures, but I <u>took</u> photos and <u>write</u> stories. **A B C D**
        A   B   C   D

22. Katia <u>live</u>, <u>studied</u>, and <u>got</u> married in Barcelona <u>in 2002</u>. **A B C D**
          A   B   C   D

23. <u>Did</u> you <u>went</u> out last night, or <u>did</u> you <u>stay</u> home? **A B C D**
     A   B   C   D

24. The T-shirts <u>didn't</u> <u>look</u> nice, so she <u>didn't</u> <u>buys</u> them. **A B C D**
             A   B   C   D

25. The boat <u>didn't</u> <u>leave</u> <u>yesterday</u> because the weather <u>were</u> bad. **A B C D**
           A   B   C   D

The Future with *Be going to*

They are going to change soon.

Next year, **we're going to have** these computer clothes in red too.

CHECK *POINT*

Circle T (True) or F (False).

T   F   They have the computer clothes in red now.

CHART CHECK 1

Circle T (True) or F (False).

T   F   ***Be going to*** does not change for different subjects.

STATEMENTS			
SUBJECT	**BE**	**(NOT) GOING TO**	**BASE FORM OF VERB**
I	**am**		
He / She / It	**is**	**(not) going to**	**change**.
We / You* / They	**are**		

*You = one person or several people.

CHART CHECK 2

Check the correct answer.

❑ *Yes/No* questions begin with ***do*** or ***does***.

❑ We use ***am***, ***is***, or ***are*** in short answers.

YES/NO QUESTIONS			
BE	**SUBJECT**	**GOING TO**	**BASE FORM OF VERB**
Am	I		
Is	she	**going to**	**change**?
Are	they		

SHORT ANSWERS					
AFFIRMATIVE			**NEGATIVE**		
Yes,	you	**are**.	**No**,	you	**'re not.** **aren't.**
	she	**is**.		she	**'s not.** **isn't.**
	they	**are**.		they	**'re not.** **aren't.**

CHART CHECK 3

Circle T (True) or F (False).

T F In *wh-* questions, ***am*, *is*,** or ***are*** goes before the subject.

WH- QUESTIONS				
WH- WORD	**BE**	**SUBJECT**	**GOING TO**	**BASE FORM OF VERB**
When	**is**	it	**going to**	**change**?

EXPRESS CHECK

Check the sentences with **be going to** *for the future.*

☐ I'm going to the store now.

☐ We're going to buy a new computer.

☐ Computers are going to change.

☐ Where does he go in the morning?

Grammar Explanations

Examples

1. Use *be going to* + **base form** of the verb (*change, be, have, . . .*) for the **future**.

Now

Past ···✗·········► Future

change

USAGE NOTE: Many people say "gonna" in conversation. Do not write *gonna*.

- Computers **are going to change**.
- They**'re going to be** cheaper.
- More cars **are going to have** computers.

SPEAKING: They're *gonna* be very small.
WRITING: They're **going to** be very small.

2. Use *be going to* to talk about **plans**.

- He**'s going to go** to college next year.
- We **aren't going to move** soon.

3. Use *be going to* when something will happen because of something you see <u>now</u>.

- Look at those dark clouds! It**'s going to rain**.

4. Begin *yes/no* **questions** with *am, is,* or *are*. Use short answers with *yes/no* questions.

Use contractions in short answers with *No*.

A: *Are* people **going to wear** computers?
B: Yes, they are. OR **Yes**.

- No, they**'re not**. OR No, they **aren't**.

5. Begin *wh-* **questions** with a **question word**. Then use the same word order as in *yes/no* questions.

- *What* are you **going to buy**?
- *Who* is she **going to ask**?

Check it out!

The Future with *Will* ►►► UNIT 15, page 64.

1 **TRUE OR FALSE •** *Look at this schedule. Circle T (True) or F (False) for each sentence.*

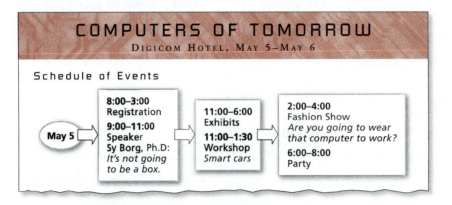

COMPUTERS OF TOMORROW
DIGICOM HOTEL, MAY 5–MAY 6

Schedule of Events

May 5

8:00–3:00
Registration
9:00–11:00
Speaker
Sy Borg, Ph.D:
*It's not going
to be a box.*

11:00–6:00
Exhibits
11:00–1:30
Workshop
Smart cars

2:00–4:00
Fashion Show
*Are you going to wear
that computer to work?*
6:00–8:00
Party

T (F) **1.** The conference is going to begin on May 6.

T F **2.** The workshop is going to be about computers in the home.

T F **3.** The exhibits are going to close at 6:00.

T F **4.** The fashion show is going to start at 4:00.

T F **5.** In the future, computers are going to look very different.

T F **6.** People are going to wear computers.

2 **COMPLETE •** *Anita is thinking about the conference tomorrow. Look at the pictures. Complete the sentences with* **be going to** *or* **not be going to** *and the words in the box.*

| be | come | eat | ~~get up~~ | rain | take |

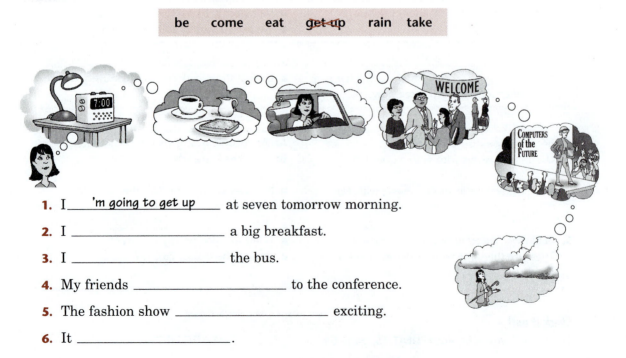

1. I _____'m going to get up_____ at seven tomorrow morning.

2. I _____ a big breakfast.

3. I _____ the bus.

4. My friends _____ to the conference.

5. The fashion show _____ exciting.

6. It _____.

3 **COMPLETE** • *Anita is talking about her plans. Complete her conversations with the words in parentheses and the correct form of* **be going to**. *Write short answers.*

LOUISE: _____Are_____ you _____going to see_____ Brian after work?
1. (see)

ANITA: _____Yes_____ , _____I am_____ . We _____ dinner
2. **3. (have)**
at Amalfi's at 7:00.

LOUISE: _____ you _____ ?
4. (drive)

ANITA: _____ , _____ . Come with us,
5.
OK? You _____ my new car.
6. (love)

[Later.]

ANITA: To Amalfi's, please.

CAR: _____ we _____ the expressway?
7. (take)

ANITA: _____ , _____ . It's the fastest way.
8.

CAR: _____ I _____ on the street?
9. (park)

ANITA: _____ , _____ . On Ninth Street.
10.

CAR: I _____ wet.
11. (get)

ANITA: Why? _____ it _____ ?
12. (rain)

CAR: _____ , _____ . In half an hour.
13.

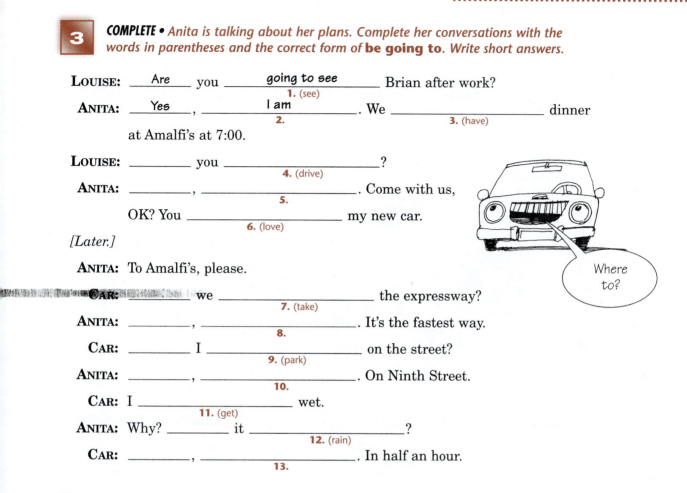

Where to?

4 **EDIT** • *Read Dr. Borg's notes for his talk at the conference. Find and correct nine mistakes in the use of* **be going to**. *The first mistake is already corrected.*

Computers are a big part of our lives now. That's ~~no~~ **not** going to change. We're going to use computers even more in the future. How your computer going to look? How are you going use it? Here are some ideas:

- Computers not going to look like boxes.
- They're going to be much smaller.
- Cameras and telephones is going to be part of many computers.
- Your car are going to talk to you.
- Your refrigerator is going buy your groceries on the Internet.
- You're no going to carry your computer. You're going to wear it. Computers are go to become part of your clothing.

The Future with *Will*

He will leave at 5:00. He won't stay.

You **will leave** very soon.

CHECK POINT

Check the correct answer.

The fortune teller is talking about the _____.

☐ past

☐ present

☐ future

CHART CHECK 1

Circle T (True) or F (False).

T F Use **will** with all subjects.

T F *I'll* is the contraction for *it will*.

STATEMENTS				
SUBJECT	**WILL**	**(NOT)**	**BASE FORM**	
I He She It We You* They	will	(not)	leave	soon.

*You = one person or several people.

CONTRACTIONS	
AFFIRMATIVE	**NEGATIVE**
I will = **I'll** he will = **he'll** she will = **she'll** it will = **it'll** we will = **we'll** you will = **you'll** they will = **they'll**	will not = **won't**

CHART CHECK 2

Check the correct answer.

In questions, **will** goes _____ the subject.

☐ before

☐ after

YES/NO QUESTIONS			
WILL	**SUBJECT**	**BASE FORM**	
Will	she	**leave**	soon?

SHORT ANSWERS	
AFFIRMATIVE	**NEGATIVE**
Yes, she **will**.	**No**, she **won't**.

WH- QUESTIONS			
WH- WORD	**WILL**	**SUBJECT**	**BASE FORM**
When	**will**	she	**leave**?

EXPRESS CHECK

Complete the chart with these words.

will • arrive • When • he

Wh- Word	Will	Subject	Base Form of Verb	
				?

Grammar Explanations

1. Use *will* + **base form** of the verb (*call, go, tell, . . .*) for the **future**.

▶ **Be careful!** The base form of the verb always follows *will*.

2. You can use *will* for future **plans**.

3. Use *will* to make an **offer**.

4. Use **contractions** in conversation, notes, and e-mail.

The negative contraction is *won't*.

5. Begin *yes/no questions* with *will*.

Use **short answers** to answer *yes/no* questions.

6. Begin *wh- questions* with a **question word**. Then use the same word order as in *yes/no* questions.

Examples

- I'**ll call** you tomorrow.
- We'**ll go** to a fortune teller.
- She'**ll tell** us about the future.

- She *will call* you tomorrow.
  Not She will ~~calls~~ . . .

- I'**ll be** at Madame Y's at 1:00.
- My sister **will come** with me.

A: I'**ll give** you a ride to Madame Y's.
B: Thanks.

A: Do you have her address?
B: Stan has it. He'**ll give** it to you.

- I *won't be* home tomorrow night.

A: *Will* you **be** home tomorrow night?

B: **Yes, I will.** OR **Yes.**
  No, I won't. OR **No.**

- *Where* will you **be** tomorrow night?
- *What* will you **do**?

Check it out!

The Future with *Be going to* ►►► **UNIT 14, page 60.**

1 **FIND** • *Read this note from Roz to her friend Jan. Underline the future with* **will**.

3:00

Hi Jan,

I won't have time to wash the dishes before dinner.

I'll be at Madame Y's.

I won't be home before 6:00.

Sorry!

I'll call you from the car phone on the way home.

Roz

P.S. I'll bring pizza.

TRUE OR FALSE • *Now write T (True) or F (False) for each statement.*

__F__ **1.** Roz is going to wash the dishes before dinner.

_____ **2.** She's going to be at Madame Y's.

_____ **3.** She's going to be home at 5:30.

_____ **4.** She's going to call Jan on the way home.

_____ **5.** She offered to bring pizza.

2 **DESCRIBE** • *Look at the pictures. Complete the sentences about what* **will** *or* **won't** *happen. Use the words in parentheses.*

1. You ___will take a trip.___
(take a trip)

2. She _____
(have only one baby)

3. He _____
(live in a big house)

4. They _____
(own a small car)

5. You _____
(be a teacher)

6. They _____
(get married)

3   **ASK & ANSWER** • *Unscramble the words to write questions to Madame Y. Write short answers.*

Q: Will I be rich?
    1. (I / be / rich / Will)

A: No , you won't . But you'll be very happy.
    2.

Q: _____
    3. (will / live / I / Where)

A: In a big house in Spain.

Q: _____
    4. (my parents / with me / Will / live)

A: _____, _____. Your parents will stay in this country.
    5.

Q: _____
    6. (Jennifer and I / get married / Will)

A: _____, _____. Congratulations!
    7.

Q: _____
    8. (we / will / get married / When)

A: Next year.

Q: _____
    9. (we / children / have / Will)

A: _____, _____. Two boys and a girl!
    10.

4   **EDIT** • *Read this ad. Find and correct six mistakes in the use of **will**. The first mistake is already corrected.*

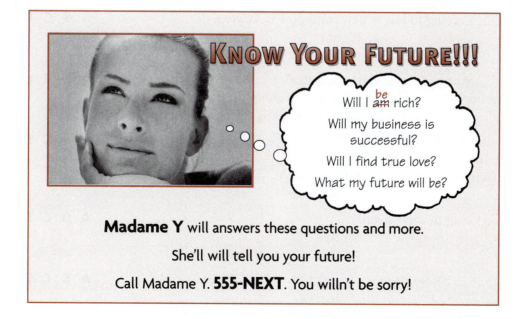

SelfTest

Circle the letter of the correct answer to complete each sentence.

> **EXAMPLE:**
> Alicia and Paulo _____ students.   A ⓑ C D
> (A) am   (C) be
> (B) are   (D) is

1. It _____ tomorrow.   A B C D
   (A) rains   (C) rained
   (B) 's raining   (D) 's going to rain

2. We _____ going to take a vacation next month.   A B C D
   (A) am   (C) is
   (B) are   (D) be

3. _____ is going to start college next fall.   A B C D
   (A) I   (C) We
   (B) She   (D) They

4. The teacher is _____ to give a test tomorrow.   A B C D
   (A) go   (C) goes
   (B) going   (D) went

5. My sister is going _____ me at 5:00.   A B C D
   (A) call   (C) calling
   (B) calls   (D) to call

6. We are _____ going to buy a new computer next year. A B C D
   (A) no   (C) not
   (B) don't   (D) won't

7. Why _____ change schools next semester?   A B C D
   (A) they are going to   (C) are they going to
   (B) they go to   (D) do they go to

8. —Is the meeting going to end at 5:00?   A B C D
   —_____. It's going to end at 4:00.
   (A) Yes, it is going to   (C) No it isn't
   (B) Yes, it is   (D) No, not

9. _____ you going to wear a suit?   A B C D
   (A) Do   (C) Are
   (B) Will   (D) Be

10. She will _____ before noon.   A B C D
    (A) leave   (C) leaves
    (B) to leave   (D) leaving

11. They _____ be home tonight.   **A B C D**
    (A) will no   (C) no will
    (B) won't   (D) don't

12. _____ you be at the meeting?   **A B C D**
    (A) Are   (C) Going
    (B) Will   (D) Do

13. Look! Those cars _____!   **A B C D**
    (A) crash   (C) will crash
    (B) crashing   (D) are going to crash

14. —Will you be at school tomorrow?   **A B C D**
    —Yes, I _____.
    (A) will   (C) won't
    (B) am   (D) be

15. —I can't go to class tonight. My car broke down.   **A B C D**
    —I _____ you a ride to class.
    (A) give   (C) 'm going to give
    (B) 'm giving   (D) 'll give

SECTION TWO

Each sentence has four underlined parts. The four underlined parts of the sentence are marked A, B, C, and D. Circle the letter of the one underlined part that is NOT CORRECT.

> **EXAMPLE:**
>
> My friends <u>is</u> here, but we <u>are</u> <u>not</u> <u>studying</u>.   **(A) B C D**
>   A   B C   D

16. <u>Will</u> you <u>going</u> to <u>finish</u> that report <u>soon</u>?   **A B C D**
    A   B   C   D

17. Dan <u>is</u> going <u>to change</u> jobs, but he <u>won't</u> <u>leaves</u> before June.   **A B C D**
       A   B   C   D

18. Sara <u>be going to</u> <u>buy</u> a new dress <u>tomorrow</u> for her sister's wedding.   **A B C D**
       A   B   C   D

19. <u>Are you</u> going to <u>watch</u> TV or <u>you are</u> going <u>to read</u>?   **A B C D**
     A   B   C   D

20. <u>When</u> <u>you will</u> <u>be</u> home <u>tomorrow</u>?   **A B C D**
     A   B   C   D

21. The sky <u>is</u> very dark—it <u>going to</u> <u>rain</u> very <u>soon</u>.   **A B C D**
        A   B   C   D

22. My sister <u>is</u> going to <u>be</u> in Rio <u>next week</u>, and will <u>calls</u> you from the hotel.   **A B C D**
        A   B   C   D

23. Is Jason <u>going</u> <u>to</u> <u>be</u> at the party <u>last night</u>?   **A B C D**
         A   B C   D

24. Why <u>you are</u> <u>going</u> to <u>take</u> the <u>train</u>?   **A B C D**
      A   B   C   D

25. <u>I'm</u> not going <u>take</u> my umbrella because it's <u>not</u> going <u>to rain</u>.   **A B C D**
    A   B   C   D

Word Order: Statements

They read the book to their children.

All over the world, children love Harry Potter.
Adults read the books to their children.
Now adults love Harry too.

CHART CHECK 1

*Circle T (True) or
F (False).*

T F The object
comes between
the subject and
the verb.

STATEMENTS WITH ONE OBJECT

SUBJECT	VERB	OBJECT
I	saw	**the movie**.
She	met	**Harry**.
We	bought	**a new book**.
They	liked	**our gift**.

CHART CHECK 2

*Check the correct
sentence.*

❐ There are two
ways to write a
statement with
two objects.

❐ Use **to** when the
indirect object
(person) comes
first.

STATEMENTS WITH TWO OBJECTS

SUBJECT	VERB	DIRECT OBJECT (THING)	To	INDIRECT OBJECT (PERSON)
He	told	**the story**		**our children**.
We	sent	**a new book**	to	**Ann**.
They	gave	**a gift**		**her**.

SUBJECT	VERB	INDIRECT OBJECT (PERSON)	DIRECT OBJECT (THING)
He	told	**our children**	**the story**.
We	sent	**Ann**	**a new book**.
They	gave	**her**	**a gift**.

EXPRESS CHECK

Check the sentences that have two objects.

☐ I bought a book last night.   ☐ We read a story in school last night.

☐ We sent a book to our friend.   ☐ They sent Phil a letter.

Grammar Explanations

Examples

1. Most statements have the word order:
subject + verb + object

subject	verb	object
■ She	wrote	**a book**.
■ They	loved	**the story**.
■ He	read	**it**.

2. Some verbs can have **two objects**.
The **direct object** is usually a <u>thing</u>.
The **indirect object** is usually a <u>person</u>.
Give, lend, send, show, and *tell* are examples of
verbs that can have two objects.

	indirect object	direct object
verb		
■ I *showed*	**Jack**	**the book**.
■ He *sent*	**me**	**a gift**.

There are two ways to make statements with
two objects:
direct object + *to* + indirect object

OR

indirect object + direct object

	direct object	indirect object
■ Harry gave	**candy** *to*	**Ron**.

	indirect object	direct object
■ Harry gave	**Ron**	**candy**.

▶ **BE CAREFUL!** Don't use *to* when the person is
the first object.

NOT Harry gave ~~to~~ Ron candy.

3. Put information about **place** and **time**
<u>after the object</u>.

	object	place
■ I read	**the book**	***at home***.

	object	time
■ We watched	**a movie**	***last night***.

NOT We watched ~~last night a movie~~.

▶ **BE CAREFUL!** Don't separate the verb and its
object.

USAGE NOTE: In sentences with place and time,
we usually give <u>place before time</u>.

	place	time
■ We watched a movie	***at home***	**last night**.

Check it out!

Some Verbs that Can Have Two Objects ▶▶▶ APPENDIX 6, page 231.

Pronouns: Subject and Object ▶▶▶ UNIT 25, page 110.

1 **FIND** • *Harry Potter lives with his Aunt Petunia and Uncle Vernon. He's a wizard (he has magic powers). Read about Harry. Circle the subjects. Underline the verbs. Put boxes around the objects.*

1. (His aunt and uncle) <u>didn't give</u> [Harry] [nice gifts] on his birthday.

2. They gave him a bed in a closet.

3. He wore old clothes.

4. Then Hogwarts School sent a letter to Harry.

5. The letter changed his life.

6. Hogwarts teaches magic to young wizards.

7. Harry made friends at Hogwarts.

8. His friends gave him gifts at Christmas.

9. He rode a broomstick.

10. He found a magic stone.

2 **DESCRIBE** • *Look at these scenes from* **Shazam School of Magic.** *Unscramble the words in parentheses. Write statements about the pictures.*

1. <u>Shazam sent Eliza a letter.</u>
   (a letter / Eliza / sent / Shazam)

2. _____
   (Olivia / a rabbit / gave / Eliza)

3. _____
   (to / showed / Liam / cards / Eliza)

4. _____
   (Eliza / Liam / her new broom / showed)

5. _____
   (to / Liam / a scarf / gave / Eliza)

6. _____
   (Hector / Liam / handed / a book)

3 **UNSCRAMBLE** • *Write facts about J. K. Rowling, the author of the Harry Potter books. Use the information in parentheses.*

1. When Rowling was a child, <u>her parents read stories to her every night.</u>
   (stories / to /every night / her parents / her / read)

2. As a child, _____
   (she / stories / all the time / wrote)

3. _____
   (to / She / read / her friends / the stories)

4. _____
   (French / in college / studied / Rowling)

5. _____
   (in Europe / English / She / taught)

6. _____
   (wrote / Rowling / in a café / her first book)

7. _____
   (finished / her book / in 1994 / She / in Scotland)

8. _____
   (in England / The book / many prizes / in 1997 / won)

4 **EDIT** • *Read this letter. Find and correct six mistakes in word order. The first mistake is already corrected.*

Dear Mum,

                                     to Harry in the morning
    Christmas was great. I gave your gifts ~~in the morning to Harry~~. He loved

the sweater. He the chocolate liked too. He was surprised. Harry's aunt and

uncle never send gifts to Harry. We ate at noon Christmas dinner. I had a lot of

turkey 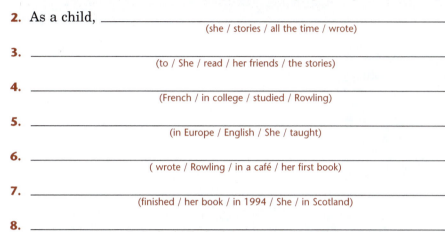, ham , potatoes, and pie . We got after dinner gifts.

I got three mice . Then we outside threw snowballs

for hours. We went to sleep early—we were so tired!

    I'll write to you another letter soon. Hogwarts is great, but I miss home.

Love,

Ron

Word Order:
Wh- Questions

Who did you ask? / Who asked you?

CHECK POINT

Check the correct answer.

In this quiz show, players _____ questions.

☐ answer   ☐ ask

CHART CHECK

Circle T (True) or F (False).

T   F   All *wh-* questions use a form of *do*.

T   F   *Wh-* questions about the subject use the base form of the verb.

WH- QUESTIONS

Wʜ- Word	Do	Subject	Verb
When	does	John	watch TV?
Where	does	he	watch?
What	did	he	break?
Who	did	John	see?

ANSWERS

ANSWERS
(He watches) **at night**.
(He watches) **in the kitchen**.
(He broke) **a glass**.
(He saw) **Alex**.

WH- QUESTIONS ABOUT THE SUBJECT

Wʜ- Word	Verb	
What	broke?	
Who	saw	John?

ANSWERS

Subject
A glass (broke).
Sara (saw him).

EXPRESS CHECK

Check all the wh- *questions about the subject.*

❐ Who asked you?   ❐ How much money did you win?   ❐ Who did you see?

❐ Where did you go?   ❐ What happened next?

Grammar Explanations	Examples
1. Use *wh-* **questions** to ask for <u>information</u>. Begin *wh-* questions with **question words**, for example, *who, what, where, when, why, which, how, how much, how many.*	■ **Who** did you like? ■ **Who** saw Sara? ■ **Which** question did she get wrong? ■ **How many** people played?

2. Many *wh-* questions are about the **object**.
 	
Wh- questions about the object and *wh-* questions with **When** and **Where** have the same word order as *yes/no* questions:
helping verb + subject + main verb
 	
Do (*do, does, did*) is a helping verb.
 	
Be can be a helping verb too.
	object
	I saw *Sara*.
	↙
	■ **Who** did you see?
	
	   Did you watch the show?
	■ What **did you watch**?
	
	   Did you see her?
	■ When **did you see** her?
	   Are you watching the show?
	■ What **are you watching**?

3. Some *wh-* questions are about the **subject**. *Wh-* questions about the subject have the same word order as statements: *wh-* **word + verb** ▶ **BE CAREFUL!** Do not use a form of **do** (*do, does, did*) for *wh-* questions about the subject.	subject *Sara* won the game. ↓ ■ **Who** won the game? *Something* happened. ↓ ■ **What** happened? *Two people* played. ↓ ■ **How many people** played? ■ **Who won** the game? NOT Who ~~did win~~ the game?

1 MATCH • *Each question has an answer. Match each question with the correct answer.*

Questions

_b_ **1.** Who asked the questions?

_____ **2.** Who did Alex ask?

_____ **3.** How many people saw Sara?

_____ **4.** How many people did Sara see?

_____ **5.** Which player answered?

_____ **6.** Which question did he answer?

Answers

a. Thousands of people saw her.

b. Alex asked the questions.

c. John answered.

d. He answered Alex's question.

e. He asked John.

f. She saw four people.

2 CHOOSE • *Circle the correct words to complete these questions.*

JEOPARDY! The #1 TV Quiz Show in the United States

Q: When began the show / (did the show begin)?
    1.

A: The first show was in 1964.

Q: Who had the idea / did the idea have for the show?
    2.

A: Merv Griffin thought of the idea.

Q: Who asked Griffin / did Griffin ask to host the show?
    3.

A: Griffin asked Art Fleming to host the first show.

Q: How many people watch / do watch *Jeopardy*?
    4.

A: Thirty-two million people watch the show every week.

Q: Who hosts / does host the show today?
    5.

A: Alex Trebek hosts the show today.

Q: How many people play / do play?
    6.

A: Three people play the game.

Today, Alex Trebek hosts the show.

Q: How much money won the #1 winner / did the #1 winner win?
    7.

A: He won $1,155,102 plus a new car!

Q: Really! How do I get / I get on the show?
    8.

A: First, you take a fifty-question test. Then you have an interview. Good luck!

3 **ASK •** *Read these statements. Then ask questions about the <u>underlined</u> words.*

1. <u>Leonardo da Vinci</u> painted the Mona Lisa.

   Who painted the Mona Lisa?

2. Leonardo da Vinci painted <u>the Mona Lisa</u>.

   Who did Leonardo da Vinci paint?

3. Gustave Eiffel completed the Eiffel Tower <u>in 1889</u>.

_____

4. John Logie Baird invented <u>color TV</u>.

_____

5. The Jin Mao building in China has <u>88</u> floors.

_____

6. <u>More than 18 million</u> people live in Mexico City.

_____

7. Einstein won the Nobel Prize <u>in 1921</u>.

_____

8. <u>Percy L. Spencer</u> invented the microwave oven.

_____

The Eiffel Tower

The Jin Mao building

4 **EDIT •** *Read this e-mail message to* Jeopardy! *Find and correct five mistakes in the use of* wh- *questions. The first mistake is already corrected.*

☐ ONLINE CONTACT FORM	_ □ ✕

Name: Lizzy Que

E-mail Address: quizzylizzy@quest.com

Subject: About the show

        do I get

I would like to be on your show. How ~~I get~~ on it? I hear there's a test. How many questions

the test has? When do I take the test? Who does give the test? Where do I take the test?

How do I prepare for the test? After I take the test, what does happen next? When people get

the results?

☐ Done   ● Internet

SelfTest

Circle the letter of the correct answer to complete each sentence.

EXAMPLE:

Alicia and Paulo _____ students.   **A (B) C D**
(A) am   (C) be
(B) are   (D) is

1. _____ last night.   **A B C D**
   (A) Sonia dinner cooked   (C) Dinner Sonia cooked
   (B) Sonia cooked dinner   (D) Dinner cooked Sonia

2. Harry mailed a gift _____ his friend.   **A B C D**
   (A) at   (C) —
   (B) on   (D) to

3. I gave the book _____.   **A B C D**
   (A) him   (C) he
   (B) to him   (D) to he

4. The teacher gave _____.   **A B C D**
   (A) to the class homework   (C) the class to homework
   (B) the class homework   (D) homework the class

5. They _____.   **A B C D**
   (A) the movie saw yesterday   (C) saw the movie yesterday
   (B) yesterday saw the movie   (D) saw yesterday the movie

6. We _____.   **A B C D**
   (A) read at home the newspaper   (C) at home read the newspaper
   (B) read the newspaper at home   (D) the newspaper at home read

7. —_____ did you go last night?   **A B C D**
   —The movies.
   (A) What   (C) Who
   (B) Where   (D) Which

8. —Which movie _____?   **A B C D**
   —*Harry Potter and the Chamber of Secrets.*
   (A) you saw   (C) did you see
   (B) saw you   (D) you did see

9. —Who _____ to the party?   **A B C D**
   —Marta invited me.
   (A) invited you   (C) you did invite
   (B) did you invite   (D) you invited

10. —Who _____ there? A B C D
—I saw Karl and his girlfriend.
(A) saw you   (C) you did see
(B) did you see   (D) you saw

11. —What _____ in class yesterday? A B C D
—The teacher gave a test.
(A) did happen   (C) does happen
(B) happened   (D) happens

12. —Who told David about the party? A B C D
—Jessica. _____ told him.
(A) Her   (C) They
(B) Him   (D) She

SECTION TWO

Each sentence has four underlined parts. The four underlined parts of the sentence are marked A, B, C, and D. Circle the letter of the one underlined part that is NOT CORRECT.

EXAMPLE:

My friends is here, but we are not studying. (A) B C D
A   B   C   D

13. Jill sent John and me last week a letter. A B C D
A   B   C   D

14. Mr. Harvey math teaches to my sister on Mondays. A B C D
A   B   C   D

15. John saw last night a movie about a magic school. A B C D
A   B   C   D

16. How many students did take the test in Ms. Rivera's class? A B C D
A   B   C   D

17. My sister sent a book me last week. A B C D
A   B   C   D

18. My family takes every year a vacation in Europe. A B C D
A   B   C   D

19. Who you saw at the movies last night? A B C D
A   B   C   D

20. I after class showed my homework to the teacher. A B C D
A   B   C   D

21. We dinner made for our friends at home. A B C D
A   B   C   D

22. Which sweater she wear to the party last night? A B C D
A   B   C   D

23. Vilma gave to Miguel a book for his birthday. A B C D
A   B   C   D

24. Who did told you about the new bookstore and café on Elm Street? A B C D
A   B   C   D

25. Who did see you with Mehmet at the airport last night? A B C D
A   B   C   D

Nouns: Common/Proper, Singular/Plural

Harrods sells pianos from Japan.

THE **world** COMES TO *Harrods*!

"All **things** for all **people** EVERYWHERE."

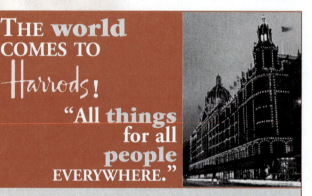

- **Gucci shoes** from **Italy**
- **Rolex watches** from **Switzerland**
- **Calvin Klein jeans** from the **United States**
- **Henckel knives** from **Germany**
- **Yamaha pianos** from **Japan**—and much more

Harrods is open six **days** a **week**: **Monday–Saturday**, 10–7

We're located at **Brompton Road, Knightsbridge, London**

Or visit our **Website** at www.harrods.com

CHECK POINT

Check the correct answers.

The ad gives the store's _____.

❑ name   ❑ business hours

❑ address   ❑ prices

❑ phone number ❑ Website address

CHART CHECK

Check the correct answers.

Common nouns begin with a _____ letter.

❑ capital (big)

❑ small

_____ nouns usually end in -**s**.

❑ Singular

❑ Plural

COMMON NOUNS	PROPER NOUNS
store	Harrods
country	England
city	London
day	Monday

SINGULAR NOUNS	PLURAL NOUNS
shoe	shoe**s**
watch	watch**es**
knife	kni**ves**
man	m**e**n

EXPRESS CHECK

Circle the correct words.

I bought one <u>watch / watches</u>, five <u>T-shirt / T-shirts</u>, and two <u>pen / pens</u>.

Grammar Explanations	**Examples**

1. Use **common nouns** for people, places, or things.

- My **sister** works from 10 to 7 in a **store**.
- She sells **shoes**.

2. Use **proper nouns** for the <u>names</u> of people, places, or things.

- **Anne** works from 10 to 7 at **Harrods**.
- She sells **Gucci** shoes.

Write proper nouns with a <u>capital</u> (big) letter.

- The store is in **L**ondon, **E**ngland.

3. Use **singular nouns** for <u>one</u> person, place, or thing.

- My **sister** has *a job* in *a store*.

4. Use **plural nouns** for <u>two or more</u> people, places, or things.

- She has *two jobs*.

Add *-s* or *-es* to make most nouns plural.

store → store**s**   glass → glass**es**
watch → watch**es**   box → box**es**

▶ **BE CAREFUL!** There are sometimes spelling changes when you add *-s* or *-es*.

city → cit**ies**
knife → kni**ves**

5. Some plural nouns are **irregular**. Do not add *-s* or *-es* to these nouns.

child → child**ren**   foot → f**ee**t
woman → wom**en**   person → **people**

6. Some nouns are always **plural**.

**clothes   pants   jeans   shorts
pajamas   glasses   scissors**

USAGE NOTE: We often use *a pair of* with these words (but not with *clothes*).

- I bought *a pair of* **jeans**.
- I bought *two pairs of* **shorts**.

7. **REMEMBER: Singular nouns** need <u>singular verbs</u> and <u>singular pronouns</u>.

- The **store** *is* open on Saturday, but *it's* closed on Sunday.

Plural nouns need <u>plural verbs</u> and <u>plural pronouns</u>.

- The **stores** *are* open on Saturday, but *they're* closed on Sunday.

Check it out!

Spelling Rules for Regular Plural Nouns ➤➤➤ APPENDIX 20, page 241.
Pronunciation Rules for Regular Plural Nouns ➤➤➤ APPENDIX 27, page 244.
Some Nouns with Irregular Plural Forms ➤➤➤ APPENDIX 8, page 232.
Proper Nouns ➤➤➤ APPENDIX 10, page 234.

1 **FIND** • *Read this information about Harrods. Circle all the singular nouns. Underline all the plural nouns.*

Harrods

It started as a small (store) in 1849.

Today it sells 1.2 million products.

4,000 people work there.

They come from more than 50 countries.

You can buy a pet there.

You can buy clothes for your pet!

You can listen to free concerts.

You can buy a real car for your children!

2 **COMPLETE** • *Order things from a store catalog. Choose the correct item from the box. Write the name of the item (singular or plural).*

~~cup~~   glass   glasses   jeans   knife   loaf   pan
pants   ~~shorts~~   strawberry   vase   watch

Order Form

	NUMBER	ITEM		NUMBER	ITEM
1.	4	cups	7.	2	Swiss _____
2.	1	pair of shorts	8.	1	
3.	1		9.	1	
4.	8		10.	1	
5.	2	_____ of bread	11.	2	
6.	12	chocolate-covered _____	12.	2	

3 **COMPLETE •** *Read these sentences. Complete them with the correct form of the noun—singular or plural—and the verb in parentheses.*

1. Harrods department ____**store**____ ____**is**____ in London.
   <small>(store)</small> <small>(be)</small>

2. The _____ _____ Brompton Place.
   <small>(address)</small> <small>(be)</small>

3. _____ always _____ to see it.
   <small>(Tourist)</small> <small>(go)</small>

4. _____ _____ to shop there.
   <small>(Person)</small> <small>(love)</small>

5. The _____ _____ products from all over the world.
   <small>(store)</small> <small>(sell)</small>

6. _____ _____ a very popular item.
   <small>(Jeans)</small> <small>(be)</small>

7. Twenty _____ _____ food to Harrods customers.
   <small>(restaurant)</small> <small>(sell)</small>

8. All their _____ _____ delicious.
   <small>(dessert)</small> <small>(taste)</small>

9. The _____ _____ a dress code! You can't wear certain clothes there.
   <small>(store)</small> <small>(have)</small>

10. Bicycle _____, for example, _____ OK to wear.
    <small>(shorts)</small> <small>(not be)</small>

4 **EDIT •** *Read this postcard. Find and correct fourteen mistakes in the use of nouns and the verbs and pronouns that go with them. The first mistake is already corrected.*

Harrods **Brompton Place, London**

London
Hi! I love England, and ~~london~~ is great. On monday we went to Harrods. There were so many persons there! I bought a lot of thing. My jean was really old, so I got two new pairs. They have great things for childs too. I bought two watch—one for my little Brother and one for Jennie.

One strange things: The store have a dress code! You can't come in if your clothes is dirty. And you can't wear bicycle shorts in the store. (But you can buy it there, of course!!)
See you in a few Weeks.   S.

68

To: Roberto García

300 Balmes

08006 Barcelona

Spain

Nouns: Count/Non-Count

Cream? Sugar? One teaspoon? Two teaspoons?

CHECK POINT

Check the correct answer.

The woman doesn't want to count _____.

☐ eggs

☐ cream

☐ calories

CHART CHECK

Circle T (True) or F (False).

T F   Count nouns can be singular or plural.

T F   Use plural verbs with non-count nouns.

SINGULAR COUNT NOUNS

	Noun	**Verb**	
An	**egg**	**is**	broken.

PLURAL COUNT NOUNS

	Noun	**Verb**	
Three	**eggs**	**are**	broken.

NON-COUNT NOUNS

Noun	**Verb**	
Sugar	**is**	sweet.

EXPRESS CHECK

Check the sentences with count nouns.

❏ Apples are cheap today.   ❏ Please buy sugar.

❏ I love ice cream.   ❏ There's only one egg in the refrigerator.

Grammar Explanations	Examples

1. **Count nouns** are things that are easy to count: *one apple, two apples, three apples, . . .*

- one **apple**   ■ two **recipes**
- three **cookies**   ■ twenty **chips**

              singular   plural

Count nouns are <u>singular or plural</u>.

- I ate an **apple**. She ate two **apples**.

2. **Non-count nouns** are things that we usually do not count. Some types of non-count nouns:

LIQUIDS AND GASES: **water, milk, air**
VERY SMALL THINGS: **rice, salt, sand**
SCHOOL SUBJECTS: **English, math, art**
IDEAS AND FEELINGS: **beauty, love, hate**

Non-count nouns have only a <u>singular</u> form.

- Did you buy **rice**?
  NOT Did you buy ~~rices~~?

3. Use <u>singular verbs</u> with **singular count nouns**.

- This **orange** *comes* from Florida.

Use <u>plural verbs</u> with **plural count nouns**.

- These **oranges** *come* from Florida.

Use <u>singular verbs</u> with **non-count nouns**.

- This **coffee** *comes* from Colombia.

4. Use a **measure word** + *of* with count and non-count nouns to talk about **quantities**.

- I had **a bowl of** soup, **two cups of** tea, and **a bag of** chips for lunch.

Some types of measure words:

SHAPES: **a loaf of** bread, **a bar of** candy
PORTIONS: **a slice of** bread, **a bowl of** soup, **a piece of** cake
CONTAINERS: **a can of** beans, **a bottle of** milk, **a container of** yogurt
MEASUREMENTS: **a teaspoon of** sugar, **a pound of** potatoes

Check it out!

Some Common Non-Count Nouns ➤➤➤ APPENDIX 9, page 233.
Some Common Measure Words ➤➤➤ APPENDIX 13, page 235.

1 **FIND** • *Read this article. Underline the nouns for food. For each food, write **N** for non-count or **C** for count.*

14 • SECTION 4 • LIFESTYLES

Good News, Bad News

Good News: Some "bad" <u>food</u> is really good for you.

N

(But remember to eat small portions.)

☺ <u>Nuts</u> are healthy. They have a lot of fat, but it's a healthy type.

C

☺ Chocolate is good! It's good for your teeth and for your heart. It makes you feel good too.

☺ Coffee isn't bad. It helps you work or study.

Bad News: Junk food *is* really bad for you.

☹ Hamburgers from fast-food restaurants are high in fat, and it's not a healthy type.

They also have a lot of salt.

☹ Soda is high in sugar. Nothing in it is good for you.

Remember, the rules for a good diet are still the same: Eat lots of vegetables, fruit, beans, fish, and chicken.

2 **DESCRIBE** • *Look at these pictures of lunches. Make a list of food for each lunch. Use the correct form of the words in the box. Use a measure word where necessary.*

bag bowl can container cup	apple banana cheese milk
glass piece ~~slice~~	noodle nut ~~pizza~~ soda tea yogurt

1. _____two slices of pizza_____
   _____
   _____

2. _____
   _____
   _____

3. _____
   _____

4. _____
   _____

3 | **COMPLETE** • *Claire is a TV chef. Read her directions for making a dessert. Complete them with the correct form of the words in parentheses.*

Welcome to Claire's Kitchen. Tonight I'm going to show you an easy dessert.

<u>Brownies</u> <u>are</u> also delicious! Let's begin
1. (Brownie)   **2.** (be)

First, we need one _____ of _____
3. (cup)   **4.** (sugar)

and a half _____ of _____.
5. (cup)   **6.** (butter)

The _____ _____ already soft. Cook together slowly.
7. (butter)   **8.** (be)

Now add two _____ of _____. Use *very* low heat because
9. (bar)   **10.** (chocolate)

_____ _____. Next, beat two _____ and add
11. (chocolate)   **12.** (burn)   **13.** (egg)

them. The _____ _____ already in this bowl. Now I'm going
14. (flour)   **15.** (be)

to add the chocolate from the pot. Mmmm. The _____ _____
16. (chocolate)   **17.** (smell)

good. Finally, I'm adding _____. _____ _____
18. (nut)   **19.** (Nut)   **20.** (taste)

great, and they're good for you. Pour into a baking pan and bake for twenty minutes.

Enjoy!

4 | **EDIT** • *Read this food quiz. Find and correct eight mistakes in the use of count and non-count nouns and the verbs that go with them. The first mistake is already corrected. Then you can take the quiz and check your answers below.*

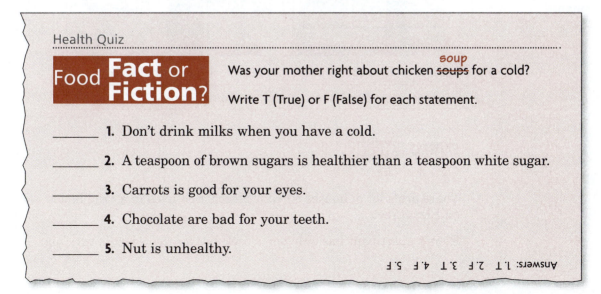

Health Quiz

Food **Fact or Fiction?**   Was your mother right about chicken ~~soups~~ ^{soup} for a cold?

Write T (True) or F (False) for each statement.

_____ **1.** Don't drink milks when you have a cold.

_____ **2.** A teaspoon of brown sugars is healthier than a teaspoon white sugar.

_____ **3.** Carrots is good for your eyes.

_____ **4.** Chocolate are bad for your teeth.

_____ **5.** Nut is unhealthy.

Answers: 1. T   2. F   3. T   4. F   5. F

Articles: *A/An* and *The*

It's not a closet. It's the kitchen!

That's **a** big closet.

That's **the** kitchen. **The** closet is much smaller!

CHECK POINT

Circle T (True) or F (False).

T   F   The apartment has one kitchen.

T   F   The kitchen is large.

T   F   The apartment has several closets.

CHART CHECK

Check the correct answer.

☐ Eleni lives in Apartment 1A.

☐ Bob's house is small.

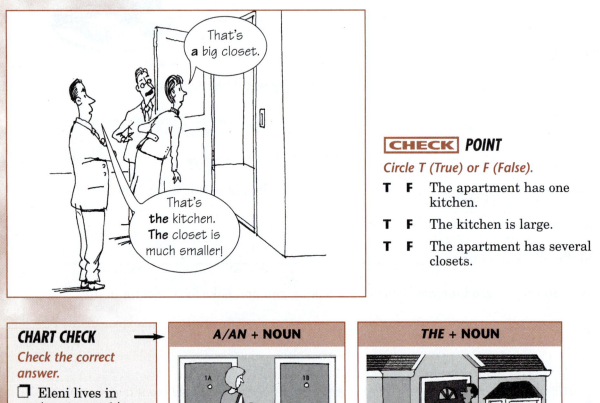

A/AN + NOUN	*THE* + NOUN
Eleni is going to open **a door**.	Bob is going to open **the door**.
She lives in **an apartment**.	**The house** is small.

EXPRESS CHECK

Circle **a** *or* **the**.

There are a lot of houses on Elm Street. Bob lives in <u>a / the</u> house on Elm Street.

Eleni's apartment has only one closet, but <u>a / the</u> closet is very big.

Grammar Explanations

Examples

1. Use *a* or *an* only with <u>singular count nouns</u>. *A* or *an* means there are several people or things, but you are <u>not</u> saying <u>which one</u>.

- Can I have *a cookie*?

  (There are several cookies. I want one. It's not important which one.)

Use *an* before <u>vowel sounds</u>.
(Vowels are *a, e, i, o, u.*)

- **an a**partment
- **an o**ld house

▶ **BE CAREFUL!** Choose *a* or *an* because of the sound, not the spelling.

- **an** hour (Say "an *our.*")
  NOT ~~a hour~~
- a university (Say "a *yew*niversity.")
  NOT ~~an university~~

2. Use *the* when it is clear <u>which person or thing you mean</u>.

- Can I have *the chocolate cookie*?

  (There is only one chocolate cookie. I want it.)

3. Use *a* or *an* <u>to say what someone or something is</u>.

- Mr. Chen is *a teacher*.
  (That's his job.)
- That's *a big closet*.

Use *the* when there is <u>only one</u> of someone or something.

- Mr. Chen is *the teacher*.
  (This class has only one teacher.)
- *The floor* is clean.
  (The room has only one floor.)
- *The sun* is hot today.
  (There is only one sun.)

4. Use *a* or *an* <u>the first time</u> you talk about something. Use *the* <u>after the first time</u> you talk about something.

- We looked at *an apartment* today.
  The apartment was too small.

5. **BE CAREFUL!** Don't use singular count nouns alone. Always use *a, an, the,* or a **possessive** *(my, Tom's)*.

- He's *a neighbor*.
- He's *the neighbor*.
- He's *our neighbor*.
  NOT ~~He's neighbor.~~

1 **MATCH** • *Look at the pictures. Check the sentence that matches each picture.*

1. ☐ Close a window.
   ☑ Close the window.

2. ☐ Have an apple.
   ☐ Have the apple.

3. ☐ It's on a shelf.
   ☐ It's on the shelf.

4. ☐ Turn off a light.
   ☐ Turn off the light.

5. ☐ I'll walk a dog.
   ☐ I'll walk the dog.

6. ☐ Take a bag.
   ☐ Take the bag.

2 **CHOOSE** • *Eleni is looking for an apartment. Read her conversations with a building owner and with a neighbor. Circle **a**, **an**, or **the**.*

1. **ELENI:** Do you have a /(an) apartment for rent?
       a.

    OWNER: Are you a / the student? We don't rent to students.
       b.

    ELENI: No. I'm a / the teacher. I teach at City College.
       c.

    OWNER: We have one apartment. It's on a / the fourth floor.
       d.

    ELENI: Can I see an / the apartment now?
       e.

    OWNER: Sure. We'll use the stairs. An / The elevator is broken.
       f.

2. **OWNER:** It's a / the nice, bright kitchen. It has a / the big window.
       a.   **b.**

    ELENI: Can I open a / the window? It's hot in here.
       c.

    OWNER: Sorry. A / The window doesn't open.
       d.

3. **TOM:** Hi. What's wrong?

    ELENI: I'm looking for a / an new apartment.
       a.

    TOM: There's a / an empty one in my building. An / The owner says it's nice.
       b.   **c.**

3 **COMPLETE** • *Eleni is giving a party. Read these conversations. Complete them with* **a**, **an**, *or* **the**.

1. **TAMMY:** I brought you _____*a*_____ plant for your new home.
   a.

   ELENI: It's beautiful. I'm going to put it in _____ living room.
   b.

   TAMMY: This is _____ great apartment. How did you find it?
   c.

   ELENI: Tom told me about it. He's _____ really nice guy.
   d.

2. **CORY:** Who is _____ man next to Tom?
   a.

   ELENI: That's Bob Chin. He teaches at _____ university in Canada.
   b.

   CORY: Is Tom _____ teacher too?
   c.

   ELENI: No. He's _____ accountant.
   d.

3. **CORY:** Please have some coffee. There are cups on _____ table.
   a.

   BOB: Can I have _____ cup of tea?
   b.

   CORY: Of course. And have _____ cookie too. I baked them this afternoon.
   c.

4. **CORY:** It was _____ fun party, Eleni. Thanks for inviting me.
   a.

   TAMMY: I enjoyed _____ party too.
   b.

   ELENI: Thanks for coming. And thank you for _____ beautiful plant, Tammy.
   c.

4 **EDIT** • *Read Eleni's note to the owner of her building. Find and correct six mistakes in the use of* **a**, **an**, *and* **the**. *The first mistake is already corrected.*

There are some problems in my apartment:

 The
 ~~A~~ refrigerator is not working.

I saw the mouse in a kitchen last night!

An ceiling in the living room is leaking. I need a umbrella when I sit on

the sofa! There was a lot of water on a living room floor this morning.

Could you please fix these problems this week?

Thank you.

E. Petras
E. Petras
Apt. 1-B

No Article (Ø) or *The*

I love music. The music here is great!

CHECK *POINT*

Circle T (True) or F (False).

T   F   The man likes only rock music.

CHART CHECK	**NO ARTICLE (Ø)**	**THE**
Check the correct answer.	**NON-COUNT NOUNS**	**NON-COUNT NOUNS**
☐ You can use no article (Ø) with singular count nouns.	She loves **music**. She saves **money** for concert tickets. She hates **traffic**.	**The music** on the radio is too loud. **The money** is on the table. **The traffic** for the concert was awful.
☐ You can use no article (Ø) with non-count nouns.		**SINGULAR COUNT NOUNS**
		I bought **the last ticket**. We have **the new CD** by Wu Bai. I like **the first song**.
	PLURAL COUNT NOUNS	**PLURAL COUNT NOUNS**
	Tickets are expensive. He collects **CDs**. He writes **songs**.	We lost **the tickets** for tonight. **The CDs** on the table are mine. He wrote **the songs** on this CD.

EXPRESS CHECK

Circle the correct words.

A: Did you buy <u>the CD / CD</u>?

B: Yes. I love <u>the music / music</u> on it.

Grammar Explanations	Examples
1. Use **no article (Ø)** for <u>general statements</u>. (You are not talking about a specific person or thing.)	**A:** Do you go to **concerts** often? **B:** Yes. I love **music**.
Use ***the*** for <u>a specific person or thing</u>. (It is clear which person or thing you are talking about.)	**A:** I enjoyed **the concert**. **B:** Me too. **The music** was great.
2. You can use **no article (Ø)** with <u>plural count nouns</u>.	■ He writes **songs**. ■ **People** enjoy his music. ■ The band gives **concerts**.
You can also use **no article (Ø)** with <u>non-count nouns</u>.	■ He loves **music**. ■ He sings about **happiness**. ■ **Money** isn't important to him. ■ He gives **advice** to new performers.
▶ **BE CAREFUL!** Don't use singular count nouns alone. Always use ***a, an, the,*** or a **possessive** (*my, Tom's*).	■ Where's ***the*** **new CD**? NOT Where's ~~new CD~~?
3. You can use ***the*** with <u>singular and plural count nouns</u>.	■ I'll meet you at **the concert**. ■ Our seats are near **the door**. ■ **The people** behind us are dancing. ■ Do you know **the words** of that song?
You can also use ***the*** with <u>non-count nouns</u>.	■ Did I give you **the money** for our tickets? ■ I really enjoyed **the music**.

Check it out!

Nouns: Count/Non-Count ▶▶▶ UNIT 19, page 84.

Some Common Non-Count Nouns ▶▶▶ APPENDIX 9, page 233.

1 **TRUE OR FALSE** • *Some people enjoyed the concert. Read their conversations. Then circle T (True) or F (False) for each statement.*

1. **CARL:** Are you enjoying the concert?
   FAYE: Yes, I am. I like this group.

   (T) **F**   Carl and Faye are at a concert.

2. **CARL:** Where do you work?
   FAYE: I'm a student. I'm studying music.

   T **F**   Faye is studying a specific song.

3. **CARL:** I write about concerts for a newspaper.
   FAYE: That sounds like an interesting job.

   T **F**   Faye knows the concerts Carl is talking about.

4. **FAYE:** Do you interview musicians?
   CARL: Sure. I interviewed Wu Bai last month.

   T **F**   Faye is asking about the musicians at this concert.

5. **FAYE:** I like the songs on his new CD.
   CARL: I like them too.

   T **F**   Faye is talking about all Wu Bai's songs.

2 **CHOOSE** • *Read about Taiwanese rock star Wu Bai. Circle the correct words.*

1. Wu Bai writes and sings the songs /(songs).

2. He often wins the awards / awards for his songs.

3. He's the leader / leader of China Blue, a Taipei band.

4. A lot of people like the music / music of Wu Bai.

5. They like the musicians / musicians of China Blue too.

6. The rock music / Rock music is very popular in Asia.

7. Wu Bai gives the concerts / concerts all over the world / world.

8. Concerts / The concerts always get good reviews.

9. A Singapore newspaper called Wu Bai "The King / King of Chinese Rock."

10. Wu Bai also acts in the action movies / action movies.

11. Rock stars / The rock stars are often the bad actors / bad actors.

12. But Wu Bai is a good actor. He was excellent in the movie / movie *Time and Tide.*

13. He played the bad guy / bad guy in the movie / movie.

3 **COMPLETE** • *Read these conversations. Write* **the** *when necessary.*

1. **NING:** Look! There's ___the___ new movie with Wu Bai.
                                        a.

  WANDA: I'm a little tired of _____ action movies
                                    b.

  NING: *Amélie* is playing. That's about _____ love.
                                              c.

2. **LON:** I think _____ stamps on that letter are beautiful.
                         a.

  INES: They're from China. Do you collect _____ stamps?
                                               b.

  LON: Yes. I get _____ mail from people all over _____ world.
                      c.   **d.**

3. **TRACY:** Did you go to _____ mall yesterday?
                                a.

  JANA: Yes, I did. I needed _____ clothes. I'm going on vacation next week.
                                 b.

  TRACY: Did you see _____ bathing suits in Sun Spot? They're on sale.
                         c.

  JANA: No, I didn't. I need _____ ski boots.
                                 d.

4. **EVA:** Where's _____ camera?
                        a.

  DOM: It's in _____ closet. Why?
                   b.

  EVA: I'm taking _____ photography this semester. My class starts today.
                      c.

  DOM: Great! You can photograph _____ musicians at _____
                                     d.   **e.**
  concert tomorrow.

  EVA: You can't take _____ pictures at _____ concerts. It's not allowed.
                         f.   **g.**

4 **EDIT** • *Read this review of a new CD. Find and correct seven mistakes in the use of* **the** *and* **no article (Ø)**. *The first mistake is already corrected.*

11 ★ ENTERTAINMENT

New Releases

BY BOB KOPKE

                    Rock
~~The rock~~ music has a great new band. The group, Far Mountain, just released its first CD. *Walking Along the River* is a good beginning. The leader, Grace Lee, has a beautiful voice, songs are very interesting, and the musicians are great. Lee wrote several songs for CD.

Her songs are about loneliness, the hope, and friendship. The friends are important to Lee. One of her best songs, "Where Are They?", is about her schoolmates in Taiwan. You can hear song on the group's Website, www.farmountain.com. Jorge Santos is the guitar player, and drummer is Zhang Teng-hui.

Quantifiers: *Some* and *Any*

Did you buy any clothes?

> We bought **some** gray sweaters last time. Do you have **any** black ones?

Young couple at a flea market

CHECK POINT

Check the correct answer.

The couple bought _____.

☐ a gray sweater

☐ more than one gray sweater

☐ black sweaters

CHART CHECK

Check the correct answer(s).

We usually use **any** in _____.

☐ questions

☐ affirmative statements

☐ negative statements

QUESTIONS			
	ANY	**NOUN**	
Did you buy	**any**	lamps dishes clothes food	at the market?

AFFIRMATIVE STATEMENTS		
	SOME	**NOUN**
I bought	**some**	lamps. dishes. clothes. food.

NEGATIVE STATEMENTS		
	ANY	**NOUN**
I didn't buy	**any**	lamps. dishes. clothes. food.

EXPRESS CHECK

Circle the correct words.

I bought <u>some / any</u> hats at the market.

I didn't buy <u>some / any</u> furniture.

Grammar Explanations

Examples

---

1. *Some* means <u>an amount</u>, but it doesn't say exactly how much or how many.

A: We need *some money* for lunch.
B: I have $5. Is that enough?

■ *Some people* go to markets every week.

Use *some* in <u>affirmative statements</u>.

A: I saw *some chairs* at the market.
B: I bought *some furniture* there last week.

Use *some* with <u>plural count nouns</u> and with <u>non-count nouns</u>.

PLURAL COUNT NOUNS	NON-COUNT NOUNS
■ some chairs	■ some furniture
■ some hamburgers	■ some food
■ some CDs	■ some music

---

2. Use *any* in <u>questions</u> and in <u>negative statements</u>.

A: Do you have *any dishes*?
B: Sorry, I don't have *any dishes* this week.

Use *any* with <u>plural count nouns</u> and with <u>non-count nouns</u>.

A: Are there *any chairs*?
B: No, there isn't *any furniture*.

---

3. You can use *some* and *any* <u>without a noun</u>.

A: I want to buy some old bowls.
B: We had *some* last week.
   (some = some bowls)

We don't have *any* this week.
(any = any bowls)

---

4. Use *some* in <u>questions</u> when you <u>offer</u> something.

■ Do you want *some coffee*?

Also use *some* in <u>questions</u> when you <u>ask for</u> something.

■ I'm thirsty. Could I have *some water*?

Check it out!

Nouns: Count/Non-Count ►►► UNIT 19, page 84.

Some Common Non-Count Nouns ►►► APPENDIX 9, page 233.

1 **FIND** • *Read this article about a flea market. Underline* **some** + **noun** *and* **any** + **noun**. *Circle* **some** *and* **any** *without a noun.*

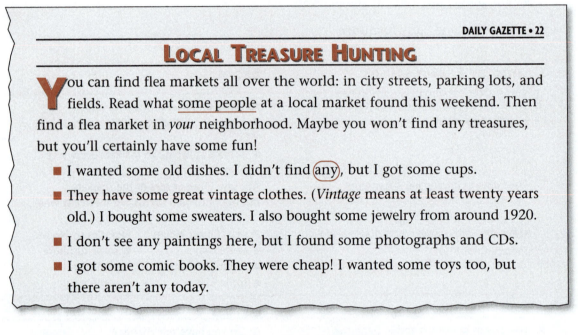

DAILY GAZETTE • 22

LOCAL TREASURE HUNTING

You can find flea markets all over the world: in city streets, parking lots, and fields. Read what <u>some people</u> at a local market found this weekend. Then find a flea market in *your* neighborhood. Maybe you won't find any treasures, but you'll certainly have some fun!

- I wanted some old dishes. I didn't find (any), but I got some cups.
- They have some great vintage clothes. (*Vintage* means at least twenty years old.) I bought some sweaters. I also bought some jewelry from around 1920.
- I don't see any paintings here, but I found some photographs and CDs.
- I got some comic books. They were cheap! I wanted some toys too, but there aren't any today.

CHECK • *What did people see at the flea market? Check all the items.*

☐ dishes ☐ vintage clothes ☐ jewelry ☐ photographs ☐ comic books
☑ cups ☐ sweaters ☐ paintings ☐ CDs ☐ toys

2 **CHOOSE** • *Read these conversations. Circle the correct words.*

1. **ANDREA:** Excuse me. I'm looking for <u>any / (some)</u> old cookbooks.
   a.

   SELLER: We had <u>any / some</u> yesterday, but I sold them all.
   b.

   ANDREA: Do you have <u>any / some</u> books about art?
   c.

   SELLER: Yes, there are <u>any / some</u> on that shelf.
   d.

2. **YASMIN:** I'm hungry. Do they sell <u>any / some</u> food at this flea market?
   a.

   GALENO: They usually have food, but I don't see <u>any / some</u> this afternoon.
   b.

   YASMIN: Wait here. I think I see <u>any / some</u> food stands over there.
   c.

   GALENO: Here's <u>any / some</u> money. Could you get me <u>any / some</u> coffee, please?
   d.   **e.**

3. **HIDEKI:** Look at those old tools! My grandfather used <u>any / some</u> just like them!
   a.

   NANAKO: Did he give you <u>any / some</u>? <u>Any / Some</u> people collect them.
   b.   **c.**

3 **COMPLETE** • *Read these conversations. Complete them with* **some** *or* **any** *and the correct form of the words in parentheses.*

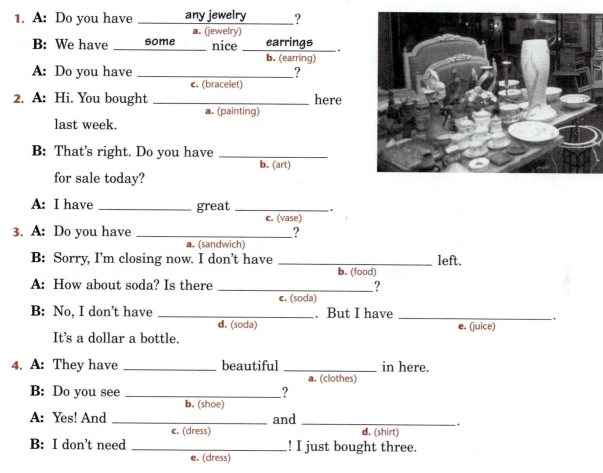

1. **A:** Do you have _____ any jewelry _____?
   a. (jewelry)
   B: We have _____ some _____ nice _____ earrings _____.
   b. (earring)
   A: Do you have _____?
   c. (bracelet)

2. **A:** Hi. You bought _____ here
   a. (painting)
   last week.
   B: That's right. Do you have _____
   b. (art)
   for sale today?
   A: I have _____ great _____.
   c. (vase)

3. **A:** Do you have _____?
   a. (sandwich)
   B: Sorry, I'm closing now. I don't have _____ left.
   b. (food)
   A: How about soda? Is there _____?
   c. (soda)
   B: No, I don't have _____. But I have _____.
   d. (soda)   **e.** (juice)
   It's a dollar a bottle.

4. **A:** They have _____ beautiful _____ in here.
   a. (clothes)
   B: Do you see _____?
   b. (shoe)
   A: Yes! And _____ and _____.
   c. (dress)   **d.** (shirt)
   B: I don't need _____! I just bought three.
   e. (dress)

4 **EDIT** • *Read this postcard. Find and correct seven mistakes in the use of* **some** *and* **any** *and the nouns that go with them. The first mistake is already corrected.*

> **Paris, France**
>
> Dear Sam,
>
> I'm having a wonderful time in Paris. I didn't have ~~some~~ **any** time to write last week because I took a tour of any flea markets. It was great. The guides are flea market experts and they gave us any good advice about shopping. Did you know that Paris has the largest flea market in the world? It's in St.-Ouen, and there are some amazing thing there! I bought some beautiful vintage clothes. I also got any interesting old books for you. I loved the old furniture, but I didn't buy some. I need any money for food! See you next week.   Love, Amy

Quantifiers: *Many, Much, A few, A little, A lot of*

He has a lot of things, but not much space.

*I'll need **a lot of** cool T-shirts in college . . .*

*. . . **a few** pairs of jeans . . .*

*. . . **a little** laundry soap . . .*

*. . . **a lot of** hair gel . . .*

*. . . but **not many** shirts.*

*Uh-oh. There's **not much** space for books!*

CHECK POINT

Check the best title for this cartoon.

☐ A Lot of Things, A Little Space   ☐ A Lot of Space, A Few Things

CHART CHECK 1

Check the correct answer.

Use _____ for count and non-count nouns.

☐ *a little*

☐ *a few*

☐ *a lot of*

AFFIRMATIVE STATEMENTS					
	QUANTIFIER	**COUNT NOUN**		**QUANTIFIER**	**NON-COUNT NOUN**
I have	a few many a lot of	books.	I have	a little a lot of	space.

NEGATIVE STATEMENTS					
	QUANTIFIER	**COUNT NOUN**		**QUANTIFIER**	**NON-COUNT NOUN**
I don't have	many a lot of	books.	I don't have	much a lot of	space.

CHART CHECK 2

Circle T (True) or F (False).

T F In questions, use *many* and *a lot of* for count nouns.

QUESTIONS					
COUNT NOUNS			**NON-COUNT NOUNS**		
Do you have	many a lot of	books?	Do you have	much a lot of	space?
How many tests do you have?			**How much time** do you have?		

EXPRESS CHECK

Circle the correct words.

I have a little <u>tests / time</u> this week. I don't have many <u>tests / time</u>.

Grammar Explanations	**Examples**
1. Use *many, a few,* and *a little* in **affirmative statements**.	■ There *are a few* students here. ■ I *have a little* time before class.
Use *many* and *a few* with <u>plural count nouns</u>.	■ **Many roommates** become friends. ■ I bought *a few CDs* today.
Use *a little* with <u>non-count nouns</u>.	■ There's only *a little paper* in the printer.
2. Use *many* and *much* in **negative statements**.	■ There *aren't* **many** students here. ■ I *don't have* **much** time before class.
Use *many* with <u>plural count nouns</u>.	■ There aren't **many *dorms***.
Use *much* with <u>non-count nouns</u>.	■ We don't have **much *homework***.
3. Use *many* and *much* in **questions**.	■ Did you have **many** tests last week? ■ **How much** time do you have?
4. Use *a lot of*:	
• in <u>affirmative and negative statements</u>	■ I *have a lot of* work. ■ I *don't have a lot of* time.
• with <u>plural count nouns</u> and <u>non-count nouns</u>	■ There are *a lot of dorms*. ■ We had *a lot of time* for the test.
• in <u>questions</u>	■ Are there *a lot of* dorms? ■ Do we have *a lot of* time?

5. You can use *a few, a little, a lot, not much,* and *not many* <u>without a noun</u>.	**A:** How many books did you buy?
	 B: *A few*. (= *a few books*)
	         OR
	 Not many. (= *not many books*)
	         OR
	 A lot! (= *a lot of books*)
	 NOT *A lot ~~of~~*!

▶ **BE CAREFUL!** Use *a lot* (not *a lot of*) without a noun.	

Check it out!

Nouns: Count/Non-Count ►►► UNIT 19, page 84.

1

TRUE OR FALSE • *Julia is a college student. Look at the picture. Then circle T (True) or F (False) for each statement.*

(**T**) **F** **1.** She has a lot of books on her desk.

T **F** **2.** She has a few books on her shelf.

T **F** **3.** There's a little water on the floor.

T **F** **4.** She doesn't have many pens.

T **F** **5.** She has a lot of CDs.

T **F** **6.** There's a lot of tea in the cup.

T **F** **7.** The test will be in a few days.

2

CHOOSE • *Circle the correct words to complete this article.*

(A Lot of) / Many Work, Just a Few / a Little Time
  1.   2.

It's your first year of college. You have a lot of / much new friends and
  3.
a lot of / many freedom. Soon, you don't have much / many time for school.
  4.   5.
You miss a few / a little classes. You don't do much / many homework. Then you
  6.   7.
get a few / a little low grades, and you wake up. It's time to make a schedule.
  8.

To start, answer a few / a little questions:
  9.

🕐 How much / many classes do you have each week?
  10.

🕐 How much / many time will you study for each class?
  11.

🕐 Do you have much / many reading assignments?
  12.

🕐 How much / many pages will you read each day?
  13.

This will take a few / a little time, but it will save you a lot of / a little headaches.
  14.   15.

3 | **COMPLETE** • *Complete these conversations. Use the words in the boxes.*

a few	~~a lot of~~	not many

ALAN: Does Professor Brown give _____a lot of_____ quizzes?
                                            1.

MAY: No, _____. He gave only _____ last semester.
                    2.   **3.**

a few	a little	a lot	much

MARCY: There isn't _____ paper in the printer.
                                4.

RENA: And there's only _____ on my desk.
                                5.

MARCY: This report is long. I'm going to need _____.
                                                            6.

RENA: I'll go to the store. I need _____ things for my art class.
                                            7.

a few	a few	A lot	How much	How many	Not much

BEV: You look tired. _____ sleep did you get last night?
                                8.

TOM: _____. Only _____ hours. I had a history test today.
                9.   **10.**

BEV: _____ pages does your teacher assign every week?
                11.

TOM: _____. More than a hundred pages!
                12.

BEV: Next time, read _____ pages every day.
                                13.

4 | **EDIT** • *Read this e-mail message. Find and correct nine mistakes in the use of quantifiers. The first mistake is already corrected.*

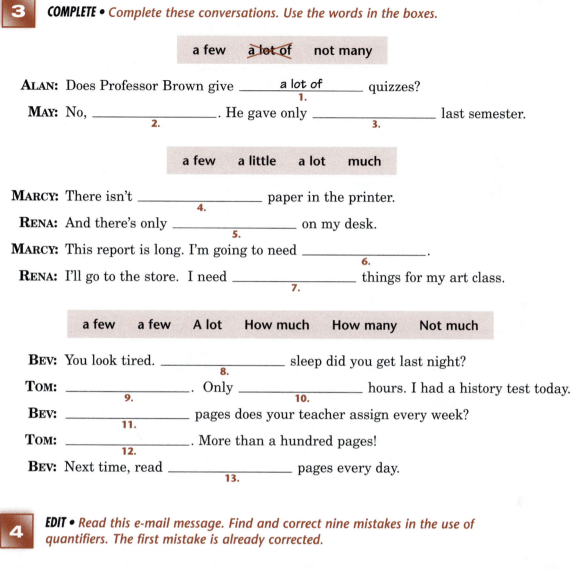

mailbox.com

Hi Donna,

 I'm going to be your roommate next semester. I'm sending *a few* ~~a little~~ photos. As you can see, I have a lot brothers and sisters. How much people are in your family? I hope we'll be good friends. I only have problems with a little things. I don't want many noise in the room at night (I need a lot of sleep). Also, I like much pictures on the walls. I didn't get many information about our dorm room. How much space do we have? Do you know? Are you packing much things? I only packed a little clothes, but I have a lot of books. Write soon!

Marcia

There is, There are

There's a fly in my soup!

Waiter! **There's** a fly in my soup!

Don't worry, Miss. The fly isn't very expensive.

CHART CHECK 1

Check the correct answers.

Use **there is** for _____.

☐ one thing

☐ several things

You can form the negative _____.

☐ in one way

☐ in more than one way

AFFIRMATIVE STATEMENTS

THERE IS/ARE	SUBJECT	
There is	a cup	on the table.
	some tea	in the cup.
There are	some cups	on the table.

NEGATIVE STATEMENTS

THERE IS/ARE + NOT/NO	SUBJECT	
There is no	cup	on the table.
There isn't	any tea	in the cup.
There aren't	any cups	on the table.

CHART CHECK 2

Circle T (True) or F (False).

T   F   Begin *yes/no* questions with **There**.

T   F   You can use contractions in affirmative short answers.

YES/NO QUESTIONS

THERE IS/ARE	SUBJECT	
Is there	a cup	on the table?
	any tea	in the cup?
Are there	any cups	on the table?

SHORT ANSWERS

AFFIRMATIVE		NEGATIVE	
Yes,	there is.	**No,**	there isn't.
	there are.		there aren't.

WH- QUESTIONS

QUESTION WORD	SUBJECT	THERE IS/ARE
How much	tea	**is there**?
How many	cups	**are there**?

EXPRESS CHECK

Circle the correct words.

A: Is / Are there a good restaurant near here?   **B:** Yes, there is / there's.

Grammar Explanations	Examples
1. Use *there is* or *there are* the first time you talk about something.	■ **There is** a new restaurant in town. *(A new restaurant is in town.)* ■ **There are** some good things on the menu. *(Some good things are on the menu.)*
After that, use a **pronoun** (*he, she, it, they* . . .) to give more information.	■ **There's** a glass on the table. *It's* a clean glass. ■ **There are** some forks in the sink. *They're* dirty.
▶ **BE CAREFUL!** There is no contraction for *there are*.	NOT There're some forks . . .
2. We often use *there is* or *there are* with: • a place • a time	■ **There's** a glass *on the table*. ■ **There's** a special breakfast *on Sundays*.
3. Use *there was* or *there were* for the past. Use *there will be* for the future.	■ **There were** a lot of people there *last night*. ■ **There will be** a lot there *tomorrow* too.
4. Use *there is (there was, there will be)*: • for one person or thing • for non-count nouns Use *there are (there were, there will be)* for two or more people or things.	■ **There's** *a menu* on the table. ■ **There was** *some water* on the table. ■ **There are** *a lot of people* here.
USAGE NOTE: In conversation, people often use *there's* for several people or things.	■ **There's** a lot of people here. NOT There is a lot of people.
5. Use *not* or *no* for the negative. ▶ **BE CAREFUL!** Do not use *not* with *no*.	■ There are**n't** any cups. OR ■ There are **no** cups. NOT There aren't no cups.
USAGE NOTE: We usually use *there is no* for one person or thing.	MORE COMMON: **There's no café** on Park Place. LESS COMMON: There isn't a café on Park Place.

Check it out!

Quantifiers: *Some* and *Any* ▶▶▶ **UNIT 22, page 96.**
Nouns: Count/Non-Count ▶▶▶ **UNIT 19, page 84.**

1 **FIND •** *Read this restaurant review. Underline all forms of* **there is** *and* **there are**.

Section 3   **Around Town**

 ## EATING OUT?
Try Jason's.

   <u>There's</u> a new restaurant in town! It's called Jason's. I ate there last night, and there were many people there. In fact, there were no empty tables. There's a good reason for that. The food is great! The menu is small, but there are always many "Specials." Last night there was grilled mushroom pizza, and it was delicious. Try Jason's, and bring the whole family. There is no special children's menu at Jason's, but there is something for everyone. Try it.

48 Park Place, 555-2163

CHECK • *Read the list. Check the things that Jason's has.*

☑ a lot of customers   ☐ great food   ☐ "Specials"

☐ empty tables   ☐ a big menu   ☐ a special children's menu

2 **DESCRIBE •** *Look at these pictures from Jason's. Complete the sentences. Use* **there is (not)** *and* **there are (not)**.

1. __There are__ some flowers on the table.

2. _____ any water in the glass.

3. _____ two chairs around the table.

4. _____ three specials today.

5. _____ any knives.

6. _____ a phone in the restaurant.

3 **COMPLETE** • *Read these conversations. Complete them with **there is** or **there are** and short answers.*

1. **Tomás:** _____Are there_____ any specials today?
   a.

   Waiter: ___Yes___, ___there are___. _____ two specials:
   b.   **c.**
   grilled mushroom pizza and roast chicken.

   Tomás: I don't eat meat. _____ any meat on the pizza?
   d.

   Waiter: _____, _____. _____ no meat. Just
   e.   **f.**
   mushrooms, tomatoes, and cheese.

2. **Doug:** _____ any special starters tonight?
   a.

   Waiter: _____, _____ one: stuffed mushrooms.
   b.

   Doug: I'm very hungry. How many mushrooms _____ in an order?
   c.

   Waiter: _____ only four, but they are very big.
   d.

3. **Olga:** Waiter, _____ a fly in my soup!
   a.

   Waiter: Oh, I'm very sorry. I'll get you another bowl.

   Olga: OK. And _____ any more rolls? These don't taste fresh.
   b.

   Waiter: _____, _____. Sorry. These are the only ones we have.
   c.

   Olga: Oh. _____ another restaurant near here?
   d.

   Waiter: _____, _____. Across the street. Our cook eats there
   e.
   every night.

4 **EDIT** • *Read this note from Jason, the owner of the restaurant. Find and correct eight mistakes in the use of **there is** and **there are**. The first mistake is already corrected.*

>   **were**
> There ~~are~~ a lot of customers last night, so this morning there're some problems. First, the
>
> food. There aren't no tomatoes. There is potatoes, but they aren't any onions. And I can't
>
> find any eggs. How many was there last night? We need these things for today's menu!
>
> Second, there isn't any clean pots this morning. There was a problem with the hot water
>
> last night? Let's work hard and keep those customers happy.
>
> Thanks! Jason

SelfTest

SECTION ONE

Circle the letter of the correct answer to complete each sentence.

> **EXAMPLE:**
> Alicia and Paulo _____ students.   A (B) C D
> (A) am   (C) be
> (B) are   (D) is

1. My jeans _____ too big.   A B C D
   (A) am   (C) be
   (B) are   (D) is

2. Todd drank two cups _____ coffee.   A B C D
   (A) a   (C) of
   (B) the   (D) Ø

3. I baked a cake. Would you like _____ piece?   A B C D
   (A) a   (C) some
   (B) the   (D) Ø

4. —What does your brother do?   A B C D
   —He writes _____ songs.
   (A) a   (C) Ø
   (B) the   (D) this

5. —What does Enrique do?   A B C D
   —He's _____ engineer at Baktor Corporation.
   (A) a   (C) the
   (B) an   (D) Ø

6. The phone is in _____ kitchen.   A B C D
   (A) a   (C) the
   (B) Ø   (D) an

7. I'll meet you at _____ party tomorrow night.   A B C D
   (A) a   (C) an
   (B) the   (D) Ø

8. Sorry I'm late. I had _____ work today.   A B C D
   (A) a few   (C) a lot of
   (B) a lot   (D) many

9. Did you find _____ nice paintings at the market?   A B C D
   (A) a little   (C) much
   (B) any   (D) that

10. —Oh, no! I don't have any money for the bus.   A B C D
      —I'll give you _____ .
   (A) a few   (C) one
   (B) any   (D) some

11. We don't have _____ time. Let's hurry.   A B C D
   (A) a little   (C) much
   (B) many   (D) some

12. There _____ two new students in our class.   A B C D
   (A) are   (C) is
   (B) has   (D) have

13. Did you buy _____ textbooks this semester?   A B C D
   (A) a little   (C) much
   (B) many   (D) ones

SECTION TWO

Each sentence has four underlined parts. The four underlined parts of the sentence are marked A, B, C, and D. Circle the letter of the one underlined part that is NOT CORRECT.

EXAMPLE:

My friends <u>is</u> here, but we <u>are</u> <u>not</u> <u>studying</u>.   (A) B C D
       A   B C   D

14. My <u>cousin</u> <u>Anne</u> lives in <u>lisbon</u>, <u>Portugal</u>.   A B C D
          A   B   C   D

15. <u>The</u> restaurant <u>are</u> open on <u>Sunday</u>, but <u>it's</u> closed on Monday.   A B C D
    A   B   C   D

16. I went to <u>any</u> flea markets, and I got <u>some</u> <u>furniture</u> and <u>a few</u> books.   A B C D
           A   B   C   D

17. <u>There</u> are <u>a lot of</u> students in my dorm, but just <u>a little</u> in yours.   A B C D
    A   B C   D

18. The <u>doctor</u> says I should drink eight <u>glasses</u> <u>of</u> <u>waters</u> every day.   A B C D
       A   B   C D

19. <u>We</u> stayed at <u>the</u> <u>party</u> for only <u>a</u> hour.   A B C D
    A   B   C   D

20. <u>I</u> bought <u>an</u> apple for <u>my</u> friend, but <u>an</u> apple was bad.   A B C D
   A   B   C   D

21. <u>My</u> roommate called <u>friend</u> last night but <u>she</u> <u>wasn't</u> home.   A B C D
   A   B   C D

22. Klaus gave <u>me</u> <u>a</u> music CD, but <u>I</u> didn't like <u>music</u> on it.   A B C D
         A B   C   D

23. <u>I</u> usually <u>don't</u> like <u>tea</u>, but this tea <u>taste</u> very good.   A B C D
   A   B   C   D

24. Would you like a <u>glass milk</u> and <u>a</u> piece <u>of</u> <u>cake</u>?   A B C D
            A   B   C D

25. There are twenty <u>people</u> in <u>my</u> class: eleven <u>men</u> and nine <u>woman</u>.   A B C D
               A   B   C   D

Pronouns:
Subject and Object

He gave her a gift. She thanked him.

It's for **you**, Mom!

Is **it** really for **me** or is **it** for **him**?!

CHECK POINT

Check the correct answers.

Who gave the gift?
❏ the son
❏ the mother

Who received the gift?
❏ the son
❏ the mother

CHART CHECK

Circle T (True) or F (False).

T   F Subject and object pronouns are sometimes the same word.

SUBJECT PRONOUNS		OBJECT PRONOUNS	
I			**me**.
You			**you**.
He			**him**.
She	looked nice.	Marta liked	**her**.
It			**it**.
We			**us**.
You			**you**.
They			**them**.

EXPRESS CHECK

Look at the picture. Check the correct sentence.

❏ He gave her a gift.
❏ She gave him a gift.
❏ He gave them a gift.
❏ She gave her a gift.
❏ He gave him a gift.

For me?

Grammar Explanations	**Examples**

1. Use **subject pronouns** (*I, you, he, she, it, we, they*) for the <u>subject</u> of a sentence.

The man bought a gift.
■ **He** bought a gift.

2. Use **object pronouns** (*me, you, him, her, it, us, them*) for the <u>object</u> of a verb.

The man bought ***a gift***.
■ The man bought **it**.

3. Use **object pronouns** <u>after prepositions</u> (*to, for, between, with, . . .*)

■ I went to the store ***with*** **him**.
■ I sat ***between*** **him** and **her**.
  NOT between ~~he and she~~

4. **USAGE NOTE:** We usually use **object pronouns** after ***be***.

A: Who's there?
B: It'**s me**.
  NOT ~~It's I~~.

5. Use ***you*** for:
  • one person or several people
  • friends and family
  • young and old people
  • strangers (people you don't know)
  • teachers, doctors, police officers, . . .

■ Thank **you,** ***Karl***.
■ Thank **you,** ***Mr. and Mrs. Rogers***.
■ Thank **you,** ***Dr. Martinez***.

6. **BE CAREFUL!** Use a **noun** <u>or</u> a **pronoun**. Don't use both.

■ **My mother** gave me a present.
            OR
■ **She** gave me a present.
  NOT ~~My mother she~~ gave me a present.

1 **FIND** • *Read about some gift-giving customs. Circle the subject and object pronouns. Draw an arrow from the pronouns to the nouns.*

GIFT GIVING

All over the world, people give gifts.

But *they* give different things in different ways.

In Japan, people often give gifts. But they never open them in front of the giver.

In the United States and Canada, a man often gives his girlfriend flowers on Valentine's Day (February 14). He sometimes gives her chocolate too.

In Korea, older people give new money to children on New Year's Day. They give it to them for good luck.

In Peru, a man gives flowers to his girlfriend. But he doesn't give her yellow flowers. They mean: The relationship is finished.

2 **DESCRIBE** • *Look at the pictures. Complete the sentences with subject pronouns and object pronouns.*

First Business Meeting, Japan

1. ___He___ gave ___it___ to ___him___.

New Year's Day, Korea

2. _____ flew _____ in the park.

Kwanzaa, USA

3. _____ gave _____ to _____.

Valentine's Day, France

4. _____ thanked _____ for _____.

Father's Day, Canada

5. BOY: _____ made _____ for _____!

Girl's 15th Birthday, Mexico

6. GIRL: _____'s dancing with _____!

3 **COMPLETE •** *Read these paragraphs. Complete them with the correct pronouns.*

1. Yesterday was my birthday. ___I___ got a present from my boyfriend, Karl. _____
   a.   **b.**
gave _____ a scarf. I love _____! _____'s blue (my favorite color) and feels
       c.   **d.**   **e.**
really soft.

2. My boyfriend, Carlos, is from Argentina. For his birthday, _____ gave _____ a
                                                                    a.   **b.**
pocket knife. _____ didn't like _____. I asked his friend Juan about it. Juan told
              c.   **d.**
_____ a knife means the person wants to end the relationship! I didn't know that!
e.

3. In Korea, older people give children money on New Year's Day. My brother and _____
                                                                                      a.
always visit our grandparents on that day. _____ always give _____ an envelope
                                            b.   **c.**
filled with new *won* (Korean money). Then _____ buy something with the money.
                                           d.

4. My friend Hassan had a beautiful painting on his wall. I said, "It's beautiful. _____
                                                                                        a.
like it very much." That was a mistake. _____ wanted to give me the painting! He
                                         b.
took _____ off the wall and handed it to _____. Of course I told _____ no, but
     c.   **d.**   **e.**
_____ were both uncomfortable. Live and learn.
f.

4 **EDIT •** *Read this thank-you note. Find and correct nine mistakes in the use of subject and object pronouns. The first mistake is already corrected.*

Dear Grandma and Grandpa,

         you
    Thank ~~yous~~ so much for the green sweater. He looks really good on me. My

girlfriend she likes the color a lot. Do you remember my girlfriend Lisa? He wanted

to wear it! (I told she, maybe next week.) Mom and Dad gave I a great party. I

invited ten of my friends. They all went to the water park. We stayed there all

afternoon. Then Mom and Dad they took us to the movies.

    I hope you're both fine. When are you going to visit we again? We miss you a lot.

                  Love,

                  Ian

UNIT 26

Possessives

Is this Amber's book? It isn't mine.

CHECK POINT

The woman is asking the man:

☐ Are you Superman?

☐ Do you own this?

CHART CHECK 1

Check the correct answer.

Possessive nouns end in _____.

☐ *-s*

☐ *-'s*

☐ *-'s* or *-s'*

POSSESSIVE NOUNS			
SINGULAR		**PLURAL**	
Kent's The **boy's**	jacket is red.	**Kent and Bill's** The **boys'**	jackets are red.

CHART CHECK 2

Circle T (True) or F (False).

T F All possessive pronouns end in *-s*.

T F The possessive adjective and possessive pronoun for *he* are the same.

T F Nouns always follow possessive adjectives.

POSSESSIVE ADJECTIVES		
	ADJECTIVE	**NOUN**
This is	**my** **your** **his** **her** **its** **our** **your** **their**	ball.

POSSESSIVE PRONOUNS	
	PRONOUN
This is	**mine**. **yours**. **his**. **hers**. — **ours**. **yours**. **theirs**.

QUESTIONS
Whose (coat) is this?

ANSWERS	
It's	**Amber's** (coat). **her** coat. **hers**.

114

EXPRESS **CHECK**
Complete the chart.

SUBJECT PRONOUN	POSSESSIVE ADJECTIVE	POSSESSIVE PRONOUN
I		mine
she	her	
	our	
they		

Grammar Explanations

1. Use **possessives** to talk about things people own.

Possessives answer the question *Whose?*

Examples

- **Superman's** cape is blue.
- **His** cape is blue.
- **His** is blue, but **hers** is red.

A: *Whose* hat is that?
B: It's **Amber's** hat.
  OR
  It's **Amber's**. / It's **her** hat. / It's **hers**.

2. To form **possessive nouns**:

- Add **-'s** to a <u>person's name</u>.

- Add **-'s** to <u>singular nouns</u>.

- Add **-'s** to <u>irregular plural nouns</u>.

▶ **BE CAREFUL!** Add only an apostrophe (**'**) to <u>plural nouns</u> that end in **-s**.

- **Kent's** jacket is brown. **Lois's** is green.

- My **sister's** car is red. My **boss's** is black.

- They're the **children's** books.

- The **boy's** books are new. (*= one boy*)
- The **boys'** books are new. (*= more than one boy*)
  NOT ~~boys's~~

3. Use **possessive adjectives** *(my, your, his, her, its, our, their)* <u>before nouns</u>.

- **His** *jacket* is blue.
- **Her** *coat* is red.
- **Their** *new house* is beautiful.

4. Use **possessive pronouns** *(mine, yours, his, hers, ours, theirs)* <u>in place of a noun</u>.

Possessive pronouns can go at the <u>beginning</u> or the <u>end</u> of a sentence.

There is no possessive pronoun for *it*.

▶ **BE CAREFUL!** Do not use nouns after possessive pronouns.

A: Is this *her jacket*?
B: No. **Hers** is red.

A: Is this Tom's jacket?
B: No. **His** is in the corner. That's **mine**.

NOT Hers ~~jacket~~.

1 FIND • *Read this article from a college newsletter. Underline all the possessives.*

COLLEGE NEWS   VOLUME III, ISSUE 2

Can't find your wallet? Don't panic! "People lose their things every day," says Ron Findler, head of the College Lost and Found office. "Our job is to help them find them again."

Jan Peterson is one happy example. "When I lost my keys, I was very worried. My teacher sent me to the

Lost and Found office. Mine weren't the only lost keys! Other people's keys were there too. I was lucky I got them back."

So, if you lose your stuff, run (don't walk!) to the College Lost and Found office.

Their hours are Monday to Friday, 9:00–5:00. Closed on weekends.

2 CHOOSE • *Circle the correct words to complete these conversations.*

1. **A:** Hi. I lost mine / <u>my</u> umbrella. I think I left it in Ms. <u>Jenkin / Jenkin's</u> class.
       a.   b.

   B: Is this <u>your / yours</u>?
               c.

   A: No, <u>mine / my</u> is black. But that one looks like my <u>roommate / roommate's</u>!
             d.   e.

2. **A:** My sister lost <u>her / hers</u> cell phone.
                          a.

   B: We have four cell phones. Is one of these <u>your / yours</u> <u>sister's / sisters'</u>?
                                                    b.   c.

   A: I'm not sure.

   B: Well, what's <u>her / hers</u> phone number? Call it! If it rings, it's <u>her / hers</u>!
                       d.   e.

3. **A:** We lost <u>our / ours</u> notebooks.
                   a.

   B: Do they have <u>your / yours</u> names in them?
                        b.

   A: <u>Mine / My</u> has <u>mine / my</u> name on the inside cover.
          c.   d.
   But <u>her / hers</u> notebook doesn't have <u>her / hers</u>.
           e.   f.

4. **A:** <u>Who / Whose</u> gloves are those?
          a.

   B: Those are <u>my / mine</u>!
                     b.

5. **A:** Are these <u>your / yours</u> keys?
                     a.

   B: No. <u>Mine / My</u> are in <u>my / mine</u> pocket.
              b.   c.

   A: Maybe they're the <u>children / children's</u>.
                                    d.

   B: Maybe. They lose <u>their / theirs</u> all the time.
                                e.

3 **COMPLETE** • *Look at these items from the Lost and Found office. Then look at the people.*
Whose items are they? Complete the sentences with the name of the items and with
mine, **yours**, **his**, **hers**, **ours**, *and* **theirs**.

| umbrella | helmet | cat | crutches | rings | shoes |

1. The
   __cat__
   is __hers__!

2. The
   _____
   is _____!

3. The
   _____
   is _____!

4. The
   _____
   are _____!

5. The
   _____
   are _____!

6. The
   _____
   are _____!

4 **EDIT** • *Read these postings from an on-line lost and found board. Find and correct*
seven mistakes in the use of possessives. The first mistake is already corrected.

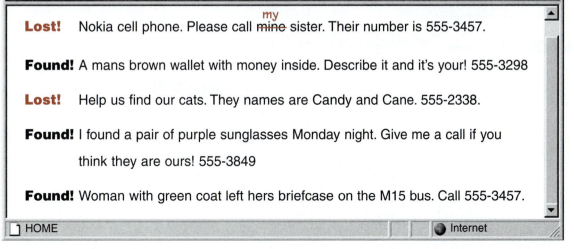

LOST AND FOUND MESSAGE BOARD _ □ ✕

Lost! Nokia cell phone. Please call ~~mine~~ ^{my} sister. Their number is 555-3457.

Found! A mans brown wallet with money inside. Describe it and it's your! 555-3298

Lost! Help us find our cats. They names are Candy and Cane. 555-2338.

Found! I found a pair of purple sunglasses Monday night. Give me a call if you
think they are ours! 555-3849

Found! Woman with green coat left hers briefcase on the M15 bus. Call 555-3457.

🗋 HOME ● Internet

This, That, These, Those

This isn't my bag. That's my bag.

Are **these** your bags?

No. **Those** are.

CHECK *POINT*

Circle T (True) or F (False).

T F   The man's bags are in front of him.

CHART CHECK 1

Check the correct answers.

Use _____ for one thing.

☐ *this*

☐ *these*

Use _____ for something near.

☐ *these*

☐ *that*

SINGULAR STATEMENTS

NEAR		FAR	
This bag **This**	**is** mine.	**That** bag **That**	**is** mine.

PLURAL STATEMENTS

NEAR		FAR	
These bags **These**	**are** mine.	**Those** bags **Those**	**are** mine.

CONTRACTION

that is = **that's**

CHART CHECK 2

Circle T (True) or F (False).

T F   Use *this* in short answers.

YES/NO QUESTIONS

Is	**this** bag **that** bag	yours?
	this **that**	your bag? yours?
Are	**these** bags **those** bags	yours?
	these **those**	your bags? yours?

SHORT ANSWERS

Yes, **it** is.
No, **it**'s not.

Yes, **they** are.
No, **they**'re not.

EXPRESS CHECK

Circle the correct words.

A: <u>This / These</u> are not my bags.

B: Sorry. Is <u>this / that</u> your bag over there?

A: Yes, <u>that / it</u> is.

Grammar Explanations	Examples
1. Use ***this*** for <u>one</u> person or thing that is <u>near</u>. Use ***that*** for <u>one</u> person or thing that is <u>far</u>.	■ **This** is the pilot of the plane. *(= here)* ■ **This** is my bag ***right here***. ■ **That**'s the pilot of the plane. *(= there)* ■ **That**'s my bag ***over there***.
2. Use ***these*** for two or more people or things that are <u>near</u>. Use ***those*** for two or more people or things that are <u>far</u>.	■ **These** are the passengers. *(= here)* ■ **These** are my bags ***right here***. ■ **Those** are the passengers. *(= there)* ■ **Those** are my bags ***over there***.

3. Use ***this, that, these, those***:
  • with a noun
    OR
  • without a noun
	■ **This** *ticket* costs $800.
	
	■ **This** costs $800.
	  (This ticket costs $800.)

4. Use ***this*** to <u>introduce people</u>. Use ***this*** <u>on the phone</u>.	**A:** Cleo, **this** is Captain Valdez. **B:** Nice to meet you, Captain. **A:** Hi, Cleo? **This** is Shao-fen. **B:** Hi, Shao-fen! How are you?

5. Use ***it*** and ***they*** in <u>short answers</u> to *yes/no* questions.
 	
Do not use *this, that, these,* or *those* in short answers.
	A: Is **this** your seat?
	B: Yes, ***it*** is.
	  NOT Yes, ~~this~~ is.
	
	A: Are **these** your seats?
	B: No, ***they*** aren't.
	  NOT No, ~~these~~ aren't.

1 **MATCH** • *Read the statements on the left. Match each one with the correct picture on the right.*

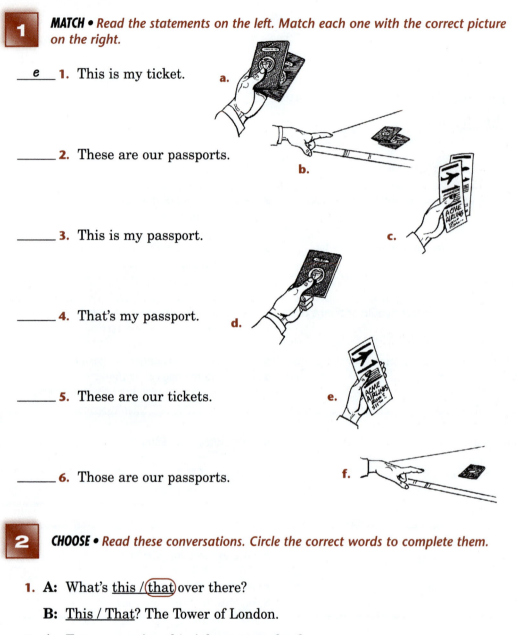

___e___ **1.** This is my ticket.

_____ **2.** These are our passports.

_____ **3.** This is my passport.

_____ **4.** That's my passport.

_____ **5.** These are our tickets.

_____ **6.** Those are our passports.

a.

b.

c.

d.

e.

f.

2 **CHOOSE** • *Read these conversations. Circle the correct words to complete them.*

1. A: What's this / that over there?

   B: This / That? The Tower of London.

2. A: Excuse me. Are this / these seats free?

   B: No, they / these aren't. Sorry. But this / that seat over there is free.

3. A: Lisa, this / that is my friend Kishana.

   B: Hi, Kishana. This / That is my roommate, Molly.

4. A: What are these / those mountains in the distance?

   B: Over there? These / Those are the Pyrenees.

5. A: This / These bus is really comfortable.

   B: And the tour guide is wonderful. This / That is a great trip!

3 | **COMPLETE** • *Look at these pictures. Complete the sentences with* **this**, **that**, **these**, *or* **those**.

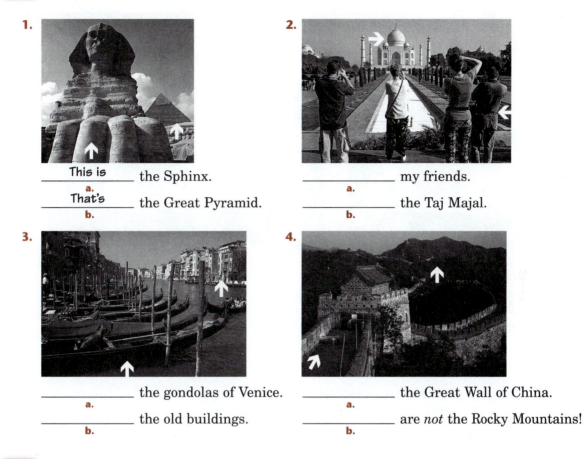

1.

__This is__ the Sphinx.
    a.
__That's__ the Great Pyramid.
    b.

2.

_____ my friends.
        a.
_____ the Taj Majal.
        b.

3.

_____ the gondolas of Venice.
    a.
_____ the old buildings.
    b.

4.

_____ the Great Wall of China.
    a.
_____ are *not* the Rocky Mountains!
    b.

4 | **EDIT** • *Read this postcard. Find and correct six mistakes in the use of* **this**, **that**, **these**, *and* **those**. *The first mistake is already corrected.*

The Leaning Tower of Pisa

This
Hi! ~~These~~ is a picture of the Leaning Tower of Pisa. I'm drinking a cup of cappuccino at a café across from it right now! That's the best cappuccino (and the best view) in the world!

Last week we were in Venice. That gondolas on the Grand Canal are beautiful! We took lots of pictures.

Italy is really beautiful. There are flowers everywhere. That café, for example, has flowers on every table. Speaking of flowers—how are these flowers in your garden?

This's a great trip! See you soon.

Carla

One, Ones

The white ones or the black ones?

> I like the white **ones**. They look great with this dress.

> The black **ones** look cool too. Can you walk with the white **ones**?

> Um . . . maybe not . . . Wear the black **ones**!

CHECK POINT

Check the correct answer.

The women are talking about _____.

☐ dresses ☐ shoes

CHART CHECK

Check the correct answers.

Use **ones** for _____.

☐ one thing

☐ two or more things

You can use **one** with _____.

☐ *this*

☐ *these*

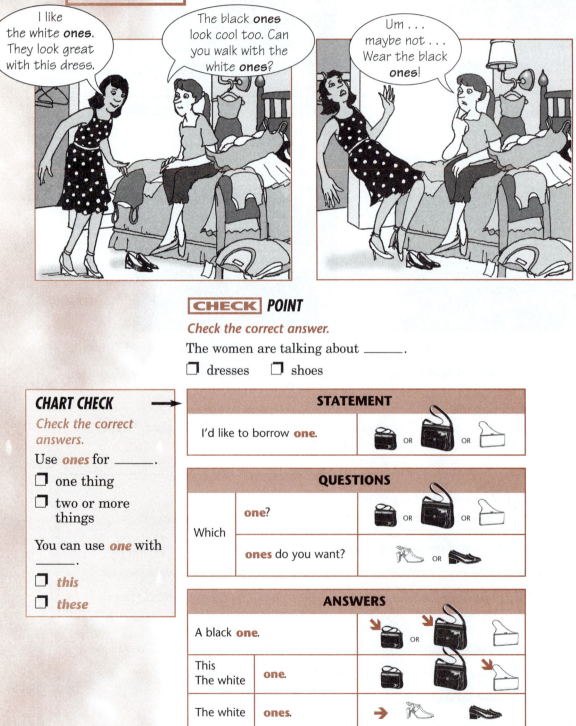

STATEMENT	
I'd like to borrow **one**.	

QUESTIONS		
Which	**one**?	
	ones do you want?	

ANSWERS	
A black **one**.	
This The white	**one**.
The white	**ones**.

EXPRESS CHECK

Circle the correct word.

I like the gray <u>one / ones</u>.

Grammar Explanations	**Examples**

1. Use **one** for <u>one</u> person or thing.

- ■ I'm looking for a salesperson. Do you see **one**?
  (Do you see a salesperson?)
- ■ Those sweaters are nice. I'd like to get **one**.
  (I'd like to get a sweater.)

▶ **BE CAREFUL!** Do not use **one** with <u>non-count nouns</u>.

A: Would you like to get some tea?
B: I had some before.
Nот I had ~~one~~ before.

---

2. Use **ones** for <u>two or more</u> people or things.

- ■ Good salespeople are important. The **ones** at Macy's are great.
  (The salespeople at Macy's are great.)
- ■ Those sweaters are nice. I like the red **ones**.
  (I like the red sweaters.)

---

3. Use **one** and **ones** to <u>identify</u> people and things. They can answer the question **Which?**

Use **one** or **ones** with:
• adjectives

A: Which bag do you want?
B: The **brown one**.

• locations

A: Which shoes do you want?
B: The **ones *on the floor***.

Use **one** with **this** or **that**.

A: Which sweater do you prefer?
B: *This* one. ***That* one** is too big.

USAGE NOTE: We usually do not use **ones** with *these* or *those*.

A: Which shoes do you like?
B: I like **these**.
Nот I like ~~these ones~~.

1 **MATCH** • *Read the sentences. Match each one with the correct picture.*

_c_ **1.** I like the one on the left.

a.

_____ **2.** I like the black one.

b.

_____ **3.** I like the black ones.

c.

_____ **4.** Wear the one on the right.

d.

_____ **5.** Buy the ones on the right.

e.

_____ **6.** I prefer the ones on the left.

f.

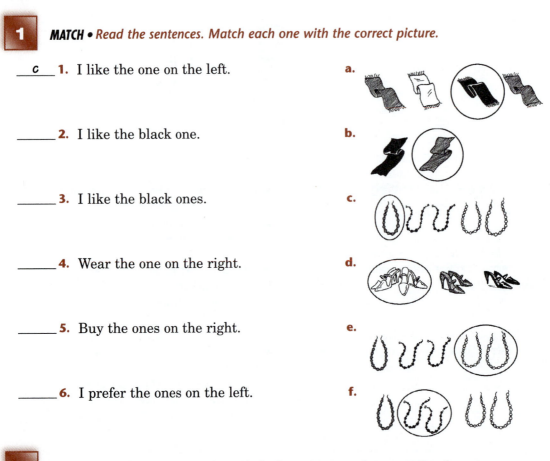

2 **CHOOSE** • *Read this conversation. Circle the correct words to complete it.*

AMY: I love New Year's Eve. I hope it's a nice party.

TODD: I'm sure it will be. The one / ones last year was a lot of fun.
   1.

   Which / Who shirt should I wear?
   2.

AMY: The blue one / ones. Blue is a great color for you.
   3.

   These shoes are really uncomfortable.

TODD: Wear the other one / ones. It's more important to be comfortable.
   4.

   Is this the right tie for this suit?

AMY: Hmmm. Let's look at some other one / ones. That one / ones on the left will
   5.   **6.**

   look better with your blue shirt.

TODD: It's almost 8:00. Let's go. We were late for the party last year. I don't want to be

   late for this one / ones too.
   7.

AMY: I'm almost ready. I found my gray gloves, but I can't find my black one / ones.
   8.

TODD: Why don't you wear your gray one / ones? They look fine.
   9.

3 **COMPLETE** • *Read these conversations. Complete them with* **one** *or* **ones**.

1. **AMY:** This is a great party. I'm going to get a glass of soda. Would you like _____one_____ ?
   a.

   TODD: Thanks. I just finished _____.
   b.

   AMY: Oh, look. That's Elena's new boyfriend over there in that group of guys.

   TODD: Which _____ is he?
   c.

   AMY: The _____ near the window.
   d.

2. **OLGA:** That's a beautiful dress. Is it new?

   AMY: No, it's an old _____. I wore it last year too.
   a.

   OLGA: Elena collects art. Some of her paintings are very old.

   AMY: Which _____? They're all beautiful.
   b.

3. **ELENA:** Could you help me carry more chairs into the living room?

   TODD: Sure. Which _____?
   a.

   ELENA: The _____ from the kitchen.
   b.

4. **JASON:** Hi. We're friends of your cousin.

   TODD: Which _____? I have more than twenty cousins!

5. **TODD:** Elena made some delicious cookies. Would you like _____?
   a.

   AMY: I just ate ten! But, sure, I'll have another _____. Thanks.
   b.

   Ow! My feet hurt. These shoes are terrible.

   TODD: I told you to wear the other _____!
   c.

4 **EDIT** • *Read this e-mail message. Find and correct six mistakes in the use of* **one** *and* **ones**. *The first mistake is already corrected.*

---

mailbox.com

Elena—That was a great party last night! Your best ~~ones~~ *one* of all! We really had a good time. The food was delicious—especially the cookies. I loved the one with the chocolate on top. I think I ate more than ten of them! Ones with the nuts were good too.

I enjoyed meeting your friends and the people you work with. I'm sorry that I didn't meet your boss. What one was she?

The only problem was my shoes. I really must buy more comfortable one!

Have a Happy New Year! And a healthy ones too. —Amy

SelfTest

Circle the letter of the correct answer to complete each sentence.

> **EXAMPLE:**
> Alicia and Paulo _____ students.   A **(B)** C D
> (A) am   (C) be
> (B) are   (D) is

1. My boyfriend gave _____ a nice sweater.   A B C D
   (A) I   (C) my
   (B) me   (D) mine

2. _____ like the sweater a lot.   A B C D
   (A) I   (C) She
   (B) Me   (D) Mine

3. Is that book for _____?   A B C D
   (A) he   (C) him
   (B) his   (D) he's

4. —Who's at the door? The Millers?   A B C D
   —Yes, it's _____. They're early.
   (A) these   (C) their
   (B) them   (D) theirs

5. —_____ hat is this?   A B C D
   —I think it's Emilia's.
   (A) Who   (C) What
   (B) Who's   (D) Whose

6. Are these _____ gloves?   A B C D
   (A) her   (C) she
   (B) hers   (D) she's

7. —Is that Donna's scarf?   A B C D
   —No. _____ is red.
   (A) Her   (C) She
   (B) Hers   (D) She's

8. Ina sat between John and _____.   A B C D
   (A) I   (C) my
   (B) me   (D) mine

9. —Is this seat free?   A B C D
   —No, _____ isn't. Sorry.
   (A) it   (C) there
   (B) that   (D) this

10. Hi! _____ Joel. Could I speak to Anna?   **A B C D**
    (A) Here is   (C) They are
    (B) There is   (D) This is

11. These hats are nice. I think I'll buy this _____.   **A B C D**
    (A) one   (C) some
    (B) ones   (D) hats

12. Excuse me. Is this book _____?   **A B C D**
    (A) you   (C) yours
    (B) your   (D) you're

13. I lost my gloves. I need _____.   **A B C D**
    (A) a glove   (C) a new one
    (B) any new   (D) new ones

14. Dan, _____ is my friend Nina.   **A B C D**
    (A) she   (C) this
    (B) these   (D) those

SECTION TWO

Each sentence has four underlined parts. The four underlined parts of the sentence are marked A, B, C, and D. Circle the letter of the one underlined part that is NOT CORRECT.

EXAMPLE:

My friends <u>is</u> here, but we <u>are</u> <u>not</u> <u>studying</u>.   **(A) B C D**
          A   B C   D

---

15. <u>My</u> <u>sister she</u> gave <u>me</u> a beautiful blouse for <u>my</u> last birthday.   **A B C D**
    A   B   C   D

16. Mr. <u>Delgado</u> <u>car</u> is in the <u>garage</u> on <u>Main</u> Street.   **A B C D**
        A   B   C   D

17. <u>These</u> <u>are</u> my sisters, and <u>that</u> people over there <u>are</u> my parents.   **A B C D**
    A   B   C   D

18. <u>These</u> <u>are</u> your tickets right here, and <u>this</u> are <u>mine</u> over there.   **A B C D**
    A   B   C   D

19. <u>Which</u> hat do you like better, this <u>one</u> or <u>that</u> <u>ones</u> over there?   **A B C D**
    A   B   C D

20. <u>I</u> see <u>Miguel's</u> umbrella and <u>your</u> umbrella, but <u>my</u> isn't here.   **A B C D**
    A   B   C   D

21. <u>Theirs</u> new house is much bigger than <u>that</u> <u>one</u> or <u>ours</u>.   **A B C D**
    A   B   C   D

22. Is <u>this</u> <u>Ana's</u> new hat over there, or is it her <u>old</u> <u>one</u>?   **A B C D**
      A   B   C D

23. <u>Those</u> <u>are</u> nice pictures, but <u>that</u> are the best <u>ones</u> right here.   **A B C D**
    A   B   C   D

24. <u>Andre</u> doesn't want to listen to <u>this</u> music because <u>he</u> heard <u>one</u> before.   **A B C D**
    A   B   C   D

25. <u>Ms. Ito</u> gave us homework, but <u>we</u> did <u>it</u> before <u>ours</u> class.   **A B C D**
    A   B   C   D

Adjectives

The dog is nice. It's a nice dog.

Pet of the Week

Cute and Friendly

"Tiger" is a **young** Doberman. He is **sweet** and **lovable**. A **great** pet for a **small** child!

For more information call 555-PETS.

CHECK *POINT*

Circle T (True) or F (False).

T F The ad gives a good description of the dog.

CHART CHECK

Circle T (True) or F (False).

T F An adjective can go before a noun.

T F An adjective can go before a verb like *be*, *look*, or *seem*.

ADJECTIVE + NOUN

	ADJECTIVE	**NOUN**
She has a	**nice** **cute** **friendly**	dog.

VERB + ADJECTIVE

NOUN	**BE/LOOK/SEEM**	**ADJECTIVE**
Her dog	is looks seems	**nice.** **cute.** **friendly.**

EXPRESS CHECK

Put these words in the correct order.

great • He's • pet • a

.

Grammar Explanations	Examples

1. Use **adjectives** to <u>describe</u> a person (or animal), place, or thing.

- Jason is a **nice** guy.
- He has a **big** dog.
- The dog is **friendly**.
- Their apartment is **small**.
- It has a **big** window.

2. Adjectives give many different kinds of **information**.

SIZE: a **small** house
AGE: a **young** man
SHAPE: a **round** table
COLOR: a **black** cat
FEELINGS: a **happy** pet
TEMPERATURE: a **hot** day
APPEARANCE: a **beautiful** garden
PERSONALITY: a **friendly** neighbor
NATIONALITY: a **Mexican** restaurant

3. Adjectives **do not change**.

- They are the same for <u>singular</u> *(one)* or <u>plural</u> *(two or more)*.

- They are the same for <u>men</u> or <u>women</u>.

- a **small** *house*
- two **small** *houses*

- a **nice** *man*
- a **nice** *woman*

4. An adjective can go:

- **before a noun**

- Jason has a **brown** *dog*.
  NOT . . . a ~~dog brown~~

- **after the verbs** *be, become, feel, get (= become), look, seem, sound, taste*

- Jason's dog *is* **brown**.
- He *looks* **cute**.
- He*'s getting* **big**.

1 **FIND** • *Read this information about pets. Circle all the adjectives. Draw arrows to the nouns they describe.*

Pets are (popular) around the world. Here are some interesting facts about pets:

• In China people think cats are lucky.

• In Arab countries people think dogs are dirty.

• Italians don't like dogs very much, but they think cats are wonderful pets.

• Pets are common in England. Fifty percent of homes have one.

• In Africa pets are uncommon.

• Dogs are very popular in the United States, but people also keep fish, hamsters, and guinea pigs.

A hamster

A guinea pig

2 **DESCRIBE** • *Choose words from the boxes to describe the pictures.*

| afraid   big   ~~gray~~   friendly   black   small | | bed   bowl   cage   ~~cat~~   pet |

1. Mindy is a
__gray__ __cat__ .

2. She sleeps in a
_____ _____ .

3. She drinks water from
a _____ _____ .

4. Mindy is a
_____ _____ .

5. Tweety lives in a
_____ _____ .

6. Tweety is _____
of Mindy.

3 **COMPLETE** • *Use the words in parentheses to complete this article about pets.*

IS A PET RIGHT FOR YOU?

Choosing a pet _____<u>is a big decision</u>_____.
1. (decision / is / big / a)

Before you get a pet, think about _____.
2. (important / questions / these)

- **Space**—Think about the size of your home. You don't want

  _____ in _____!
  3. (a / dog / big)   **4.** (small / a / apartment)

- **Time**—_____. They don't need a lot of attention.
  5. (are / independent / Cats)

  But _____ on you for many things.
  6. (dogs / dependent / are)

- **Money**—How much will your pet's food and doctor bills cost?

  _____, but some _____.
  7. (cheap / is / goldfish / A)   **8.** (expensive / pets / are)

Remember! Pets _____, but they are also
9. (are / friends / wonderful)

_____!
10. (responsibility / big / a)

4 **EDIT** • *Read this e-mail message. Find and correct six mistakes in the use of adjectives. The first mistake is already corrected.*

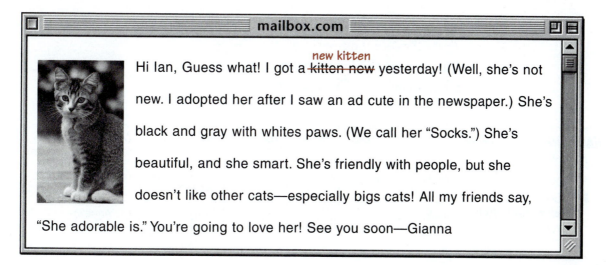

mailbox.com

Hi Ian, Guess what! I got a ~~kitten new~~ ^{new kitten} yesterday! (Well, she's not

new. I adopted her after I saw an ad cute in the newspaper.) She's

black and gray with whites paws. (We call her "Socks.") She's

beautiful, and she smart. She's friendly with people, but she

doesn't like other cats—especially bigs cats! All my friends say,

"She adorable is." You're going to love her! See you soon—Gianna

Comparisons: *As . . . as*

Ryoko is as short as Anne.

Sister Cities: Friendships between cities are **as important as** friendships between people.

Wow! Anne is only 5 feet tall. She's **as short as** me!

JAPAN

YOKOHAMA

Wow! Ryoko's hair is **as long as** mine!

CANADA
VANCOUVER

Ryoko and Anne live far apart, but soon they'll be **as close as** sisters.

CHECK POINT

Check the correct answer.

The girls are thinking about how they are _____.

☐ the same   ☐ different

CHART CHECK

Circle T (True) or F (False).

T F You can use **as** before and after an adjective.

	VERB	(NOT)	AS	ADJECTIVE	(AS)
Ryoko	is		as	short	(as Anne).
		not	as	athletic	
Ryoko's hair	is		as	long	(as Anne's).

EXPRESS CHECK

Check the correct answer.

☐ Ukon is as tall as Aki.

☐ Ukon isn't as tall as Aki.

☐ Aki isn't as tall as Ukon.

Grammar Explanations

Examples

1. Use *as* + **adjective** + *as* to talk about how two people, places, or things are **the same**.

- Jin is **as tall as** Keizo.
- The black T-shirt is **as big as** the white T-shirt.
- It's **as cheap as** the white shirt too.

Usage Note: We often use *just* before *as*.

- The black T-shirt looks *just* **as nice as** the white T-shirt.

2. Use *not as* + **adjective** + *as* to talk about how two people, places, or things are **not the same**.

- Todd is**n't as tall as** Ian.
- The white T-shirt is**n't as expensive as** the black one.
- It is**n't as nice as** the black one.

3. After the **second as**, you can use:

- an **object pronoun** (*me, you, him, her, it, us, them*)

  OR

- a **subject pronoun** (*I, you, he, she, it, we, they*) + **verb**.

Usage Note: We usually use object pronouns after *as* in conversation, notes, and e-mail.

- Todd is as tall **as *me***.

  OR

- Todd is as tall **as *I am***.

4. You **don't need the second as** + person, place, or thing when the meaning is clear.

- Anne is a fast runner. Ryoko isn't **as fast**. (*Ryoko isn't as fast as Anne.*)

1 **READ** • *"Sister" cities have a special relationship. The goal is friendship between two cities in different parts of the world. Look at this information about two "sister" cities.*

Vancouver, Canada

Became city: 1886
Population: 560,000 people
Size: 113 km² (44 sq mi)
Rain: 1,219 mm (48 in) per year
January temperature: 3°C (37°F)
July temperature: 18°C (64°F)

Yokohama, Japan

Became city: 1889
Population: 3,500,000 people
Size: 435 km² (168 sq mi)
Rain: 1,630 mm (64 in) per year
January temperature: 5°C (42°F)
July temperature: 24°C (76°F)

TRUE OR FALSE • *Read these statements. Circle T (True) or F (False).*

(T) F **1.** Yokohama is almost as old as Vancouver.

T F **2.** In population, Vancouver is as large as Yokohama.

T F **3.** In size, Vancouver isn't as big as Yokohama.

T F **4.** Vancouver is as rainy as Yokohama.

T F **5.** In winter, Yokohama isn't as cold as Vancouver.

T F **6.** In summer, Vancouver is as warm as Yokohama.

2 **DESCRIBE** • *Look at these family pictures. Complete the sentences with* **as** + *adjective* + **as** *or* **as** + *adjective. Use the correct form of the verbs in parentheses.*

Ryoko and her family

1. Ryoko ___isn't as tall as___ her brother.
　　　　(be / tall)

2. Ryoko _____ her brother.
　　　　(look / just / thin)

3. She _____ her mother.
　　　　(be / short)

4. Anne's family _____
　　　　　　　　　　(be / big)
Ryoko's family.

5. Anne _____ her sister.
　　　　(be / thin)

6. Anne _____ her mother.
　　　　(be / tall)

7. Anne's brother has long hair, but

it _____ Anne's.
　　(be / long)

Anne and her family

3 | **CHOOSE & COMPLETE** • Read this information about two hotels in Yokohama. Complete the sentences with **as** + **adjective** + **as** or **as** + **adjective**. Choose the correct adjective from the box.

~~big~~   expensive   good   far   tall

Yokohama Hotels

	Pan Pacific	**Grand**
Number of rooms	485	600
Number of floors	25	31
Room rate (1 person)	¥35,000	¥28,000–38,000
Distance from airport	100 km (62 mi)	106 km (66 mi)
Rating	★★★★★	★★★★★

1. With 485 rooms, the Pan Pacific is ___*n't as big as*___ the Grand.

2. With 25 floors, the Pan Pacific is _____ the Grand.

3. At ¥35,000 a night, the Pan Pacific is _____ some of the rooms at the Grand.

4. The Grand is 106 km from the airport. The Pan Pacific is almost _____.

5. The Grand is a five-star hotel. The Pan Pacific is just _____.

4 | **EDIT** • Read Anne's postcard to a friend. Find and correct six mistakes in the use of **as** + **adjective** + **as**. The first mistake is already corrected.

Dear Megan,

I'm spending the summer in Yokohama. It's a very big city, but not
                    as
as big ~~than~~ Tokyo. But it is as international as. It's a very modern city—
as just modern as Vancouver.

I'm living with a Japanese family—the Watanabes. They're great.
Their daughter Ryoko is my age. We are very similar, and we're now
almost close as sisters. Her little sister is as funny like Emmy.

I'm studying Japanese! It isn't as easier as French, but I'm learning
a little every day. Please write. Anne

Comparative Adjectives

He's older than me.

Brotherly love

CHECK POINT

Check the correct answers.

The brothers are talking about how they are _____.

☐ the same   ☐ different

CHART CHECK

Circle T (True) or F (False).

T F Comparative adjectives always end in **-er**.

T F Comparative adjectives always need **than**.

	COMPARATIVE ADJECTIVE	(THAN)
Jason is	older heavier	(than Taylor).
	better	
	more intelligent more athletic	

EXPRESS CHECK

Check all the sentences with comparative forms.

☐ My brother is tall.   ☐ She's a very good athlete.

☐ He's older than me.   ☐ She's more athletic than us.

☐ My sister is younger.   ☐ Tennis is her favorite sport.

Grammar Explanations	Examples

1. Use **comparative adjectives** to talk about <u>differences</u> between two people, places, or things.

- Mike's **taller** than his brother.
- He's **friendlier** than him.
- He's **more popular** than him.
- He gets **better** grades.

2. For <u>short adjectives</u>, use:
adjective + -er

▶ **BE CAREFUL!** There are often <u>spelling changes</u> when you add **-er**.

ADJECTIVE	COMPARATIVE
old	old**er**
tall	tall**er**
short	short**er**
nice	nic**er**
hot	hot**ter**
happy	happ**ier**

3. The comparatives for **good, bad,** and **far** are <u>irregular</u>.

ADJECTIVE	COMPARATIVE
good	**better**
bad	**worse**
far	**farther**

4. For <u>long adjectives</u>, use:
more + adjective

ADJECTIVE	COMPARATIVE
intelligent	**more** intelligent
interesting	**more** interesting

5. Use **than** before the second part in the comparison.

You **don't need than** when the meaning is clear.

- **She**'s more athletic **than** her sister.
- **They** are stronger **than** us.

- Her brother is fast, but she's **faster**.
  (She's faster than her brother.)

6. **After than**, you can use:

- an **object pronoun** (*me, you, him, her, it, us, them*)

  OR

- a **subject pronoun** (*I, you, he, she, it, we, they*) + **verb**

USAGE NOTE: We usually use object pronouns after *than* in conversation, notes, and e-mail.

- He's faster **than** *me*.

  OR

- He's faster **than** *I am*.

Check it out!

Spelling Rules for the Comparative of Adjectives ▶▶▶ **APPENDIX 21, page 241.**
Irregular Comparisons of Adjectives ▶▶▶ **APPENDIX 11, page 234.**

1 **READ** • *Read about tennis sisters Venus and Serena Williams.*

Venus Williams
Date of birth: 6/17/1980
Height: 6 ft 1 in (186 cm)
Weight: 168 lb (76 kg)
Serve* speed: 100 mph (161 km/h)
Rank in 2002: 2

Serena Williams
Date of birth: 9/26/1981
Height: 5 ft 10 in (178 cm)
Weight: 145 lb (66 kg)
Serve speed: 101 mph (163 km/h)
Rank in 2002: 1

*serve = throwing the ball into the air and hitting it to start a game

TRUE OR FALSE • *Read these statements. Circle T (True) or F (False).*

T **F** **1.** Venus is older than Serena.

T **F** **2.** Serena is taller than Venus.

T **F** **3.** Venus is heavier than Serena.

T **F** **4.** Venus has a faster serve.

T **F** **5.** In 2002, Serena was more successful.

2 **DESCRIBE** • *Look at these pictures. Circle the correct adjective and complete the comparisons. Use* **than** *when necessary.*

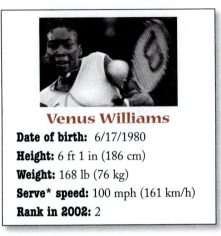

1. (big / small)
Andre's racket is
_____**bigger than**_____ Igor's.

2. (clean / dirty)
The shoes on the left
are _____ .

3. (cheap / expensive)
4A is _____
28Z.

4. (low / high)
The ball on the left is
_____ .

5. (good / bad)
Andre's score is
_____ Igor's.

6. (happy / sad)
Igor is _____
Andre.

3 | **CHOOSE & COMPLETE** • *Read about these brothers and sisters. Complete the comparisons with the correct form of the words in the box. Use **than** when necessary.*

| expensive   good   large   popular   short   slow   heavy   ~~young~~ |

1. Ava is 18. Her sister is 21. Ava is ___younger than___ her sister.

2. Elio gets 80s on his tests. Paz gets 90s. Paz is a _____ student.

3. Lev runs 1 mile in 7 minutes. Dorit needs 8 minutes. Dorit is _____.

4. Annika has a lot of friends. Her brother has only one. Annika is _____.

5. Jan pays $50 for his running shoes. His brother pays $100. Jan's brother buys _____ running shoes.

6. Lea's room is 200 square feet. Her sister's is 120 square feet. Lea's room is _____ her sister's.

7. Todd weighs 125 pounds. His brother weighs 110 pounds. Todd is _____.

8. Natalie is 5 feet 4 inches tall. Her sister is 5 feet 6. Natalie is _____.

4 | **EDIT** • *Read this student's essay. Find and correct eight mistakes in the use of comparative adjectives. The first mistake is already corrected.*

> Sibling rivalry is competition between brothers and sisters.
> smarter
> Which brother is ~~more smart~~? Which sister is popularer? Who gets
> good grades than the other? Sibling rivalry is not unusual in
> families. It is *more* unusual on the tennis court.
>
> The Williams sisters, Venus and Serena, are star tennis
> players. They often compete. Is it difficulter or more easier to
> play against your own sister? The sisters say the *game* is
> important—not the other player. Does their relationship make
> their game more interestinger? Some people think the game is not
> as exciting when sisters play. I don't agree. I think their games
> are more excitinger. Venus and Serena are both better as most
> other players in the world—sisters or not.

Superlative Adjectives

It's the longest noodle in the world.

On June 2, 2001, Michael Sorge cooked **the longest** noodle in the world. It was 418 feet (127.4 meters) long.

SOURCE: *Guinness Book of World Records, 2002.*

CHECK POINT

Check the correct answer.

All other noodles are _____ than 418 feet.

☐ longer

☐ shorter

ADJECTIVE	COMPARATIVE	SUPERLATIVE

long	longer	the longest

CHART CHECK

Circle T (True) or F (False).

T F Use *the* with all superlative adjectives.

T F All superlative adjectives end with *-est*.

	THE	SUPERLATIVE ADJECTIVE	
He cooks	the	longest hottest	noodles in the world.
		best worst	
		most amazing most delicious	

EXPRESS CHECK

Check the sentences with superlative adjectives.

☐ Sorge's is the best restaurant in town.

☐ Their food is better than Roma's.

☐ It's not the most expensive restaurant.

☐ They serve great noodles.

☐ It's on the busiest street.

Grammar Explanations

Examples

1. Use **superlative adjectives** to compare one person, place, or thing with other people, places, or things in a group. (a group = three or more)

A   B   C

■ C is **the biggest** bowl. *(bigger than A and B)*

2. For <u>short adjectives</u>, use:
the* + adjective + *-est

▶ **BE CAREFUL!** There are often <u>spelling changes</u> when you add ***-est***.

ADJECTIVE	SUPERLATIVE
old	**the** old**est**
fast	**the** fast**est**
long	**the** long**est**
nice	**the** nic**est**
hot	**the** hot**test**
salty	**the** salt**iest**

3. The superlatives for ***good, bad,*** and ***far*** are <u>irregular</u>.

ADJECTIVE	SUPERLATIVE
good	**the best**
bad	**the worst**
far	**the farthest**

4. For <u>long adjectives</u>, use:
***the most* + adjective**

ADJECTIVE	SUPERLATIVE
amazing	**the *most* amazing**
interesting	**the *most* interesting**
difficult	**the *most* difficult**

5. **After superlatives**, you can use expressions like ***in the world, on earth,*** and ***of all***.

■ It's **the longest** noodle *in the world*.
■ What's **the highest** place *on earth*?
■ She's **the best** teacher *of all*.

Check it out!

Spelling Rules for the Superlative of Adjectives ▶▶▶ **APPENDIX 21, page 241.**
Irregular Comparisons of Adjectives ▶▶▶ **APPENDIX 11, page 234.**

1 **MATCH** • *Look at this family picture. Match each name with the description.*

Name	Description
c **1.** Jesse	**a.** the tallest
_____ **2.** Sharon	**b.** the heaviest
_____ **3.** Mike	**c.** the oldest
_____ **4.** Patty	**d.** the most athletic
_____ **5.** Ron	**e.** the youngest
_____ **6.** Doug	**f.** the most serious

Sharon

Jesse Mike Patty Ron Doug

2 **DESCRIBE** • *Look at these pictures and complete the sentences. Use the superlative form of the correct word.*

WORLD RECORDS (2001)

Born 1990

1. The ___youngest___
(old / young)
chef is Justin Miller. He
works for a hotel company.

**Heels: 16 inches
(41 cm)**

2. The shoes with the

_____
(high / low)
heels cost $1,062.

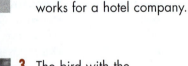

**Puck knew
1,724 words.**

3. The bird with the

_____
(big / small)
vocabulary died in 1994.

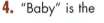

**403 pounds
(182 kg)**

4. "Baby" is the

_____
(heavy / light)
snake in the world.

$46,532

5. The _____
(cheap / expensive)
pair of jeans today cost
only $1 in the 1800s.

Born 1875

6. Jeanne Calment was the

_____ person.
(old / young)
She died at age 122.

3 **CHOOSE & COMPLETE** • *Complete these sentences with the superlative form of the words in the box. Then you can take the quiz and check your answers below.*

~~big~~ dry fast heavy high hot intelligent

1. _____The biggest_____ piece of ice on earth is three miles thick. It's in:
   a. Antarctica **b.** Canada **c.** Russia

2. The Sahara is _____ place in the world. Its highest temperature is:
   a. 200°F (93°C) **b.** 105°F (41°C) **c.** 130°F (57°C)

3. _____ animals of all weigh almost 200 tons (181 metric tons). They are:
   a. blue whales **b.** elephants **c.** lions

4. Cheetahs are _____ animals in the world. They can run:
   a. 40 mph (64 km/h) **b.** 100 mph (161 km/h) **c.** 70 mph (113 km/h)

5. At 29,035 ft (8,850 m), Everest is _____ mountain on earth. It's in:
   a. Australia **b.** Europe **c.** Asia

6. It isn't as smart as us, but it is one of _____ animals in the world.
   a. a cat **b.** a monkey **c.** a tiger

7. The Atacama Desert is _____ place on earth. It never rains. It's in:
   a. Africa **b.** South America **c.** North America

Answers: 1. a 2. c 3. a 4. c 5. c 6. b 7. b

4 **EDIT** • *Read this review of* The Guinness Book of World Records. *Find and correct eight mistakes in the use of superlative adjectives. The first mistake is already corrected.*

The ~~Amazingest~~ Facts on Earth
Most Amazing

Who is the oldest person in the world? Who bought the expensive shoes? What is the smaller TV? Where is the baddest air on earth? You will find all these facts and many more in *The Guinness Book of World Records*—the popularest book of modern times. Kids call it the greatest birthday gift of all. Parents love it too. For you, maybe the facts about movie stars will be the interesting. But for me, the goodest chapter is "Amazing Nature." *Please* ask me, "What's the long river in the world?"

Adjectives with *Very, Too,* and *Enough*

Is it big enough? It's too small.

Is it **big enough?**

CHART CHECK

Check the correct answers.

Which words go before an adjective?

☐ *enough*

☐ *too*

☐ *very*

VERY + ADJECTIVE			
	VERY	**ADJECTIVE**	
The car is	very	**small**.	
The suitcase is		**big**.	

TOO + ADJECTIVE			
	TOO	**ADJECTIVE**	
The car is	too	**small**.	
The suitcase is		**big**.	

ADJECTIVE + ENOUGH			
	ADJECTIVE	**ENOUGH**	
The car is	**big**	enough.	
The suitcase is	**small**		

EXPRESS CHECK

Look at this picture.
Check the correct name.

	Bozo	**Zombo**	**Sparkles**
1. His shoes are too small.	☐	☐	☐
2. His shoes are big enough.	☐	☐	☐
3. His shoes are too big.	☐	☐	☐

Grammar Explanations

Examples

1. Use *very, too,* and *enough* with adjectives.	■ New cars are *very* **expensive**. ■ This car is *too* **small** for us. ■ That one is **big** *enough*.
2. *Very* makes an adjective <u>stronger</u>.	■ Our car is *very* **big**. Six people can ride in it. ■ It's raining hard. The roads are *very* **wet**.

3. *Too* and *not . . . enough* mean that there is a <u>problem</u>.	■ The Jaguar is *too* **expensive**.
	■ It is*n't* **cheap** *enough*.
	  (We can't buy it.)
	
	■ The seats are *too* **hard**.
	■ They are*n't* **soft** *enough*.
	  (They're not comfortable.)

4. *Enough* and *not too* mean that there is <u>no problem</u>.	■ The Toyota is **cheap** *enough*.
	■ It is*n't* *too* **expensive**.
	  (We can buy it.)
	
	■ The seats are **soft** *enough*.
	■ They are*n't* *too* **hard**.
	  (They're comfortable.)

5. *Very* and *too* <u>go before the adjective</u>.	■ It's *very* **noisy** in the car. ■ The radio is *too* **loud**.
▶ **Be careful!** *Enough* goes <u>after the adjective</u>.	■ This car isn't **quiet** *enough*. Not This car isn't ~~enough quiet~~.

1   **READ •** *Read this review of a new car. Underline all examples of* **very**, **too**, *and* **enough** *with adjectives.*

MINI Cooper

Last week we looked at a MINI Cooper. First I said, "This car is too small for us." The MINI Cooper is for four people, but we are four very large people! Then we got in. Surprise! The front seat was big enough for my tall husband. The back seat was wide enough for two teenagers with backpacks. The MINI Cooper is only 14.6 feet long, and I parked it in a very small space. ("Too small," said my daughter. She was wrong.) Most important, it's a very safe car. And we're lucky: It isn't too expensive for us.

TRUE OR FALSE • *Circle T (True) or F (False).*

T **(F)** **1.** The car is big enough for six.   T   F   **4.** The parking space was too small.

T   F   **2.** It wasn't too small for this family.   T   F   **5.** It is safe enough.

T   F   **3.** It isn't very long.   T   F   **6.** The family can buy the car.

2   **CHOOSE •** *Look at these pictures. Circle the correct words to complete the sentences.*

3 **COMPLETE •** *Read this information about two cars. Complete the sentences with* **too** *or* **enough** *and the adjectives in parentheses. Use the correct form of* **be**.

1. Bryan can spend $20,000 on a car.

   The Honda ___*isn't too expensive*___ for him.
   <u>(expensive)</u>

2. Safety is very important to the Ruiz family.

   The Jeep _____ for them.
   <u>(dangerous)</u>

3. Pam can't spend a lot on gas. The Honda

   _____ for her.
   <u>(expensive)</u>

4. There are five people in the Smith family. The

   Jeep _____ for them.
   <u>(big)</u>

5. Eva travels a lot. The Jeep _____.
   <u>(comfortable)</u>

6. Dan doesn't need a quiet car. The Jeep _____ for him.
   <u>(quiet)</u>

7. Lin wants a car for under $30,000. The Jeep _____.
   <u>(cheap)</u>

8. Paz and Maria have one child. The Honda _____ for them.
   <u>(small)</u>

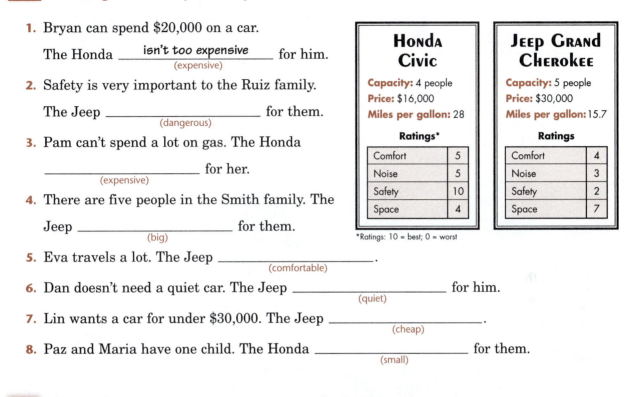

Honda Civic	
Capacity: 4 people	
Price: $16,000	
Miles per gallon: 28	
Ratings*	
Comfort	5
Noise	5
Safety	10
Space	4

Jeep Grand Cherokee	
Capacity: 5 people	
Price: $30,000	
Miles per gallon: 15.7	
Ratings	
Comfort	4
Noise	3
Safety	2
Space	7

*Ratings: 10 = best; 0 = worst

4 **EDIT •** *Read this ad for a new car. Find and correct nine mistakes in the use of* **very**, **too**, *and* **enough**. *The first mistake is already corrected.*

Is your car "almost ~~enough good~~?"
good enough

• Is it big enough for your family, but too much big for city parking?

• Do you feel too safe, but not very comfortable on long trips?

Test-drive a new Beep today. It's very big for big families. It's enough safe for your teenage driver. Drive it to the mall or across the country—it's too comfortable for every trip. Nothing can stop the Beep—the worst road isn't too bad for this car. The smallest parking spot isn't small enough. But don't wait—the new Beep is a too popular car, and it's selling fast. For you, "too not bad" really isn't good enough. Buy a Beep. Today.

Adjectives and Adverbs

The music is nice. They skate nicely.

Canadian ice dancers David Pelletier and Jamie Salé

Speech bubbles:
- They skate **beautifully**.
- The music is **nice**.
- That was a **bad** jump.
- She jumped **perfectly**. I'll give her a 10.
- I'm getting **cold**.

CHECK POINT

Check the correct answer.

Which judges will probably give the skaters the highest score?

☐ 1 and 3   ☐ 2 and 3

☐ 1 and 4   ☐ 4 and 5

CHART CHECK

Circle T (True) or F (False).

T F An adjective can go after a form of *be*.

T F All adverbs end in *-ly*.

ADJECTIVES	ADVERBS
The music is **nice**.	They skate **nicely**.
That jump wasn't **easy**.	They won **easily**.
We have **perfect** seats.	We can see **perfectly**.
They're **good** skaters.	They skate **well**.
That was a **hard** jump.	They practiced **hard**.

EXPRESS CHECK

Write sentences with the words in parentheses.

(music / The / slow / is) _____   (slowly / skate / They) _____

148

Grammar Explanations

Examples

1. Adjectives describe <u>people</u>, <u>places</u>, and <u>things</u>.

- Jamie and David are **good** skaters.
- They're **young**.

Adjectives can go <u>before a noun</u>.

adjective + noun

- That was a **nice jump**.

Adjectives can go <u>after the verbs</u> *be, become, feel, get (= become), look, seem, sound,* and *taste.*

verb + adjective

- The show ***was good***.
- They ***looked*** **happy**.

---

2. Some **adverbs** describe <u>actions</u>. They often answer the question *How?*

A: *How* did they skate?
B: They skated **nicely**.

These adverbs usually go <u>after a verb</u>.

verb + adverb

- He ***jumped*** **badly** today.
- They ***dance*** **perfectly** together.

REMEMBER! Use adjectives, not adverbs, after the verbs *be, become, feel, get (= become), look, seem, sound,* and *taste.*

- The music ***sounds*** **nice**.
  NOT The music sounds ~~nicely~~.

---

3. Many **adverbs** have the form:
adjective + -ly

ADJECTIVE	**ADVERB**
careful	careful**ly**
nice	nic**ely**
easy	eas**ily**
terrible	terrib**ly**
fantastic	fantastic**ally**

▶ **BE CAREFUL!** There are sometimes <u>spelling changes</u> when you add *-ly*.

---

4. BE CAREFUL!

a. Some adjectives also end in *-ly*. *Friendly, lonely,* and *lovely* are adjectives, <u>not</u> adverbs.

adjective

- My coach is **friendly**.
  NOT He talks ~~friendly~~.

b. The adverb form of ***good*** is ***well***.

adjective   adverb

- He's a **good** skater. He skates **well**.

c. Some **adjectives** and **adverbs** have the <u>same form</u> (*early, fast, hard, late, wrong*).

adjective   adverb

- He's a **fast** learner. He learns **fast**.
- It's a **late** show. It starts **late**.

d. The adjective ***hard*** and the adverb ***hard*** have <u>different meanings</u>.

- It's a **hard** dance. *(It's a difficult dance.)*
- They practiced **hard**. *(They practiced a lot.)*

Check it out!
Spelling Rules for Adverbs Ending in *-ly* ▶▶▶ APPENDIX 22, page 241.

1 **FIND** • Ice Dancer Magazine (ID) *interviewed Tyler Miller (TM), a famous skater. Circle the adjectives. Put a box around the adverbs. Draw arrows to the words they describe.*

I N T E R V I E W

ID: Why did you start skating?

TM: As a kid, I played ball badly, but I skated well. It was a good sport for me.

ID: Were you always a serious skater?

TM: No. I didn't want to work hard, and prizes weren't important to me.

ID: You skate seriously now.

TM: I watched the Olympics a few years ago. My feelings changed fast after that.

ID: You looked great today on the ice. Maybe I'll see you at the Olympics.

TM: Sure! Maybe I'll be lucky!

---

2 **CHOOSE** • *Look at these pictures. Complete the sentences with the words from the box.*

cold   friendly   perfect   terribly   terrible   well

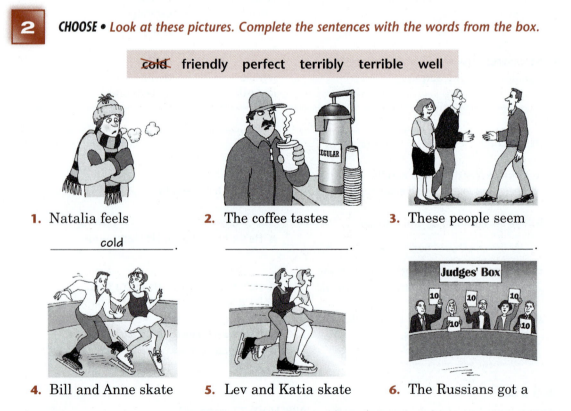

1. Natalia feels

_____cold_____.

2. The coffee tastes

_____.

3. These people seem

_____.

4. Bill and Anne skate

_____.

5. Lev and Katia skate

_____.

6. The Russians got a

_____ score.

3 **COMPLETE** • *Read this diary of a young skater. Complete it with the correct form of the words in parentheses.*

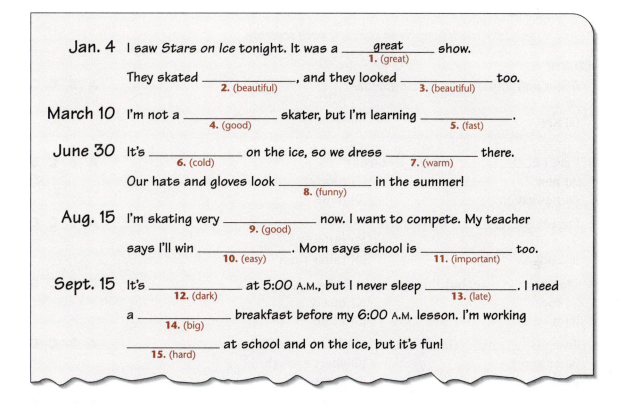

Jan. 4 I saw *Stars on Ice* tonight. It was a ___great___ show.
1. (great)

They skated _____, and they looked _____ too.
2. (beautiful) **3. (beautiful)**

March 10 I'm not a _____ skater, but I'm learning _____.
4. (good) **5. (fast)**

June 30 It's _____ on the ice, so we dress _____ there.
6. (cold) **7. (warm)**

Our hats and gloves look _____ in the summer!
8. (funny)

Aug. 15 I'm skating very _____ now. I want to compete. My teacher
9. (good)

says I'll win _____. Mom says school is _____ too.
10. (easy) **11. (important)**

Sept. 15 It's _____ at 5:00 A.M., but I never sleep _____. I need
12. (dark) **13. (late)**

a _____ breakfast before my 6:00 A.M. lesson. I'm working
14. (big)

_____ at school and on the ice, but it's fun!
15. (hard)

4 **EDIT** • *Read this movie review. Find and correct eight mistakes in the use of adjectives and adverbs. The first mistake is already corrected.*

The Cutting Edge **Rating: ★★★ out of ★★★★**

Skating fans, listen up! *The Cutting Edge* is a romantic movie with ~~greatly~~ ^{great} skaters. The stars are practicing for the Winter Olympics. Kate Mosely looks beautifully on the ice, but she isn't a nicely person. All her partners leave quickly. Then her coach introduces her to Doug Dorsey. Doug was a hockey star, so he skates good. At first, they argue. To Kate, Doug is the wrong choice (he's not a dancer). To Doug, ice dancing isn't a seriously sport. But Doug learns fastly, and they are well partners. Do they get to the Olympics? Rent the movie and see. The conversation is funnily, and the story moves quickly.

SelfTest

Circle the letter of the correct answer to complete each sentence.

> **EXAMPLE:**
> Alicia and Paulo _____ students.   A **B** C D
> (A) am   (C) be
> (B) are   (D) is

1. I got two _____ kittens yesterday.   A B C D
   (A) new   (C) newly
   (B) newest   (D) news

2. I'm not as _____ my sister.   A B C D
   (A) tall   (C) tallest
   (B) tall as   (D) taller than

3. That shirt is nice, but this one looks just as _____.   A B C D
   (A) nice   (C) nicely
   (B) nice as   (D) nicer

4. Jason is _____ than I am.   A B C D
   (A) as short   (C) short enough
   (B) more short   (D) shorter

5. The weather is bad today, but yesterday it was _____.   A B C D
   (A) more bad   (C) worse than
   (B) worse   (D) worst

6. Is baseball _____ popular than football?   A B C D
   (A) as   (C) the
   (B) more   (D) very

7. Bill is fast, but Cory is the fastest runner _____.   A B C D
   (A) as Bill   (C) than Bill
   (B) on the team   (D) than the team

8. Hondas are _____ popular cars.   A B C D
   (A) enough   (C) too
   (B) most   (D) very

9. This car isn't _____. We need more room.   A B C D
   (A) big enough   (C) small enough
   (B) enough big   (D) too small

10. They look _____ together.   A B C D
    (A) as happy as   (C) happily
    (B) enough happy   (D) happy

11. She skates _____.　　　　　　　　　　　　**A B C D**
　　(A) as beautiful　　　　　　　(C) beautiful
　　(B) beautifully　　　　　　　　(D) more beautiful

12. Are those _____ dogs?　　　　　　　　　**A B C D**
　　(A) friend　　　　　　　　　　(C) friendly
　　(B) friendliest　　　　　　　　(D) friends

13. Uma is just _____ as Renée.　　　　　　**A B C D**
　　(A) as intelligent　　　　　　(C) intelligently
　　(B) intelligent　　　　　　　　(D) more intelligent

14. Carla drives _____. I always feel safe with her.　**A B C D**
　　(A) good　　　　　　　　　　　(C) well
　　(B) too good　　　　　　　　　(D) worse

15. Patrick works very _____.　　　　　　　**A B C D**
　　(A) hard　　　　　　　　　　　(C) hardly enough
　　(B) hardly　　　　　　　　　　(D) too hard

SECTION TWO

Each sentence has four underlined parts. The four underlined parts of the sentence are marked A, B, C, and D. Circle the letter of the one underlined part that is NOT CORRECT.

> **EXAMPLE:**
> My friends <u>is</u> here, but we <u>are</u> <u>not</u> <u>studying</u>.　　**(A) B C D**
> 　　　　　　A　　　　　　　B　　C　　D

16. The <u>car new</u> was <u>too</u> <u>expensive</u>, so I bought an <u>older</u> one.　**A B C D**
　　　　A　　　　B　　C　　　　　　　　　D

17. Sylvie is <u>very</u> <u>smart</u> and she studies <u>hard</u>, but her grades aren't as　**A B C D**
　　　　　　A　　B　　　　　　　　C
　　<u>good than</u> Anne's.
　　　D

18. A goldfish is <u>cheaper</u> <u>that</u> a dog, but it's not <u>friendly</u> <u>enough</u> for me.　**A B C D**
　　　　　　A　　B　　　　　　　　C　　D

19. Rob is <u>a youngest</u> boy, and his <u>brothers</u> are <u>bigger</u> and <u>stronger</u>.　**A B C D**
　　　　A　　　　　　　　B　　　　C　　　　D

20. Those cats are <u>cutes</u>, but my <u>apartment</u> is <u>too</u> <u>small</u> for pets.　**A B C D**
　　　　　　A　　　　　B　　　C　D

21. Rosa isn't <u>as old as</u> Fiona, <u>but</u> she's <u>as just</u> <u>tall</u>.　**A B C D**
　　　　　A　　　　　　B　　　C　　D

22. Scott <u>plays</u> football <u>well</u>, but soccer is <u>more</u> <u>interestinger</u> to him.　**A B C D**
　　　　A　　　　　B　　　　　C　　D

23. This is the <u>goodest</u> <u>restaurant</u> in town, and the <u>food</u> is <u>delicious</u>.　**A B C D**
　　　　　A　　　B　　　　　　　C　　D

24. Today was <u>the</u> <u>worse</u> day of the week—it rained <u>hard</u>, then it was <u>hot</u>.　**A B C D**
　　　　A　　B　　　　　　　　C　　　　D

25. My roommates are <u>too</u> <u>nice</u>, but our dorm is the <u>most crowded</u> one <u>of all</u>.　**A B C D**
　　　　　A　　B　　　　　　　C　　　　D

UNIT 35

Ability: *Can, Could*

He can run, but he can't fly.

Wow! That guy can run fast!

Yes! But he can't fly! Or can he . . . ?

Yes, he can! Wow! Awesome!

CHECK *POINT*

Check the correct answer.

The people are suprised because the man _____.

☐ doesn't run fast

☐ flies

CHART CHECK 1

Circle T (True) or F (False).

T F Use *can* and *could* with all subjects.

T F Use *could* with *now*.

STATEMENTS

SUBJECT	CAN (NOT)/ COULD (NOT)	BASE FORM OF VERB	
I You* He She It We They	**can** **cannot** **can't**	**run**	fast now.
	could **could not** **couldn't**		fast last year.

*You = one person or several people.

CONTRACTIONS

cannot = **can't**
could not = **couldn't**

YES/NO QUESTIONS

CAN/ COULD	SUBJECT	BASE FORM	
Can	he	**run**	fast?
Could			

SHORT ANSWERS

AFFIRMATIVE			NEGATIVE		
Yes,	he	**can**. **could**.	**No**,	he	**can't**. **couldn't**.

154

CHART CHECK 2 ➝

Check the correct answer.

Form questions with:

☐ *can* or *could*

☐ *do*

WH- QUESTIONS			
QUESTION WORD	CAN/ COULD	SUBJECT	BASE FORM OF VERB
How fast	**can** **could**	he	**run**?

EXPRESS CHECK

Circle the correct words.

In 2001, I <u>can't / couldn't</u> swim. I took swimming lessons. Now I <u>can / could</u> swim!

Grammar Explanations

Examples

1. Use *can* + **base form** of the verb (*run, fly, speak,* . . .) for <u>abilities</u> people have <u>now</u>.

The <u>negative</u> of *can* is **cannot**. Use *can't* in conversation, notes, and e-mail.

- He **can run** fast.
- She **can fly** a plane.

- I **can't speak** French.

2. Use *could* + **base form** for <u>abilities</u> people had in the <u>past</u>.

The <u>negative</u> of *could* is **could not**. Use *couldn't* in conversation, notes, and e-mail.

- He **could swim** at the age of three.
- He **could** also **run** really fast.

- He **couldn't understand** me.

3. Begin *yes/no questions* with *can* or *could*.

Use **short answers** to answer *yes/no* questions.

Use *can't* and *couldn't* in negative short answers.

- **Can** you **drive** a car?
- **Could** you **understand** the movie last night?

A: *Can* you speak Spanish?
B: **Yes,** I **can**. OR **Yes**.

A: *Could* you understand the movie?
B: **No,** I **couldn't**. OR **No**.

4. Begin *wh- questions* with a **question word**. Then use the same word order as in *yes/no* questions.

- *Which* languages **can** you **speak**?
- *How* well **could** you **understand** the movie last night?

Check it out!

Requests with *Can, Could* ➤➤➤ UNIT 37, page 162.
Permission with *Can, Could* ➤➤➤ UNIT 38, page 166.
Possibility with *Could* ➤➤➤ UNIT 40, page 176.

1 **FIND** • *Read about triathlete Eduardo Martín Sturla. Underline all the words for ability.*

Swim, Bike, Run!

Eduardo Martín Sturla is a professional triathlete from Argentina. He <u>can swim</u>, he can ride a bike, and he can run. Many people can do these things too. But most people can't do them as fast (or for as long) as triathletes. In a triathlon, athletes compete in all three sports without a break.

In his first triathlon, Sturla couldn't bike or run fast enough. He finished almost last, but he didn't quit. In 2001 he wanted to compete in Brazil, but he couldn't pay for a plane ticket. Then his girlfriend returned his ring. No girlfriend and no money—it was a very hard time for Eduardo! A friend gave him an airplane ticket so he could fly to Brazil. He finished first! He couldn't win his girlfriend's heart, but he could win a triathlon!

2 **DESCRIBE** • *Look at these pictures. Complete the sentences with* **can, can't, could,** *or* **couldn't** *and the verbs in parentheses.*

Then   **Now**

1. She ___*couldn't ride*___ a bike then.
(ride)

2. Now she _____ a bike.
(ride)

3. He _____ beautifully now.
(skate)

4. He _____ beautifully then too.
(skate)

5. They _____ fast now.
(run)

6. They _____ very fast then.
(run)

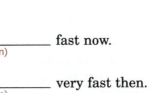

3 **ASK & ANSWER** • *Look at the information about athlete Lizel Schmidt. Then complete the questions and answers. Use* **can, can't, could,** *and* **couldn't.**

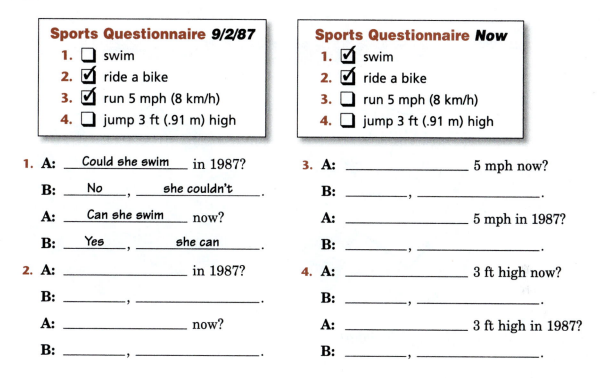

Sports Questionnaire 9/2/87
1. ☐ swim
2. ☑ ride a bike
3. ☑ run 5 mph (8 km/h)
4. ☐ jump 3 ft (.91 m) high

Sports Questionnaire *Now*
1. ☑ swim
2. ☑ ride a bike
3. ☐ run 5 mph (8 km/h)
4. ☐ jump 3 ft (.91 m) high

1. **A:** _____Could she swim_____ in 1987?

   B: _____No_____, _____she couldn't_____.

   A: _____Can she swim_____ now?

   B: _____Yes_____, _____she can_____.

2. **A:** _____ in 1987?

   B: _____, _____.

   A: _____ now?

   B: _____, _____.

3. **A:** _____ 5 mph now?

   B: _____, _____.

   A: _____ 5 mph in 1987?

   B: _____, _____.

4. **A:** _____ 3 ft high now?

   B: _____, _____.

   A: _____ 3 ft high in 1987?

   B: _____, _____.

4 **EDIT** • *Read this athlete's journal entry. Find and correct seven mistakes in the use of* **can** *or* **could**. *The first mistake is already corrected.*

I'm so tired! I'm surprised I can ~~to~~ write!! I just finished my first triathlon!
(Sara was in the race too, but she couldn't finishes.) This morning I got up at
5:30 (I'm glad I could slept!). I took a quick shower and put on my swim suit.
The race started at 7:30. I can still feel the cold water! It was very green, and
I could no see very well. But I finished the first part of the race. I got out of the
water and ran to my bike. I can usually biking very fast. This time I had trouble.
But, again, I finished. After the bike race, I went for the run. The big question was
this: I could continue to run fast? Well, I didn't win the triathlon, but I finished.
And I learned an important lesson. A year ago I thought: Me in a triathlon?
Never! Now I know I can to do it!

UNIT 36

Suggestions:
Why don't, Let's, How about

Let's go to the cafeteria.

CHECK POINT

Check the correct answer.

The student _____.

☐ has a good idea   ☐ wants information

CHART CHECK 1

*Circle T (True) or
F (False).*

T   F Suggestions
with *Why don't*
can have
different
subjects.

SUGGESTIONS WITH *WHY DON'T*

WHY DON'T	SUBJECT	BASE FORM OF VERB	
Why don't	we you	**eat**	now?
Why doesn't	he she	**get**	pizza?

CHART CHECK 2

*Check the correct
answer.*

☐ Suggestions with
Let's can be
affirmative or
negative.

☐ Suggestions with
Let's end in a
question mark.

SUGGESTIONS WITH *LET'S*

LET'S (NOT)	BASE FORM OF VERB	
Let's	**eat**	now.
Let's not	**get**	pizza.

158

<table>
<tr><td rowspan="3">

CHART CHECK 3

Circle T (True) or F (False).

T F After *How about* you need the base form of the verb.
</td></tr>
</table>

SUGGESTIONS WITH *HOW ABOUT*		
How about	**Verb + -ing**	
How about	eating	now?
	getting	pizza?

EXPRESS CHECK

Check all the suggestions.

☐ Let's go to the cafeteria.

☐ How's the food there?

☐ Why do you bring your own lunch?

☐ How about getting some coffee?

☐ Why don't we get some dessert?

☐ Let's not stay here.

Grammar Explanations

Examples

1. Use *Why don't* or *Why doesn't* + **base form** of the verb (*go, ride, come, . . .*) for <u>suggestions</u>.

- It's a beautiful day. **Why don't** we *go* to the park?
- Good idea! **Why don't** we *ride* our bikes there?
- **Why doesn't** your brother *come* with us?

Suggestions with **Why don't** or **Why doesn't** end in a <u>question mark</u>.

- **Why don't** you get something to eat**?**

2. You can also use *Let's* or *Let's not* + **base form** of the verb to make <u>suggestions</u>.

- **Let's go** to the park.
- **Let's ride** our bikes there.
- **Let's not ride** our bikes. It's too cold.
- **Let's not walk**. We don't have enough time.

Let's means *Why don't we?*

- **Let's** go to the movies. (*Why don't we go to the movies?*)

Usage Note: *Let's* is the <u>contraction</u> for *Let us.* We almost always use the contraction.

- **Let's** take the bus. Not ~~Let us~~ take the bus.

Suggestions with **Let's** end in a <u>period</u>.

- **Let's** invite Mehmet to go with us**.**

3. You can also use *How about* + verb + *-ing* to make <u>suggestions</u>.

- **How about** *going* to the park?
- **How about** *taking* the bus?

Suggestions with **How about** end in a <u>question mark</u>.

- **How about** walking**?**

1 **FIND** • *Read this conversation. Underline all the suggestions.*

KARL: I'm hungry.

EVA: Me too. <u>How about getting something to eat?</u>

KARL: OK. But let's not go to the school cafeteria. I hate that place.

EVA: Why do you hate the school cafeteria?

KARL: The food is terrible. <u>Why don't we go to Joe's for pizza?</u>

EVA: Good idea. But <u>how about leaving now?</u> I have a 1:00 class.

KARL: Fine. <u>Let's go.</u>

TRUE OR FALSE • *Read the statements. Circle T (True) or F (False).*

(T) **F** **1.** Eva wants to get something to eat.

T **F** **2.** Karl wants to eat in the school cafeteria.

T **F** **3.** Karl wants to have pizza.

T **F** **4.** Eva doesn't want to go to Joe's for pizza.

T **F** **5.** Karl and Eva want to leave now.

2 **CHOOSE** • *Read these suggestions from the Suggestion Box in the school cafeteria. Circle the correct words or punctuation to complete them.*

1. I hate waiting in line just for drinks. Why don't you get a soda machine .

2. Why <u>don't / doesn't</u> the cafeteria have more desserts? Ice cream and cake every day is boring.

3. Let's <u>get / getting</u> comfortable chairs. The ones we have are terrible.

4. Many students don't eat meat. How about <u>have / having</u> some more non-meat choices?

5. Let's have pizza as a lunch choice <u>. / ?</u> Everyone loves pizza!

6. There aren't enough vegetables. Why don't you <u>make / making</u> a salad for lunch?

7. Why <u>do / don't</u> you have a salad bar? That way we can make our own salad.

8. <u>Why don't / Let's</u> you have music in the cafeteria?

9. <u>Let's / Let's not</u> have spinach! I hate spinach!

10. <u>Let's / Let's not</u> have spinach! I love spinach!

3 **CHOOSE & COMPLETE** • *Read these conversations. Complete them with the correct form of the words from the box. Add the correct punctuation.*

> ~~bring your own lunch~~   get tickets   go to the library   see a serious film
> make that suggestion   get some dessert

1. **TOMÁS:** I hate the food here.

   ANA: Why don't you ___bring your own lunch?___

2. **TOMÁS:** I'm still hungry.

   ANA: Me too. How about _____

3. **TOMÁS:** There's a concert on campus tomorrow night.

   ANA: Really? Let's _____

4. **TOMÁS:** Do you want to go to the movies Friday night?

   ANA: Sure. But let's not _____ I need a good laugh.

5. **TOMÁS:** I have some homework to do before my next class.

   ANA: Me too. How about _____ We can do it there.

6. **TOMÁS:** The library needs a coffee machine.

   ANA: Why don't you _____ There's an online suggestion box.

4 **EDIT** • *Read this online library suggestion box. Find and correct seven mistakes in the use of suggestions. Check punctuation! The first mistake is already corrected.*

📄 ONLINE LIBRARY SUGGESTION BOX _ ▫ ✕

Suggestion:

I think the library is great, but I have several suggestions:

        getting
1. How about ~~get~~ new copying machines? The old ones don't work well.

2. A lot of students want to study on the weekend. Why don't the library have longer hours on Sunday.

3. Why you don't get coffee machines?

4. Let's having a special room for cell phone users. The library needs to be quiet!

5. The study rooms are too dark. Why don't you getting more lights?

6. How about put the library phone number on this Web page? I can't find it!

Send it now!   **Thank you for your suggestions!**

📄 Library Services   🌐 Internet

UNIT 37

Requests:
Will, Would, Can, Could

Could you open the door for me?

CHECK POINT

Check the correct answer.

❑ Brenda is asking about Tina's plans.

❑ Brenda wants Tina to help her.

CHART CHECK

Circle T (True) or F (False).

T F You can make a request with a question.

T F You can use *would* and *could* in short answers to requests.

QUESTIONS		
WILL/WOULD CAN/COULD	**YOU**	**BASE FORM OF VERB**
Will **Would** **Can** **Could**	you	**help** me?

SHORT ANSWERS	
AFFIRMATIVE	**NEGATIVE**
Of course. Certainly. Sure. No problem.	Sorry, **I can't**.

EXPRESS CHECK

Check all the requests.

❑ Can you drive a car?   ❑ Can you help me?

❑ Could you give me a ride?   ❑ Could you understand her?

❑ Will you be home after work? ❑ Will you please explain this?

❑ Would you like a cup of coffee? ❑ Would you call me tomorrow?

Grammar Explanations	**Examples**
1. Use *will, would, can,* or *could* + **base form** of the verb (*buy, help, lend, . . .*) for <u>requests</u> (asking someone to do something for you).	■ **Will** you please **buy** some soda? ■ **Would** you **help** me clean the living room? ■ **Can** you **lend** me $10? ■ **Could** you **answer** the phone?
USAGE NOTES: *Will* and *can* are <u>informal</u>. We use them with friends.	■ Hey, Sandy. **Can** you **drive** me to class?
Would and *could* are more <u>formal</u>. We use them with teachers and adults we don't know.	■ **Could** you **explain** the homework, Professor Smith?

2. Use *please* to make requests <u>more polite</u>.	■ **Will** you *please* open the door? ■ **Would** you *please* come here? ■ **Could** you *please* explain this?

3. Use *of course, certainly, sure,* and *no problem* for <u>Yes</u> answers. Do not use *will, would, can,* and *could*.	**A:** *Would* you please close the window? **B:** **Certainly**. NOT ~~Yes, I would~~.
	A: *Could* you call me tomorrow morning? **B:** **Of course**. NOT ~~Yes, I could~~.
USAGE NOTE: We usually use *Sure* and *No problem* in <u>informal</u> situations (with friends, children).	**A:** *Will* you help me with my homework? **B:** **Sure**. NOT ~~Yes, I will~~.
	A: *Can* you open the door for me? **B:** **No problem**. NOT ~~Yes, I can~~.

4. Use *can't* for <u>No</u> answers. Do not use *won't, wouldn't,* and *couldn't.*	**A:** *Could* you lend me $10? **B:** I'm sorry, I **can't**. I have only $5. NOT ~~No, I couldn't~~.
USAGE NOTE: When we say *No* to a request, we usually start with an <u>apology</u> (*I'm sorry*) and add an <u>explanation</u>.	apology explanation **B: I'm sorry,** I can't. **I have only $5**.

Check it out!

Ability with *Can, Could* ➤➤➤ UNIT 35, page 154.
Permission with *Can, Could* ➤➤➤ UNIT 38, page 166.
Possibility with *Could* ➤➤➤ UNIT 40, page 176.
The Future with *Will* ➤➤➤ UNIT 15, page 60.

1 **CHOOSE** • *Circle the correct words to complete the requests and short answers.*

1. **EMMA:** <u>Do</u> / (Will) you wash the dishes, please? We need clean plates for the party.

2. **BRIAN:** Can you <u>help / to help</u> me with these glasses?

3. **EMMA:** Would you <u>buy please / please buy</u> some soda on the way home?

4. **EMMA:** Would you drive me to the supermarket?

   BRIAN: <u>No, I wouldn't / Sorry, I can't</u>. My car is at the mechanic's.

5. **BRIAN:** Could you invite Antonio to the party?

   EMMA: <u>Sure / Yes, I could</u>.

6. **EMMA:** Can you mail these invitations for the party?

   BRIAN: <u>No, I can't / No problem</u>. I'm going to the post office before class.

2 **CHOOSE & COMPLETE** • *Look at these pictures. Write a request with the correct words from the box. Add* **please**.

answer the phone   buy more soda   check the oven
close the window   ~~open the window~~   wash the dishes

1. Could __you please__ __open the window?__

2. Would _____

3. Will _____

4. Could _____

5. Can _____

6. Would _____

3 **CHOOSE & COMPLETE** • Look at the "to do" list. Complete the conversation with requests and short answers. There are several ways to complete the sentences.

EMMA: The party is tomorrow. _____Could you buy_____
                                    1.
    the chips and soda, Brian?

BRIAN: _____No problem_____. I'll get them on the way home.
              2.

EMMA: Good. And Sara, _____ a dessert?
                             3.

SARA: _____. I'll bake brownies.
           4.

EMMA: Great. Tyler, _____ the living room?
                     5.

TYLER: _____. I'll do it tonight. Anything else?
           6.

EMMA: Yes. _____ the dishes too?
              7.

TYLER: _____.
       8.

EMMA: Thanks. And we need chairs. Sara, _____ Ana for chairs?
                                                  9.

SARA: _____. Ana needs all her chairs. Her party is tomorrow night too!
           10.

Before Party
Buy chips
Buy 10 bottles of soda
Wash dishes
Clean living room
Make dessert
Ask Ana for chairs

4 **EDIT** • Read these notes. Find and correct five mistakes in the use of **will**, **would**, **can**, and **could**. The first mistake is already corrected.

Emma,
I bought the soda, but I forgot the chips. Could you ~~got~~ get them?
Thanks.
Brian

Tyler,
Would you choosing some CDs for the party tonight?
Sara

Sara,
We still need more chairs! Will you ask please José to bring some?
Emma

Brian,
I made some brownies for dessert. Could you get some ice cream. S.
Yes, I could.
Vanilla or chocolate? B.

UNIT 38

Permission:
May, Can, Could

Can we swim here? No, you can't!

Can we **swim** here?

No, you **can't**!

CHECK *POINT*

Circle T (True) or F (False).

T F   It's OK to swim here.

CHART CHECK 1

Check the correct answer.

Begin a question about permission with _____.

☐ *do* or *does*

☐ *may, can,* or *could*

QUESTIONS			
MAY/CAN/COULD	**SUBJECT**	**BASE FORM OF VERB**	
May **Can** **Could**	I we she	**swim**	here?

CHART CHECK 2

Check the correct answer.

Don't use _____ in answers.

☐ *may*

☐ *can*

☐ *could*

ANSWERS					
AFFIRMATIVE			**NEGATIVE**		
Yes,	you* she	**may**. **can**.	**No,**	you she	**may not**. **can't**.
Sure. **Certainly**.			**No**, **please don't**.		

*You = one person or several people.

166

EXPRESS CHECK

Check all the questions about permission.

☐ Can she drive safely?

☐ May I use the computer now?

☐ Could he speak Spanish last year?

☐ Can we start the test?

☐ Could I come in?

Grammar Explanations	**Examples**
1. Use *may, can,* or *could* + **base form** of the verb (*ask, leave, sit,* . . .) to ask for <u>permission</u>.	■ **May** I **ask** a question? *(Is it OK to ask a question?)* ■ **Can** I **leave** now? ■ **Could** I **sit** here?
Usage Note: *May* is more <u>formal</u> than *can* or *could.*	■ **May** I start the test now, Mr. Silva?
Use *please* to be more polite.	■ **Could** I *please* open the window?
2. Use *can* or *may* for <u>Yes answers</u>. Don't use *could.*	**A: Could** I use the phone? **B: Yes,** you **can**. It's on the table. Not Yes, you ~~could~~. **A: May** I use this phone? **B: Yes**, you **may**.
3. Use *can't* or *may not* for <u>No answers</u>. Don't use *couldn't.*	**A: Could** I park here? **B: No**, you **can't**. Please read the sign. Not No, you ~~couldn't~~.
▶ **Be careful!** Don't use a contraction for *may not.*	**A: May** I park here? **B: No**, you **may not**. Not No, you ~~mayn't~~.
4. We often use **polite expressions** in <u>answers</u>.	**A: Could** I use my cell phone now? **B: Certainly**. OR **Of course**. OR **Sure**. OR **No, please don't**.
Usage Note: We usually <u>apologize</u> for a *No* answer. Then we <u>give a reason</u>.	apology reason **B: I'm sorry**, but **it's dangerous**. The plane is going to land soon.

Check it out!

Ability with *Can, Could* ➤➤➤ UNIT 35, page 154.
Requests with *Can, Could* ➤➤➤ UNIT 37, page 162.
Possibility with *May, Could* ➤➤➤ UNIT 40, page 176.

1

MATCH • *Each question has an answer. Match the questions and answers.*

Questions

_**d**_ **1.** Can I carry these bags on the plane?

_____ **2.** Can we travel with our bikes?

_____ **3.** May I carry my cat on the plane?

_____ **4.** Could I change my seat?

_____ **5.** Can I use my cell phone now?

_____ **6.** This is Jan. Could I talk to Maria?

Answers

a. Yes. We have large boxes for them.

b. Sure. One minute. I'll get her.

c. No, but you can use it in a few minutes.

d. Sorry. You can take only two bags.

e. Go ahead. Seat 27A is free.

f. Yes, you may. Small animals are OK.

2

CHOOSE & COMPLETE • *Look at these pictures. Complete the questions with words from the box. Check the correct answer to each question.*

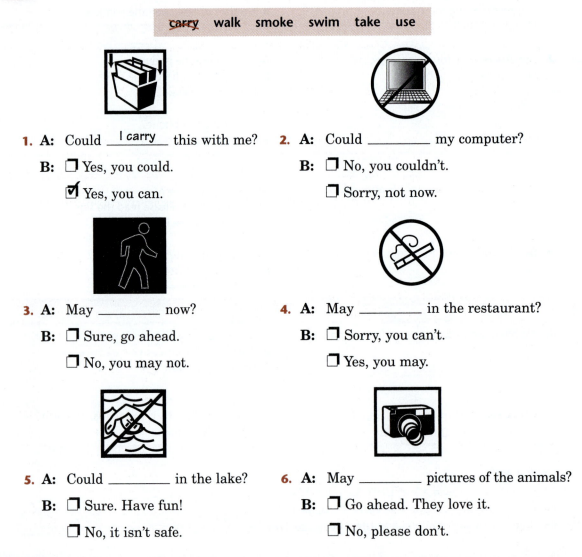

~~carry~~   walk   smoke   swim   take   use

1. A: Could _I carry_ this with me?

  B: ❏ Yes, you could.

  ☑ Yes, you can.

2. A: Could _____ my computer?

  B: ❏ No, you couldn't.

  ❏ Sorry, not now.

3. A: May _____ now?

  B: ❏ Sure, go ahead.

  ❏ No, you may not.

4. A: May _____ in the restaurant?

  B: ❏ Sorry, you can't.

  ❏ Yes, you may.

5. A: Could _____ in the lake?

  B: ❏ Sure. Have fun!

  ❏ No, it isn't safe.

6. A: May _____ pictures of the animals?

  B: ❏ Go ahead. They love it.

  ❏ No, please don't.

3 | **COMPLETE** • *Read the FAQ (Frequently Asked Questions). Complete the questions with the words in parentheses. Write short answers.*

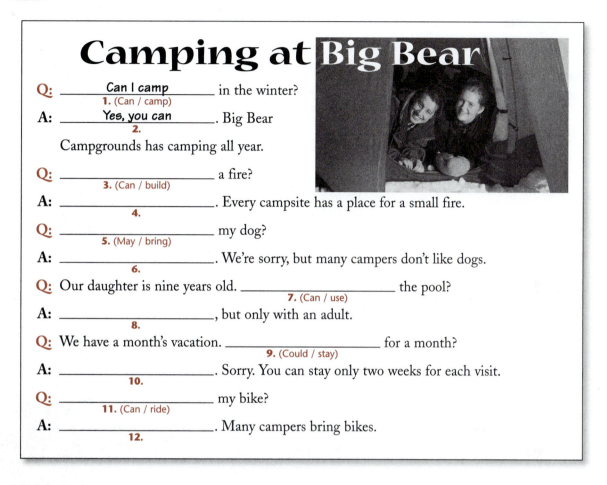

Camping at Big Bear

Q: _____Can I camp_____ in the winter?
          1. (Can / camp)

A: _____Yes, you can_____. Big Bear
           2.
Campgrounds has camping all year.

Q: _____ a fire?
    3. (Can / build)

A: _____. Every campsite has a place for a small fire.
      4.

Q: _____ my dog?
    5. (May / bring)

A: _____. We're sorry, but many campers don't like dogs.
      6.

Q: Our daughter is nine years old. _____ the pool?
                           7. (Can / use)

A: _____, but only with an adult.
      8.

Q: We have a month's vacation. _____ for a month?
                   9. (Could / stay)

A: _____. Sorry. You can stay only two weeks for each visit.
      10.

Q: _____ my bike?
    11. (Can / ride)

A: _____. Many campers bring bikes.
      12.

4 | **EDIT** • *Read these e-mail messages. Find and correct six mistakes in the use of **may**, **can**, or **could**. The first mistake is already corrected.*

Intermail.com

                                     listen
This place has a million rules! We can't ~~listening~~ to music after 9 P.M. We can no swim

alone. We can't do anything! Could I to come home, please? ☹   Tommy

Hi Tommy—No, you couldn't. You just got there! You'll have fun soon—we're sure of it!

Dear Mr. and Mrs. Jones—May Tommy goes on a boat trip? Please mail permission.

Hi Mom and Dad—The boat trip was really fun! Can I came here again next year? ☺

SelfTest

Circle the letter of the correct answer to complete each sentence.

> **EXAMPLE:**
> Alicia and Paulo _____ students.   A Ⓑ C D
> (A) am   (C) be
> (B) are   (D) is

1. How about _____ pizza?   **A B C D**
   (A) do we get   (C) getting
   (B) get   (D) to get

2. Let's _____ to the movies.   **A B C D**
   (A) go   (C) going
   (B) goes   (D) we go

3. Why _____ Anna come with us?   **A B C D**
   (A) doesn't   (C) no
   (B) don't   (D) not

4. How about _____ tonight?   **A B C D**
   (A) don't we eat out   (C) eating out
   (B) eat out   (D) let's eat out

5. —Would you answer the phone?   **A B C D**
   —_____.
   (A) No, I wouldn't   (C) Yes, I do
   (B) Sure   (D) Yes, I would

6. —_____ you lend me some money?   **A B C D**
   —Certainly. How much do you need?
   (A) Are   (C) Did
   (B) Can   (D) Please

7. Could you _____ me home?   **A B C D**
   (A) drive   (C) drove
   (B) driving   (D) to drive

8. —_____ we take pictures here?   **A B C D**
   —Sure. No problem.
   (A) Did   (C) May
   (B) Let's   (D) Why not

9. —Could I get on the plane now?   **A B C D**
   —_____.
   (A) No, you couldn't   (C) Sorry, you can't
   (B) No, you won't   (D) Yes, you could

10. _____ you swim in 2001?   **A B C D**
    (A) Can   (C) May
    (B) Could   (D) Will

11. I couldn't _____ very well then.   **A B C D**
    (A) swam   (C) swimming
    (B) swim   (D) to swim

12. —Can you drive?   **A B C D**
    —Yes, _____.
    (A) I can   (C) you can
    (B) I could   (D) you could

13. —Who can run fast?   **A B C D**
    —_____.
    (A) Ahmed   (C) Yes, he can
    (B) At school   (D) Yesterday

SECTION TWO

Each sentence or pair of sentences has four underlined parts. The four underlined parts of the sentence are marked A, B, C, and D. Circle the letter of the one underlined part that is NOT CORRECT.

EXAMPLE:

My friends <u>is</u> here, but we <u>are</u> <u>not</u> <u>studying</u>.   (**A**) **B C D**
         A   B   C   D

14. <u>Could</u> <u>you please</u> <u>call</u> me <u>yesterday</u>?   **A B C D**
   A   B   C   D

15. It's cold, so <u>let's</u> <u>not</u> <u>walking</u> to work <u>today</u>.   **A B C D**
        A   B   C   D

16. <u>Is</u> that a bus stop, or <u>can</u> <u>we</u> <u>parking</u> here?   **A B C D**
 A   B   C   D

17. We <u>can't</u> <u>parking</u> here, so why <u>don't we</u> park across the street<u>?</u>   **A B C D**
    A   B   C   D

18. Last year, I <u>couldn't</u> <u>use</u> a computer, but now I <u>can</u> <u>sending</u> e-mail.   **A B C D**
            A   B   C   D

19. <u>I'm sorry</u>, but passengers <u>mayn't</u> <u>leave</u> their seats <u>now</u>.   **A B C D**
  A   B   C   D

20. We <u>can't</u> <u>use</u> our cell phones on the plane, so <u>let's</u> call home now<u>?</u>   **A B C D**
   A   B   C   D

21. <u>Would</u> you <u>help</u> Jen? She <u>can't</u> <u>opens</u> this window.   **A B C D**
  A   B   C   D

22. <u>Sure</u>. <u>Will</u> <u>please you</u> ask her to wait a few minutes<u>?</u>   **A B C D**
  A   B   C   D

23. <u>Could</u> you <u>understood</u> Mr. Brown, or did he <u>talk</u> <u>too fast</u>?   **A B C D**
   A   B   C   D

24. I <u>could</u> <u>understand</u> him, but now I <u>couldn't</u> <u>read</u> my notes!   **A B C D**
    A   B   C   D

25. <u>How about</u> <u>to ride</u> our bikes to the park and <u>playing</u> basketball<u>?</u>   **A B C D**
  A   B   C   D

Desires:
Would like, Would rather

Would you like fruit? I'd rather have cake.

CHECK POINT

Check the correct answer.

The mother is asking:

☐ "Do you want fruit?" ☐ "Do you like fruit?"

CHART CHECK 1

Check the correct answer(s).

Use _____ after **would like**.

☐ a noun

☐ an infinitive

☐ the base form of a verb

STATEMENTS WITH *WOULD LIKE*		
SUBJECT	***WOULD LIKE***	**NOUN OR INFINITIVE**
I/You*/He/She/It/We/They	**would like**	**cake**. **to have** cake.

*You = one person or several people.

CHART CHECK 2

Circle T (True) or F (False).

T F Use the base form of the verb after **would rather**.

T F Put **not** before **rather**.

STATEMENTS WITH *WOULD RATHER*			
SUBJECT	***WOULD RATHER***	**BASE FORM OF VERB**	
I/You/He/She/It/We/They	**would rather**	**(not) have**	cake.

CONTRACTIONS
would like = **'d like**
would rather = **'d rather**

QUESTIONS
Would you **like cake**?
Would you **like to have** cake?
Would you **rather have** cake?

SHORT ANSWERS			
Yes,	please.	**No**,	thank you.
	I **would**.		I'**d rather not**.

EXPRESS CHECK

Circle the correct words.

A: Would you like <u>have / to have</u> coffee?

B: No, thanks. I'd rather <u>have / to have</u> tea.

Grammar Explanations

Examples

1. Use *would like* + **noun** or **infinitive** (*to have, to go, . . .*) to talk about things people <u>want</u>.	**A: Would** you **like** *coffee*? **B:** No, thanks. We'**d like** *to have* the check, please.
Use the contraction *'d like* in conversation, notes, and e-mail.	▪ I'**d like** some chocolate cake. ▪ They'**d like** to take a vacation.
2. *Would like* is more polite than *want*. Use *would like* for <u>offers</u> and <u>invitations</u>.	▪ **Would** you **like** a glass of water? ▪ We're going to lunch now. **Would** you **like** to join us?
Use *would like* <u>to ask for something</u>.	▪ I'**d like** more coffee, please. ▪ I'**d like** to have more coffee.
▶ **BE CAREFUL!** *Would like* and *like* have <u>different meanings</u>.	▪ **Would** you **like** coffee? *(Do you want coffee now?)* ▪ **Do** you **like** coffee? *(Do you enjoy coffee?)*
3. Use *would rather* + **base form** of the verb (*have, eat, get, . . .*) to talk about things people <u>want more than other things</u>.	**A: Would** you **like** *cake*? **B:** Thanks, but I'**d rather have** *pie*.
Use the contraction *'d rather* in conversation, notes, and e-mail.	**A: Would** you **rather** eat at home or eat out? **B:** I'**d rather** eat at home.
The <u>negative</u> is *would rather not* or *'d rather not.*	▪ I'**d rather not** eat out tonight. NOT I'd not rather eat out tonight.
We often use *would rather not* as a polite way to say *No* to an offer.	**A:** Would you like another piece of pie? **B:** Thanks, but I'**d rather not**.

1 | **READ** • *Look at this airplane traveler's menu choices.*

> ### EFL Airlines Welcomes You!
>
> Please check (✓) your dinner choices.   Name: <u>Lauren Helms</u>
>
> **First Course**   **Main Course**
> ❑ Black bean soup   ☑ Salad   ❑ Baked fish   ☑ Roast chicken
>
> **Desserts**   **Beverages**
> ☑ Chocolate cake   ❑ Apple pie   ❑ Coffee   ☑ Tea

TRUE OR FALSE • *Read the statements about Lauren's choices. Circle T (True) or F (False).*

T **(F)** **1.** Lauren would like soup.   T F **5.** She'd rather not have cake.

T F **2.** She'd rather have salad.   T F **6.** She'd like apple pie.

T F **3.** She'd rather not have fish.   T F **7.** She'd like to have tea.

T F **4.** She'd like roast chicken.   T F **8.** She'd rather have coffee.

2 | **CHOOSE** • *Circle the correct words to complete these conversations.*

1. **NICK:** Would you rather (eat)/ to eat   **2.** **NICK:** Would you like <u>move / to move</u>?
    at Apollo's?   **DANA:** Yes, I'd <u>like / rather not</u>
   DANA: Yes, I'd rather <u>not wait / wait</u>.   <u>move / to move</u>.

3. **DANA:** <u>Do / Would</u> you like the soup?   **4.** **NICK:** <u>Do / Would</u> you <u>like / like to</u> cake?
   NICK: No, <u>thanks / I don't</u>.   **DANA:** I'd rather <u>not / not have</u>. Thanks.

3 **COMPLETE** • *Read this survey. Complete it with the words in parentheses or a short answer. Use* **would like** *or* **would rather**.

Customer Survey

We ___'d like your help___. What _____ you _____
       1. (like / your help)   **2.** (rather / eat)

on your next long airplane trip? Please fill out this questionnaire.

✈ Would you rather have soup or salad?

❑ I _____ soup.   ❑ I _____ salad.
    3. (rather / have)   **4.** (like)

✈ _____ you _____ pasta as a main course?
                5. (like / have)

❑ Yes, I _____.   ❑ No, I _____.
           6.   **7.**

✈ _____ you _____ more vegetables on the menu?
                8. (like / see)

OR _____ you _____ more choices for the main course?
                 9. (rather / have)

❑ I _____ more vegetables.   ❑ I _____ more choices.
   10. (rather / see)   **11.** (like / have)

✈ Which new desserts _____ you _____?
                              12. (like)

❑ I _____ ice cream.   ❑ I _____ fresh fruit.
    13. (like)   **14.** (rather / eat)

4 **EDIT** • *Read this report about the survey in Exercise 3. Find and correct six mistakes in the use of* **would like** *and* **would rather**. *The first mistake is already corrected.*

Survey Report

                                     would

We received 150 surveys. Only one person ~~woulds~~ like soup! All other

passengers would rather to have salad. About half (78 people) would

like have pasta, and the rest would rather not. Only a few people want

more vegetables. More than 100 would like to more choices. For the

dessert choices, 75% would not rather have fruit for dessert. It seems

most people would liking ice cream.

Possibility:
May, Might, Could

The wind could be dangerous.

This tornado **could be** dangerous.

It **might travel** for miles. But it **might not**.

It **may disappear** in minutes.

You can never be sure with tornadoes.

CHECK *POINT*

Circle T (True) or F (False).

T   F   The tornado will definitely be dangerous.

CHART CHECK 1

Check the correct answer.

In sentences about possibility, use **could** to talk about _____.

☐ the past
☐ the future

STATEMENTS			
SUBJECT	**MAY (NOT)/ MIGHT (NOT)/COULD**	**BASE FORM OF VERB**	
I/You*/He/She/It/We/They	**may (not) might (not) could**	**get**	cold later.

*You = one person or several people.

CHART CHECK 2

Circle T (True) or F (False).

T   F   Use **may** and **might** in questions about possibility.

YES/NO QUESTIONS
Is it going to rain soon?
Will it rain soon?

SHORT ANSWERS	
It	**may (not)**. **might (not)**. **could**.

WH- QUESTIONS
When is it going to rain?
How long will it rain?

ANSWERS			
It	**may might could**	**rain**	tomorrow. all day.

EXPRESS CHECK

Check the sentences about possibility.

☐ It could snow next week.

☐ May I turn on the TV?

☐ We might not have class tomorrow.

☐ I couldn't speak English last year.

Grammar Explanations

Examples

1. Use *may, might,* or *could* + **base form** of the verb (*snow, leave, close,* . . .) to talk about things that <u>will possibly happen</u> in the future.	■ It **may snow** tomorrow. There's a 60% chance. ■ I **might leave** work early. I'll decide tomorrow. ■ Schools **could close**. They usually close for heavy snow.
2. Use *may not* and *might not* to talk about things that <u>possibly will not happen</u> in the future. Don't use contractions for *may not* or *might not*. ▶ **BE CAREFUL!** *Couldn't* means that something is <u>not possible</u>.	**A:** I **may not pass** the quiz. I didn't study. **B:** Don't worry. It **might not be** hard. NOT It ~~mightn't~~ be hard. ■ It **couldn't be** hard. *(It won't be hard. That's not possible.)*
3. We usually use the future (*be going to, will*) for <u>questions about possibility</u>. We do not usually use *may, might,* or *could*.	■ **Are** you **going to watch** TV tonight? ■ **Will** you **be** home? NOT ~~May~~ you watch TV?
4. *May (not), might (not),* and *could* in <u>short answers</u> mean, *"It's not certain, but it's possible."* We usually <u>don't use *Yes* or *No*</u> in short answers with *may, might,* or *could*. We often use *be* in short answers to <u>questions with *be*</u>.	**A:** Will it snow tomorrow? **B:** It **may**. There's a 60% chance of snow. *(It's possible that it will snow.)* OR It **may not**. There's only a 20% chance. *(It's possible that it won't snow.)* **A:** Will it rain? **B:** It **might not**. NOT ~~No~~. It might not. **A:** Will it **be** cold? **B:** It **could be**.

Check it out!

Permission with *May* ►►► UNIT 38, page 166.
Ability with *Could* ►►► UNIT 35, page 154.
Requests with *Could* ►►► UNIT 37, page 162.

1 **FIND** • *Read this story. Underline all the words for possibility.*

Storm Chasers

"Hi, it's Jill. There's going to be a big storm. There <u>could be</u> several tornadoes."

Jill Lee and Cy Davis are weather scientists. Today they are going to follow a storm and study it.

"We may find tornadoes to the north," says Jill. She's looking at a computer in the car. Suddenly, they see a dark cloud to the east—a tornado! Jill calls the weather station. Her report might save lives.

"Hurry Cy! It could get here in minutes," Jill says. "We may not get away in time."

YES OR MAYBE • *Now answer these questions with* **Yes** *or* **Maybe**.

<u> Yes </u> **1.** Will there be a storm?   _____ **4.** Will there be tornadoes to the north?

_____ **2.** Will they see tornadoes?   _____ **5.** Will they save lives?

_____ **3.** Will they follow the storm?   _____ **6.** Will the tornado hit them?

2 **CHOOSE** • *Circle the correct words to complete this conversation. Use the information in the weather forecast.*

WEDNESDAY	THURSDAY	FRIDAY	SATURDAY	SUNDAY

40°F (4.4°C) Cloudy. 60% chance of rain.	20°F (−6.6°C) Cold. Winds may be 10–15 mph (24–32 km/h).	15°F (−9.4°C) 90% chance of snow. 12 in. (30 cm) possible.	35°F (1.6°C) Sunny with no chance of rain.	50°F (10°C) Sun early, 70% chance of rain.

DAN: Did you see the forecast for Wednesday? It (<u>'s going to</u>) / <u>might</u> be cloudy.
        1.

OLA: I know. It <u>might / might not</u> rain. You <u>may / may not</u> need an umbrella.
        2.   **3.**

DAN: I didn't exercise today. I <u>may / may not</u> walk to work Thursday.
        4.

OLA: That <u>may not / might</u> be a good idea. Look at Thursday's forecast. It
        5.

    <u>might / 's going to</u> be very cold and it <u>could / may not</u> be very windy.
        6.   **7.**

DAN: It <u>could / may not</u> snow Friday. We <u>could / may not</u> get 12 inches.
        8.   **9.**

OLA: I just heard the forecast for Saturday. We <u>may / may not</u> see the sun all day!
        10.

DAN: It <u>might / might not</u> be a good day for a walk. It <u>'s not going to / might not</u> rain.
        11.   **12.**

OLA: I have some free time on Sunday. I <u>might / might not</u> go the park.
        13.

DAN: It <u>might / may not</u> be nice in the afternoon. Check the forecast.
        14.

3 **CHOOSE & COMPLETE** • *Complete these conversations with* **may**, **might**, *or* **could** *and a verb from the box. Write short answers to the questions.*

follow   go   invite   order   ~~see~~   take

1. **OLA:** I _____ may see _____ *The Perfect Storm* tonight. Do you want to come?
   (may)
   DAN: I don't know. I _____ might _____. I'll call you later and let you know.

2. **OLA:** I _____ Lucia to the movies. Do you think she'll come?
   (might)
   DAN: I'm not sure. She _____. She's studying for a test.

3. **DAN:** I _____ spaghetti. Is it good here?
   (might)
   OLA: It _____. Most of the food is good here.

4. **OLA:** I _____ the weather course next fall. Who's going to teach it?
   (may)
   DAN: Professor Davis _____. He usually teaches in the fall.

5. **LUCIA:** Are you going to go to Florida in January?
   OLA: We _____ there. We're not sure.
   (may)

6. **OLA:** Hi, Professor Davis. Are you going to be in your office at school tomorrow?
   DAVIS: I _____. They're forecasting a big storm. I _____ it.
   (might)

4 **EDIT** • *Read this information. Find and correct seven mistakes in the use of* **may**, **might**, *and* **could**. *The first mistake is already corrected.*

GET READY!

                                                                         be
Are you ready for weather emergencies? Many people might not˄ They think, "It won't

happen here." Wrong. It *could* happened here. Get ready now!

⚡ You might to lose electricity. Have plenty of batteries—you will need them for your

radio and flashlights.

⚡ There mayn't be clean water for some time. Buy bottled water.

⚡ Your supermarket may closes. You should have plenty of canned food.

⚡ Stay calm. Remember—your first idea not might be the best idea. Think before you act.

A storm or tornado could hit tomorrow! You never know! Might you be ready?

Advice: *Should, Ought to*

Should I shake her hand?

There's Cho-Mi's mother! **Should** I **kiss** her?

Should I **shake** her hand?

Should I **bow**?

I really don't know, Ana. Maybe you **should leave** now!

CHECK POINT

Circle T (True) or F (False).

T F Ana doesn't know the right way to say hello to Cho-Mi's mother.

CHART CHECK 1

Circle T (True) or F (False).

T F Use *should* and *ought to* with all subjects.

T F We usually use *not* with *ought to*.

STATEMENTS

SUBJECT	*SHOULD (NOT)/ OUGHT TO*	BASE FORM OF VERB
I/You*/He/She/It/We/They	**should (not) ought to**	**leave**.

*You = one person or several people.

YES/NO QUESTIONS

SHOULD	SUBJECT	BASE FORM
Should	we	**leave**?

SHORT ANSWERS

AFFIRMATIVE	NEGATIVE
Yes, you **should**.	**No**, you **shouldn't**.

CONTRACTION

should not = **shouldn't**

CHART CHECK 2

Circle T (True) or F (False).

T F   Use *ought to* in questions.

WH- QUESTIONS			
WH- WORD	**SHOULD**	**SUBJECT**	**BASE FORM OF VERB**
When	should	we	leave?
Why			

EXPRESS CHECK

Circle the correct words.

A: There's Tony. What <u>ought to / should</u> I do? <u>Ought to / Should</u> I shake hands?

B: No, you <u>ought to not / shouldn't</u>. Just say hello.

Grammar Explanations

1. Use *should* or *ought to* + **base form** of the verb (*leave, stay, call, . . .*) to give <u>advice</u>.

The <u>negative</u> of *should* is *should not*. Use *shouldn't* in conversation, notes, and e-mail.

USAGE NOTE: We usually don't use *ought to* for the negative.

2. Begin *yes/no questions* with *should*.

USAGE NOTE: We usually don't use *ought to* in questions.

Use **short answers** to answer *yes/no* questions.

Use *shouldn't* in short answers with *No*.

3. Begin *wh- questions* with a **question word**. Then use the same word order as in *yes/no* questions.

4. **USAGE NOTE:** We often use *maybe* or *I think* to be <u>more polite</u>.

Examples

■ It's late. We **should leave** soon.
OR
■ We **ought to leave** soon.

■ We **shouldn't stay** late.

■ She **shouldn't call** him by his first name.
NOT She ~~ought not to~~ call . . .

■ **Should** I **shake** hands with her?

■ **Should** Kim **wear** a suit?
NOT ~~Ought Kim to~~ wear . . . ?

A: *Should* I call her tomorrow?
B: **Yes**, you **should**. OR **Yes**.

A: *Should* I kiss her hello?
B: **No**, you **shouldn't**. OR **No**.

■ *What* **should** I **say**?
■ *Where* **should** we **meet**?

■ *Maybe* you **should arrive** a little earlier.
■ *I think* he **should smile** a little more.

1 **FIND** • *Read this magazine article. Underline all the expressions for advice.*

"When in Rome do as the Romans do." This means travelers <u>should learn</u> the customs of the place they are visiting. Well, what if you really *are* going to Rome? What should you do? What shouldn't you do?

◎ You should shake hands when you meet someone for the first time.

◎ You should say hello and goodbye to people in restaurants and stores.

◎ You shouldn't chew gum in public (for example, in stores and restaurants).

◎ And finally, you ought to learn a little Italian. *Buon viaggio!* ("Have a nice trip!")

Chew gum

ANSWER • *Check the things that are OK to do in Italy.*

☑ **1.** Shake hands with new people.

☐ **2.** Say hello to people in a store.

☐ **3.** Chew gum in school.

☐ **4.** Speak Italian with Italians.

2 **COMPLETE** • *Look at these pictures. Complete the sentences with **should** or **shouldn't** and the words in parentheses.*

Brazil

1. You ___shouldn't yawn___
(yawn)
in public places.

Russia

2. You _____
(look)
at someone's eyes.

Germany

3. You _____
(say)
hello in a store.

Canada

4. You _____
(give)
a long answer.

France

5. You _____
(point)
at someone.

China

6. You _____
(arrive)
on time.

3 **UNSCRAMBLE & COMPLETE •** *Read this Q and A (Question and Answer) article from a magazine. Complete it with the words in parentheses in the correct order. Write short answers.*

Q: I'm going to take a business trip to Egypt next month. I hear people often

come late to meetings there. _____Should I come_____ late too?
                                    1. (I / should / come)

A: _____No, you shouldn't_____ . Other people may arrive late, but _____ on time.
            2.   **3.** (be / ought to / you)

Q: My daughter is going to take a trip to Germany. _____ some
                                                          4. (study / should / she)

German before her trip?

A: _____ . People are happy when you try to speak their language.
            5.

_____ a little German.
    6. (learn / should / she)

Q: My Korean boss invited me to his house for dinner. _____ as a gift?
                                                              7. (what / bring / I / should)

A: _____ chocolate, fruit, or very good tea.
            8. (should / you / bring)

And remember: _____ a gift with both hands.
                   9. (give / you / should)

Q: For a first-time meeting in Spain, _____?
                                            10. (I / should / bow)

A: _____ . People in Spain don't bow. _____ hands.
            11.   **12.** (shake / you / should)

4 **EDIT •** *Read this quiz. Find and correct five mistakes with* **should** *and* **ought to***. The first mistake is already corrected. When you are finished, you can take the quiz!*

> should you
> # What ~~you should~~ do in these situations?
>
> **1.** You're in the U.S. talking to your teacher. How far you should stand from her?
>
> **a.** 1.5 ft (45.72 cm) **b.** 3 ft (91.44 cm) **c.** 5 ft (152.4 cm)
>
> **2.** Todd is in Saudi Arabia. He meets a Saudi businessman. He should _____.
>
> **a.** shake hands **b.** bows **c.** kiss
>
> **3.** You're sitting in a restaurant in Turkey. You should no show _____.
>
> **a.** the inside of your wallet **b.** your gloves **c.** the bottom of your shoes
>
> **4.** You're in Taiwan. You shouldn't to touch the _____ of another person's child.
>
> **a.** arm **b.** head **c.** hand
>
> Answers: 1.b 2.a 3.c 4.b

Necessity: *Have to, Must, Don't have to, Must not*

You have to wear a tie.

CHECK *POINT*

Circle T (True) or F (False).

The father is saying:

☐ You own a white shirt and a tie.

☐ A white shirt and a tie are necessary.

CHART CHECK 1

Circle T (True) or F (False).

T F In affirmative statements, use ***have to*** with all subjects.

T F In negative statements, use ***doesn't*** with *he, she,* and *it.*

AFFIRMATIVE STATEMENTS WITH *HAVE TO*

SUBJECT	HAVE TO	BASE FORM OF VERB
I/You*/We/They	**have to**	**leave**.
He/She/It	**has to**	

*You = one person or several people.

NEGATIVE STATEMENTS WITH *HAVE TO*

SUBJECT	DO NOT	HAVE TO	BASE FORM
I/You/We/They	**don't**	**have to**	**leave**.
He/She/It	**doesn't**		

QUESTIONS WITH *HAVE TO*

DO	SUBJECT	HAVE TO	BASE FORM
Do	I/you/we/they	**have to**	**leave**?
Does	he/she/it		

CHART CHECK 2

Circle T (True) or F (False).

T F Use the base form of the verb after **must**.

STATEMENTS WITH *MUST*		
SUBJECT	**MUST (NOT)**	**BASE FORM**
I/You/He/She/It/We/They	must (not)	leave.

EXPRESS CHECK

Circle the correct words.

Gary <u>have / has</u> to get dressed for school.

All boys must <u>wear / to wear</u> ties.

Grammar Explanations

Examples

1. Use **have to** and **must + base form** of the verb *(wear, do, go, . . .)* to talk about things that are <u>necessary</u>.

- Men **have to wear** suits in my office. It's a rule.
- Sue **must wear** a uniform to school.

Must is stronger than **have to**. A parent or a teacher can use **must** with a child or a student.

MOTHER: Tina, you **must do** your homework.

USAGE NOTE: We usually use **have to** in speaking and writing.

A: My daughter **has to wear** a white blouse to school.
B: A lot of children **have to wear** school uniforms.

2. Use **has to** with *he, she,* and *it* in affirmative statements.

- He **has to change** for the party.
- She **has to leave** by six o'clock.

Use **have to** (not **must**) in questions.

- **Does** Tina **have to go** home now?
- **Do** you **have to wear** a tie to the restaurant?

3. BE CAREFUL! *Don't have to* and *must not* have very different meanings.

Don't have to and **doesn't have to** mean something is <u>not necessary</u>. You have a choice.

A: Men **don't have to wear** suits in our office. Why does Tom always wear one?
B: He likes suits.

Must not means something is <u>against the rules</u>. There is no choice.

- Students **must not leave** the building during school hours. It's against the rules.

USAGE NOTE: In conversation, we usually use **can't** (not *must not*).

- Students **can't leave** the building.

1 **READ** • *Look at these school rules.*

DRESS CODE

The Lewis School does not have a uniform, but there is a dress code.

🧢 Dark blue pants and white shirts for boys

🧢 Dark blue skirts and white blouses for girls

🧢 All shirts and blouses must have collars (no T-shirts)

🧢 No blue jeans

🧢 No sport shoes

← COLLAR →

TRUE OR FALSE • *Circle T (True) or F (False).*

(T) **F** **1.** Boys have to wear dark blue pants.

T **F** **2.** Girls must not wear white blouses.

T **F** **3.** They have to wear skirts.

T **F** **4.** Students have to wear T-shirts.

T **F** **5.** Students must not wear jeans.

T **F** **6.** They have to wear running shoes.

2 **COMPLETE** • *Look at this dress code for another school. Complete the sentences with the correct form of the words in parentheses. Use affirmatives and negatives.*

Students ___*don't have to*___ wear a uniform.
  1. (have to)

They _____ dress neatly.
  2. (have to)

A boy _____ wear a tie.
  3. (have to)

Students _____ wear shirts with collars.
  4. (have to)

Their clothes _____ fit (not too big or too small).
  5. (must)

Girls _____ wear skirts.
  6. (have to)

Shirts _____ have words or pictures.
  7. (must)

Students _____ wear clothes with holes in them.
  8. (must)

3 **COMPLETE** • *Read these conversations. Complete them with **have to**, **must**, or **can't** and the correct form of the verb in parentheses. Use affirmatives and negatives.*

1. **CARI:** My sister _____has to wear_____ a uniform to school this year.
   a. (wear)

   RENÉE: Really? What _____ she _____?
   b. (wear)

   CARI: Girls _____ a white blouse and a dark skirt. It's really boring.
   c. (wear)

   RENÉE: Well, now she _____ about clothes. She knows what to wear.
   d. (think)

2. **TARIQ:** _____ I really _____ this tie? It looks stupid.
   a. (put on)

   AZIZA: It's a rule: Students _____ to school without a tie.
   b. (come)

   TARIQ: OK, but I _____ it in the car. I'll put it on at school.
   c. (wear)

3. **VAN:** My wife _____ to work in a suit. She hates that rule.
   a. (go)

   BARRY: We _____ suits in my office, but we _____
   b. (wear)   **c. (come)**
   in jeans or sports shoes. That's the only rule.

   VAN: I _____ relaxed at work. That's the reason I work at home!
   d. (feel)

4 **EDIT** • *Read these online comments about dress codes. Find and correct six mistakes in the use of **have to** and **must**. The first mistake is already corrected.*

---

schoolforum.com

My son ~~musts~~ **must** wear a white shirt and tie and dark pants to school. He is more comfortable

in jeans and T-shirts, but the dress code says he doesn't have to wear them. I think kids

have to feeling comfortable or they won't learn.

---

schoolforum.com

I love my school dress code. I must not spend a lot of money on new clothes. I don't have

to look different every day. I'm a better student with a dress code.

OfficeMail.net

My office has a new dress code—office workers must to wear suits. People look great in

my office now, but I need a raise! I have buy three or four business suits.

SelfTest

Circle the letter of the correct answer to complete each sentence.

> **EXAMPLE:**
> Alicia and Paulo _____ students.   A (B) C D
> (A) am   (C) be
> (B) are   (D) is

1. _____ you like some coffee? I just made some.   A B C D
   (A) Are   (C) Will
   (B) Do   (D) Would

2. Would Sally like _____ dinner with us?   A B C D
   (A) had   (C) have
   (B) has   (D) to have

3. The cake looks good, but I _____ have ice cream.   A B C D
   (A) 'd like   (C) like
   (B) 'd rather   (D) rather

4. It _____ rain tomorrow. There's a 50% chance.   A B C D
   (A) couldn't   (C) will
   (B) doesn't   (D) might

5. _____ it snow tomorrow?   A B C D
   (A) Does   (C) May
   (B) Is   (D) Will

6. _____ he have to leave now?   A B C D
   (A) Can   (C) Does
   (B) Do   (D) Must

7. That _____ be Maria. It's impossible.   A B C D
   (A) couldn't   (C) may not
   (B) isn't   (D) might not

8. Leo shouldn't _____ so much.   A B C D
   (A) be worry   (C) worries
   (B) to worry   (D) worry

9. We _____ to go now. It's late.   A B C D
   (A) may   (C) ought
   (B) must   (D) should

10. What _____ wear to the party?   A B C D
    (A) I have to   (C) should I
    (B) I ought to   (D) I should

11. You _____ do that. It's not polite.　　　　　　　　A B C D
    (A) not have to　　　　　(C) rather not
    (B) ought to not　　　　　(D) shouldn't

12. Does he _____ wear a tie to school?　　　　　　　A B C D
    (A) has to　　　　　(C) must
    (B) have to　　　　　(D) ought to

13. I _____ pass the test tomorrow. I didn't study.　　A B C D
    (A) could　　　　　(C) must
    (B) might not　　　　　(D) must not

14. I'm not sure, but I _____ late for work. The traffic is terrible.　　A B C D
    (A) couldn't be　　　　　(C) may be
    (B) 'll be　　　　　(D) maybe

SECTION TWO

Each sentence or pair of sentences has four underlined parts. The four underlined parts of the sentence are marked A, B, C, and D. Circle the letter of the one underlined part that is NOT CORRECT.

> **EXAMPLE:**
>
> My friends <u>is</u> here, but we <u>are</u> <u>not</u> <u>studying</u>.　　Ⓐ B C D
>   A　　　　　　　　B　　C　　D

15. Students <u>don't have to</u> <u>smoke</u>, but they <u>can</u> <u>chew</u> gum.　　A B C D
          A　　　　B　　　　　　　C　　D

16. I <u>don't have to</u> <u>dress</u> up, but <u>I'd</u> <u>not rather</u> wear jeans.　　A B C D
     A　　　　　　B　　　　　　C　　D

17. <u>Would</u> you like <u>to have</u> coffee, or <u>do</u> you <u>rather</u> have tea?　　A B C D
     A　　　　　　B　　　　　　C　　D

18. In Argentina <u>you</u> <u>not ought to</u> <u>eat</u> on the bus <u>.</u>　　A B C D
          A　　B　　　　C　　　　　D

19. <u>Should</u> I <u>leave</u> my umbrella home, or <u>may</u> it <u>rain</u> today?　　A B C D
     A　　B　　　　　　　　　　C　　D

20. I <u>must not</u> <u>take</u> math, but my teacher said I <u>should</u> <u>take</u> it.　　A B C D
       A　　B　　　　　　　　　　C　　D

21. <u>Shoulds</u> Roberto <u>call</u> you tonight, or <u>would</u> you <u>rather</u> call him?　　A B C D
     A　　　　　　B　　　　　　C　　D

22. I <u>like</u> <u>the food</u> at Casa del Sol, but I'd <u>rather</u> Thai food <u>tonight</u>.　　A B C D
     A　　B　　　　　　　　　　C　　　　　　D

23. Passengers must <u>to</u> <u>wear</u> belts, or the driver <u>could</u> <u>get</u> a ticket.　　A B C D
         A　　B　　　　　　　　C　　D

24. It <u>can</u> <u>be</u> cold on the plane, so you <u>ought to</u> <u>bringing</u> a sweater.　　A B C D
     A　　B　　　　　　　　　　C　　D

25. We <u>should</u> <u>be</u> at the airport by 2:00. What time <u>have we</u> <u>to leave</u>?　　A B C D
     A　　B　　　　　　　　　　　　C　　D

Gerunds and Infinitives

She enjoys exercising. / She wants to exercise.

Let's keep **going**. We're almost there!

I think you need **to rest**, Grandma.

CHECK *POINT*

Circle T (True) or F (False).

T F   The grandmother wants to stop.

CHART CHECK 1

Circle the correct answers.

Gerunds / Infinitives end in **-ing**.

Gerunds / Infinitives begin with **to**.

AFFIRMATIVE STATEMENTS					
	VERB	**GERUND**		**VERB**	**INFINITIVE**
She He	keeps enjoys	**walking**. **exercising**.	She He	wants needs	**to walk**. **to exercise**.

CHART CHECK 2

Check the correct answer.

Not goes _____ the gerund or infinitive.

☐ before

☐ after

NEGATIVE STATEMENTS					
	VERB	***NOT* + GERUND**		**VERB**	***NOT* + INFINITIVE**
I We	suggest discussed	**not smoking**. **not going**.	I We	decided promised	**not to smoke**. **not to go**.

EXPRESS CHECK

Circle the correct words.

I enjoy <u>to visit / visiting</u> my grandfather. He promised <u>to tell / telling</u> me about his life.

Grammar Explanations	Examples

1. Form the **gerund** with:
base form of the verb + **-ing**

BASE FORM	GERUND
walk	walk**ing**
rest	rest**ing**

▶ **BE CAREFUL!** There are often <u>spelling changes</u> when you add **-ing**.

hike	hik**ing**
stop	stop**ping**

■ I enjoy **walking**.

Notice the difference between the **gerund** and the **present progressive**.

gerund
■ I enjoy **walking**.
present progressive
■ I**'m walking** in the park.

2. Form the **infinitive** with:
to + **base form** of the verb

BASE FORM	INFINITIVE
walk	**to** walk
rest	**to** rest

■ We plan **to walk** more.

3. Put **not** <u>before</u> the gerund or infinitive for negatives.

■ My doctor suggests **not eating** much fat.
■ We decided **not to eat** dessert.

4. Use the **gerund** <u>after these verbs</u>:

avoid	enjoy	quit
deny	finish	recommend
discuss	keep	regret
dislike	practice	suggest

■ Don't **avoid going** to the doctor.
■ We **discussed moving**.
■ In Florida, we **enjoy not wearing** coats.
■ Did you **finish writing** that letter?

5. Use the **infinitive** <u>after these verbs</u>:

agree	expect	plan
ask	hope	promise
choose	learn	refuse
decide	need	want

■ She **agrees to go** to the doctor.
■ We **decided to move**.
■ He **promised not to wear** those jeans.
■ Where did you **learn to write** Chinese?

Check it out!

Common Verbs Followed by the Gerund ➤➤➤ APPENDIX 3, page 230.
Common Verbs Followed by the Infinitive ➤➤➤ APPENDIX 4, page 230.
Common Verbs Followed by the Gerund or the Infinitive ➤➤➤ APPENDIX 5, page 230.
Spelling Rules for Base Form of Verb + **-ing** ➤➤➤ APPENDIX 17, page 239.

1 **READ** • *Look at this information about four centenarians (people 100 years old or more). Circle the verbs + gerunds. Underline the verbs + infinitives.*

Parker Yia-Som McKenzie, born 1897 in the USA

McKenzie (enjoys talking) about the history of his people. He's writing a dictionary of Kiowa, his Native American language. He started it in 1911, and he hopes to finish soon.

Rose Freedman, born 1893 in Vienna, Austria

Freedman enjoys learning languages. She already speaks five, and she's studying Spanish. She didn't quit working until her 80s. Now she paints and watches a lot of basketball.

Daisy Nakada, born 1900 in Osaka, Japan

Nakada taught English in Japan and traveled to schools all over the world for her work. She keeps trying new things and she hopes to stay active many more years.

Leo Ornstein, born around 1893 in Russia

Ornstein became a famous pianist as a teenager. In his 20s he decided to start a music school. He quit performing, but he continued to write music. Ornstein died at the age of 109.

2 **COMPLETE** • *Read this article about centenarians. Complete it with the gerund or infinitive form of the words in parentheses.*

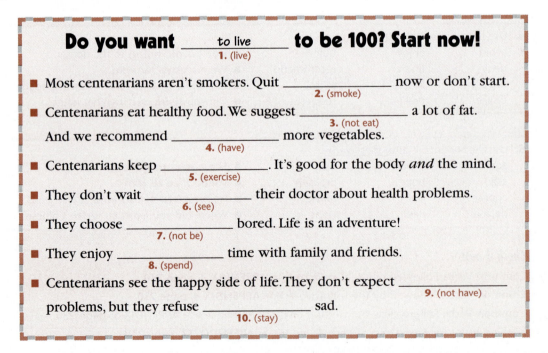

Do you want ___to live___ to be 100? Start now!

1. (live)

■ Most centenarians aren't smokers. Quit _____ now or don't start.
   2. (smoke)

■ Centenarians eat healthy food. We suggest _____ a lot of fat.
   3. (not eat)

   And we recommend _____ more vegetables.
   4. (have)

■ Centenarians keep _____. It's good for the body *and* the mind.
   5. (exercise)

■ They don't wait _____ their doctor about health problems.
   6. (see)

■ They choose _____ bored. Life is an adventure!
   7. (not be)

■ They enjoy _____ time with family and friends.
   8. (spend)

■ Centenarians see the happy side of life. They don't expect _____
   9. (not have)

   problems, but they refuse _____ sad.
   10. (stay)

3 **COMPLETE** • *Read each statement or question. Then complete the summary. Use gerunds and infinitives. Choose between affirmative and negative.*

1.   **ANNA:** Can we hike to the lake, Grandma?

    (summary) Anna enjoys _____hiking_____ .

2.   **GRANDMA:** Yes, we can. I'll take you soon.

    (summary) Grandma promised _____ her soon.

3.   **DOCTOR:** No more desserts, Paula. You really must lose some weight.

    (summary) Paula needs _____ weight.

4.   **PAULA:** I don't eat desserts!

    (summary) Paula denied _____ desserts.

5.   **FRANK:** Thanks for the CD. I listen to it all the time.

    (summary) Frank keeps _____ to the CD.

6.   **SYLVIE:** I think I'll watch a movie on TV tonight.

    (summary) Sylvie plans _____ a movie.

7.   **CELINE:** Hi, Grandpa. I'm sorry I'm not at your party today. I'm sick.

    (summary) Celine regrets _____ at her grandfather's party.

8.   **GRANDPA:** That's OK. Let's have dinner together next week.

    (summary) Grandpa suggested _____ dinner together.

4 **EDIT** • *Read this article about a centenarian's birthday. Find and correct six mistakes in the use of gerunds and infinitives. The first mistake is already corrected.*

100 YEARS YOUNG

                                                    to give
Jack Delano's family wanted ~~giving~~ him a big birthday party, but they didn't expect see all sixty-seven relatives. "People kept to come," Jack's granddaughter Myra said. "It was amazing."

Jack was born in 1895 in Salerno, Italy. He went to Canada in 1920, but he didn't plan to stay. Then in 1921, he met Celia in his night school class. That same night, Jack decided not going back to Salerno. "Two months later, I visited Celia's parents and I asked to marry their daughter," he said.

Jack sold his business a few years ago. He enjoys no working, but he stays active. He recommends to keeping close to family and friends.

Infinitives of Purpose

I use it to send e-mail.

At an Internet café

CHECK *POINT*

Check the correct answer.

The people are answering this question: _____ do you come here?

☐ How often   ☐ When   ☐ Why

CHART CHECK

Circle T (True) or F (False).

T F You must always use a noun or a pronoun before the infinitive.

T F For the negative, *not* goes before the infinitive.

AFFIRMATIVE STATEMENTS

SUBJECT	VERB	(NOUN/ PRONOUN)	INFINITIVE	
I	came		**to use**	a computer.
He	uses	a computer / it	**to send**	e-mail.

NEGATIVE STATEMENTS

SUBJECT	VERB	(NOUN/ PRONOUN)	IN ORDER NOT	INFINITIVE	
She	left			**to miss**	her class.
We	took	photos / them	**in order not**	**to forget**	our trip.

EXPRESS CHECK

Check all the sentences with infinitives of purpose.

☐ We went to an Internet café.

☐ Roberto left early in order not to miss the train.

☐ Ellie wants to go to Nepal next year.

☐ I can use my computer to watch movies.

☐ She sent an Instant Message to say *hi*.

☐ The computers at school are too slow.

Grammar Explanations

Examples

1. Use an **infinitive** (*to + base form* of the verb) to explain someone's <u>purpose</u> (*why* someone does something).	■ I logged on **to check** my e-mail. ■ Amy called **to ask** a question about her computer. ■ They left **to go** to class.
An infinitive of purpose often answers the question **Why?**	**A:** *Why* did you go to the store? **B:** I went **to buy** a computer.
2. You can use a **noun** or **pronoun** before the infinitive.	■ We use *the Internet* **to pay** bills. ■ She made *a Web page* **to tell** her family history.
	A: What do you use your computer for? **B:** I use *it* **to send** e-mail.
3. **Usage Note:** In conversation, we often answer with **just the infinitive**.	**A:** Why did you leave early? **B:** **To catch** the bus.
	A: What do you use the Internet for? **B:** **To find** information.
4. Use *in order not + infinitive* to explain <u>a negative purpose</u>. **Usage Note:** We usually use *in order not + infinitive* in writing or formal speaking.	■ In my office, we use e-mail *in order not to have* a lot of meetings. Not We use e-mail ~~not to have~~ . . .
In conversation, we often use *because* and give a reason.	■ We use e-mail *because* we don't want to have a lot of meetings.

1 **MATCH** • *Look at the ways people use the Internet. Match each action with a purpose.*

Action	Purpose
__d__ 1. Maria took a language course	a. to buy a plane ticket.
_____ 2. Jerry went to www.tickets.com	b. in order not to write checks.
_____ 3. Pedro visits a chat room	c. to write her geography paper.
_____ 4. Laila found facts about Nepal	d. to learn French.
_____ 5. Luc pays his bills online	e. to show photos of her trip.
_____ 6. Carla made a Web page	f. to talk to people on the Internet.

2 **COMPLETE** • *Read this online bulletin board about Internet cafés. Complete the information with the words in parentheses. Use infinitives of purpose.*

TRAVELERS' GUIDE

_____Use_____ this bulletin board _____to share_____
1. (use / share)
information with other travelers.

Dot.Com Café in Turku, Finland. I'm here on vacation.
I _____ _____ my e-mail.
2. (came / read)
But I _____ _____ games!
3. (stayed / play)

Surf-City in Tapei, Taiwan. I _____ here _____ Chinese.
4. (am / study)
I _____ e-mail _____ a lot of money on phone calls.
5. (send / not spend)

Calculus Café, New Delhi, India. I _____ a Web cam _____
6. (used / make)
a video for my parents. I _____ it _____ them I'm really OK!
7. (sent / show)
They _____ that _____ about me.
8. (needed / not worry)

Internet House, Rio de Janeiro, Brazil. This is a really great place.

I only _____ 16 *reais* _____ a computer for two hours.
9. (spent / use)
People _____ here _____ and _____ coffee too.
10. (meet / talk) **11.** (drink)

HOME   Internet

3 **CHOOSE & COMPLETE** • *Read this article about an Internet café. Complete it with words from the box. Use infinitives of purpose.*

| call   carry   check   clean up   help   play   practice   send   ~~use~~   use |

World's Highest Internet Café

From Tokyo to Toronto, people are going to Internet cafés ___*to use*___ computers.
1.
Travelers look for cafés _____ e-mail
2.
to friends and family. Young people go there
_____ computer games. And—believe
3.
it or not—there's now a café near Mount Everest! The owner, Tsering Gyalzen,
built it _____ climbers. He needed yaks _____ the equipment to
4.   5.
the 17,400-foot-high café. Now climbers can use the Internet _____ the
6.
weather or _____ someone for help.
7.

a yak

Visitors to Everest pay a lot _____ the café.
8.
Gyalzen uses the money _____ the mountain.
9.
(The visitors leave thousands of pounds of trash every year.) Local people go to the café too. They log on for the news, and use it _____ computer skills.
10.

4 **EDIT** • *Read this e-mail message. Find and correct seven mistakes in the use of infinitives of purpose. The first mistake is already corrected.*

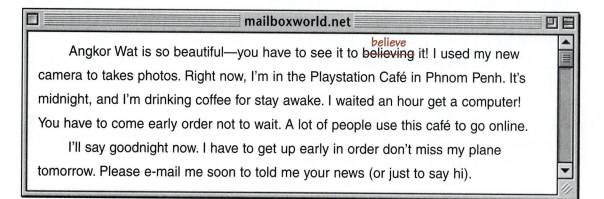

| mailboxworld.net |

Angkor Wat is so beautiful—you have to see it to ~~believing~~ *believe* it! I used my new camera to takes photos. Right now, I'm in the Playstation Café in Phnom Penh. It's midnight, and I'm drinking coffee for stay awake. I waited an hour get a computer! You have to come early order not to wait. A lot of people use this café to go online.

I'll say goodnight now. I have to get up early in order don't miss my plane tomorrow. Please e-mail me soon to told me your news (or just to say hi).

SelfTest

Circle the letter of the correct answer to complete each sentence.

EXAMPLE:

Alicia and Paulo _____ students.   A ⓑ C D
(A) am   (C) be
(B) are   (D) is

---

1. When did he quit _____?   A B C D
   (A) smoked   (C) smokes
   (B) smoking   (D) to smoke

2. I use my computer _____ pay bills online.   A B C D
   (A) for   (C) in order
   (B) I   (D) to

3. I left home early _____ be late for class.   A B C D
   (A) for not   (C) in order not to
   (B) in order not   (D) so I don't

4. Tom's doctor suggests _____ a lot of sweets.   A B C D
   (A) doesn't eat   (C) not eating
   (B) not eat   (D) not to eat

5. Jim called _____ about his new job.   A B C D
   (A) for talking   (C) to talk
   (B) he talked   (D) to talking

6. Where did you learn to _____ English so well?   A B C D
   (A) speak   (C) speaks
   (B) speaking   (D) spoke

7. They decided _____ for two years.   A B C D
   (A) not move   (C) not to move
   (B) not moving   (D) won't move

8. She's sick, but she avoids _____ to the doctor. A B C D
   (A) going   (C) not to go
   (B) not going   (D) to go

9. I _____ to exercise every day.   A B C D
   (A) advise   (C) keep
   (B) enjoy   (D) want

10. We _____ buying a new computer.   A B C D
    (A) decided   (C) hope
    (B) discussed   (D) promised

11. I regret _____ calling you sooner.   **A B C D**
    (A) didn't   (C) no
    (B) don't   (D) not

12. Cyril went to the library _____.   **A B C D**
    (A) because study   (C) studying
    (B) studied   (D) to study

13. Marcie refuses _____ e-mail. She prefers the phone.   **A B C D**
    (A) send   (C) sends
    (B) sending   (D) to send

SECTION TWO

Each sentence has four underlined parts. The four underlined parts of the sentence are marked A, B, C, and D. Circle the letter of the one underlined part that is NOT CORRECT.

> **EXAMPLE:**
>
> My friends <u>is</u> here, but we <u>are</u> <u>not</u> <u>studying</u>.   Ⓐ **B C D**
>   A   B C   D

14. I suggest <u>to write</u> down your password <u>in order</u> <u>not</u> <u>to forget</u> it.   **A B C D**
              A   B   C   D

15. I <u>bought</u> a camera <u>to</u> <u>took</u> pictures, but it <u>broke</u>.   **A B C D**
      A   B C   D

16. I <u>went</u> to Paris <u>for studying</u> French, and then I <u>decided</u> <u>to stay</u>.   **A B C D**
      A   B   C   D

17. Carol <u>wanted</u> <u>to call</u>, <u>but</u> I suggested <u>to send</u> an e-mail message.   **A B C D**
         A   B   C   D

18. My parents <u>enjoy</u> <u>to hiking</u>, so they <u>plan</u> <u>to go</u> to the Alps.   **A B C D**
           A   B   C   D

19. I <u>need</u> <u>to work</u> today, so I <u>asked</u> <u>to taking</u> the test tomorrow.   **A B C D**
      A   B   C   D

20. Do you go to the Internet café <u>for</u> <u>meet</u> your friends, or do you <u>use</u> the   **A B C D**
                               A   B   C
    computers <u>to play</u> games?
               D

21. My grandfather disliked <u>not</u> <u>to be</u> busy, so he decided <u>not to retire</u>.   **A B C D**
                       A   B   C   D

22. My computer <u>keeps</u> <u>breaking down</u>, so I copy disks <u>in order no</u>   **A B C D**
              A   B   C
    <u>to lose</u> information.
      D

23. This article recommends <u>getting</u> enough sleep and <u>to exercise</u> every   **A B C D**
                       A   B
    day <u>in order not to get</u> sick.
        C   D

24. I <u>use</u> the computer to <u>pay</u> bills, but I <u>avoid</u> <u>play</u> games.   **A B C D**
      A   B   C   D

25. Tara wanted <u>to</u> <u>improves</u> her English, so her teacher <u>suggested</u>   **A B C D**
             A   B   C
    listening to the news and <u>joining</u> some clubs at school.
                         D

Prepositions of Time

We'll arrive on Monday at 8:00 A.M.

Across the Atlantic in 3 Hours and 50 Minutes!

By Joel Abdo
Gazette International Reporter

On Monday May 24, 1976, two Concorde jets crossed the Atlantic Ocean **in** three hours and fifty minutes. The planes took off and landed **at** the same time.

CHECK *POINT*

Circle T (True), F (False), or ? (The information isn't in the newspaper article).

T   F   ?   The flights were less than four hours.

T   F   ?   The flights were on a weekend.

T   F   ?   The flights landed at 3:50.

MONDAY MAY 1976	**24**
8:00 A.M.	
9:00 A.M.	
10:00 A.M.	*10:30 take off*
11:00 A.M.	
12:00 P.M.	*Work!*
1:00 P.M.	
2:00 P.M.	*arrive NYC*

CHART CHECK 1

Check the correct answer.

Use **at** with _____.

☐ July 5

☐ 2:15 P.M.

WHEN . . . ?	
It was	**in** 1976.
	on May 24.
The flight left	**at** 10:30 A.M.
I had breakfast	**after** takeoff.
I worked	**during** the flight.
I finished	**before** landing.
We got to NYC	**in** less than four hours.

CHART CHECK 2

Check the correct answer.

Use **for** with _____.

☐ Friday to Sunday

☐ three weeks

HOW LONG . . . ?	
We stayed	**for** five days.
	from Monday **to** Friday.
	until Friday.

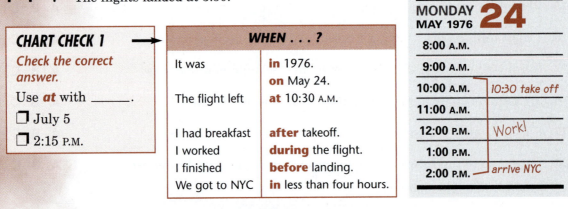

Sunday	Monday	Tuesday	Wednesday	Thursday	Friday	Saturday
	arrive				*leave*	

EXPRESS CHECK

Check all the sentences with prepositions of time.

☐ They are at the airport.

☐ Their plane is going to leave at 5:15.

☐ They'll eat on the plane.

☐ They'll arrive on Monday morning.

Grammar Explanations

Examples

---

1. Use **prepositions of time** to talk about **when** something happens.

A: *When* does your flight leave?
B: At *9:00*.

Use *at* with an <u>exact point of time</u>.

■ **at** 9:13, **at** midnight

Use *on* with <u>days</u> and <u>dates</u>.

■ **on** Tuesday, **on** New Year's Day, **on** May 6

USAGE NOTE: We often say or write days and dates without *on*.

■ I'll call you **on** Monday. OR
■ I'll call you Monday.

Use *in* with <u>years</u>, <u>seasons</u>, <u>months</u>, and <u>parts of the day</u>.

■ **in** 2004, **in** the summer, **in** January, **in** the afternoon

▶ **BE CAREFUL!** Use *at* with *night*.

■ I work **at** *night*.
NOT I work ~~in the~~ night.

---

2. Use *in* to mean *from a point of time.*

■ The flight leaves **in** 10 minutes.
(= 10 minutes from now)

Use *by* to mean *no later than.*

■ I'll get there **by** 9:00.
(= no later than 9:00)

---

3. We often use *before, during,* and *after* with nouns that show a <u>period of time</u>.

■ We left **before** *lunch*.
■ We slept **during** *the flight*.
■ We returned **after** *the concert*.

---

4. Use **prepositions of time** to talk about **how long** something happens.

A: *How long* did you stay in Paris?
B: For *three days*.

Use *for* to talk about <u>how much time</u>.

■ I traveled **for** a month.

Use *from . . . to* OR *from . . . until* for the <u>beginning and end</u> of a length of time.

■ They stayed **from** June **to** May. OR
■ They stayed **from** June **until** May.

Use *until* for the <u>end of a length of time</u>.

■ We'll stay **until** 11:00.

Check it out!

Some Common Prepositions ►►► **APPENDIX 15, page 236.**

1 **FIND** • *Read these facts about the Concorde. Underline all the prepositions + time.*

➤ England and France began the Concorde project <u>in 1962.</u>

➤ The first test flight was on April 9, 1969.

➤ In 1976 flights began between London and Bahrain and between Paris and Rio.

➤ By 2000 most flights traveled between New York City and Paris or London.

➤ The Concorde crossed the Atlantic in 3 hours and 50 minutes.

➤ A flight left Paris on Wednesday at 10:30 A.M. Paris time. It arrived in New York on Wednesday *before* 10:30 A.M. New York time!

➤ The last flight was in 2003.

2 **CHOOSE** • *Look at the pictures. Circle the correct prepositions.*

1. **a.** The flight is in / (on) Sunday.

    b. It leaves <u>at</u> / in 10:30.

    c. Get to the airport <u>at</u> / <u>by</u> 8:30.

2. **a.** We're going to the theater <u>on</u> / <u>at</u> Sunday, the day we arrive!

    b. The play is <u>at</u> / <u>in</u> the evening.

    c. It starts <u>at</u> / <u>before</u> 8:00 P.M.

JANUARY						
SUNDAY	**MONDAY**	**TUESDAY**	**WEDNESDAY**	**THURSDAY**	**FRIDAY**	**SATURDAY**
1	2	3	4	5	*Today* 6	7
New York 8	9	10	11	12	13	14
15	16	17	18	19	20	21
22	23	24	25	26	27	28

3. **a.** We'll be in New York <u>in</u> / <u>for</u> two days.

    b. We'll stay there <u>in</u> / <u>for</u> a week.

    c. We'll be there <u>for</u> / <u>from</u> January 8 <u>in</u> / <u>to</u> January 14.

3 **CHOOSE & COMPLETE** • *Read these conversations. Complete them with the correct prepositions from the boxes.*

during   until   ~~at~~   at   in   by

1. YVES: Our flight leaves _____*at*_____ 10:30. When is check-in?
   a.

   ZARA: We have to check in _____ 9:45. That's the latest possible time.
   b.

   YVES: No problem. The airport bus gets there _____ 9:04.
   c.

2. YVES: There's a magazine store. I want to get something to read _____
   a.

   the flight. There's no movie.

   ZARA: Is there enough time? Our flight is going to leave _____ twenty minutes.
   b.

   YVES: It's OK. I can shop _____ 10:00. That's when we start boarding.
   c.

on   on   until   in   for

3. YVES: The lounge is nice. Let's stay here _____ a few minutes.
   a.

   ZARA: Sure. I hear that New York is cold _____ January.
   b.

   YVES: Maybe we can go ice skating _____ Thursday.
   c.

   ZARA: OK. Or maybe _____ the weekend. We're going to be there
   d.

   _____ January 14.
   e.

4 **EDIT** • *Read this postcard. Find and correct nine mistakes in the use of prepositions of time. The first mistake is already corrected.*

1/8/02

Here I am—18,000 meters (about 49,000 feet) above the ground. My first Concorde
                              at
flight! We boarded the plane ~~in~~ 10:00 A.M. —a half hour after takeoff. In a few

seconds we were high in the sky. There's no movie at the flight. It's too short! But I

listened to music during our wonderful lunch. We're going to land on twenty minutes.

That's at 8:24 A.M. New York time—in the same day we left Paris! Because of the time

difference, we're going to arrive BEFORE our departure time! It's great to arrive early

on the morning. We're going to see a play on the evening. I'll call you at Monday, and

I'll see you in Thursday!

Love, Zara

Prepositions of Place

It's in the living room, on the table.

They aren't **on** the shelf.

They aren't **under** the magazines.

They aren't **behind** the computer.

Look **in** the mirror! They're **on** your head!

CHECK *POINT*

Check the correct answer.

The woman can't find her _____.

☐ magazines   ☐ computer   ☐ glasses   ☐ mirror

CHART CHECK

Check the correct answer.

Prepositions of place answer the question _____.

☐ **When?**

☐ **Where?**

in	**on**	**under**	**over**
in front of	**in back of / behind**	**to the right of / next to**	**to the left of / next to**
across from / opposite	**between**	**near**	**far (from)**

EXPRESS CHECK

Look at the picture. Circle the correct words.

I found my keys <u>on / under</u> the night table

<u>behind / next to</u> the lamp <u>in / next to</u> the bedroom.

Grammar Explanations

Examples

1. Use **prepositions of place** to talk about **where** someone or something is.	**A:** *Where* are my keys? **B:** They're **on** *the table*.
We often use prepositions of place after verbs like *be, have,* and *keep*.	■ The pen *is* **next to** the phone. ■ I *have* ice cream **in** the freezer. ■ I *keep* my money **in** the drawer.

2. Use *in* with: • continents • countries • provinces • states • cities • buildings • rooms • some types of transportation (usually small)	■ **in** Asia, **in** South America, **in** Africa ■ **in** Korea, **in** Brazil, **in** Sudan ■ **in** Ontario, **in** Normandy ■ **in** California, **in** Texas, **in** Florida ■ **in** Seoul, **in** Rio, **in** Khartoum ■ **in** the UN Building, **in** the bank ■ **in** the kitchen, **in** the living room ■ **in** a car, **in** a taxi, **in** a small boat

3. Use *on* with: • streets • some types of transportation (usually big)	■ **on** Main Street, **on** First Avenue, **on** the corner ■ **on** a train, **on** a bus, **on** a ship, **on** a plane, **on** a bike

4. Use *at* with: • addresses • events • places someone goes to in everyday life	■ **at** 26 Main Street, **at** 10 Park Place ■ **at** a party, **at** a meeting, **at** a concert ■ **at** school, **at** work, **at** home, **at** church, **at** the post office, **at** the doctor's

5. Use **object pronouns** *(me, you, him, her, it, us, them)* <u>after prepositions</u>.	■ Sit **between** *him* and *me*. NOT ~~between he and I~~.

Check it out!

Some Common Prepositions ➤➤➤ APPENDIX 15, page 236.

1 **FIND** • *Read this article. Underline the prepositions of place + nouns or pronouns.*

It's Not Always <u>in the Bank</u>!

Do you keep your money in the bank? Some people don't. Some people keep their money at home. But where is it safe? On a table? I don't think so! Under a pillow? Not really! Experts say: The best place for your money *is* in the bank. But if you really want to keep it near you all the time, hide it in an unusual place. And write it down, so you don't forget where! One day you'll want to find it again!

2 **DESCRIBE** • *Look at some places people keep money. Describe the location. Choose the correct preposition from the box.*

| behind | between | between | ~~in~~ | in | on | near | under | under |

1. ___in___ a sock

2. _____ the mattress

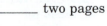

3. _____ two pages

4. _____ the refrigerator

5. _____ the front door

6. _____ a high shelf

7. _____ a piggy bank

8. _____ the floor

9. _____ the cushions

3 **CHOOSE & COMPLETE** • *Look at the map. Complete the sentences with the correct prepositions from the box.*

> across from   across from   across from   ~~at~~   at   between
> in   in   in   on   next to   to the left   to the right

My bank is _____at_____ 35 Main Street
                    1.
_____ Centerville. Centerville
   2.
is a small city _____ Canada. The
                        3.
bank is _____ the bookstore and
          4.
the pharmacy. It's _____ the café.
                          5.
   There's a pizza place _____ the
                              6.
corner of Main and First. It's
_____
   7.
the bookstore. The clothing shop is
_____ 39 Main. The pharmacy is
   8.
_____ of the clothing shop. The
   9.
bakery is _____. There's a great shoe store _____ the bakery. It's
             10.   **11.**
_____ the post office. Centerville is a nice place. I think it's one of the nicest
   12.
places _____ North America!
          13.

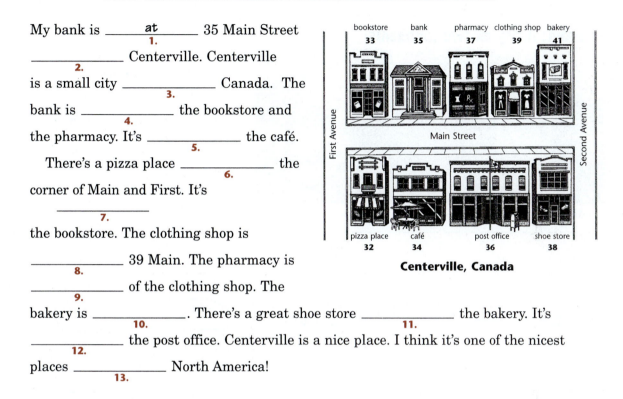

bookstore   bank   pharmacy   clothing shop   bakery
  33   35   37   39   41

First Avenue   Second Avenue

Main Street

pizza place   café   post office   shoe store
   32   34   36   38

Centerville, Canada

4 **EDIT** • *Read this journal entry. Find and correct ten mistakes in the use of prepositions of place. The first mistake is already corrected.*

> Last week I received a big check for my birthday. I hid it ~~in~~ home, but then I couldn't
>   *at*
> remember where! I looked everywhere. It wasn't on my desk drawer (I often keep money
>
> there). Maybe it was in the dictionary. I have a large dictionary over a bookshelf next
>
> my desk. I sometimes keep money in two pages. But it wasn't there! Maybe it fell
>
> between the two cushions on my couch. But I looked, and it wasn't between they.
>
> I looked in the floor over the couch. Not there. Then I remembered! The check was
>
> on the bank at Main Street!!

Prepositions of Movement

Go across the bridge. Walk along the river.

Istanbul: A city on two continents

We drove **across** this bridge—**from** Asia **to** Europe!

CHART CHECK

Check the correct answer.

Prepositions of movement show people or things _____.

☐ in one place

☐ going from one place to another place

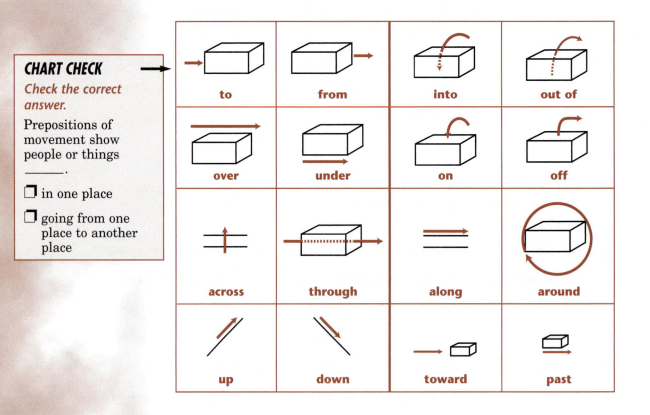

to	from	into	out of
over	under	on	off
across	through	along	around
up	down	toward	past

EXPRESS CHECK

Look at the map and circle the correct words.

Bob walked <u>along / across</u>

Front Street. He went

<u>into / past</u> the bank.

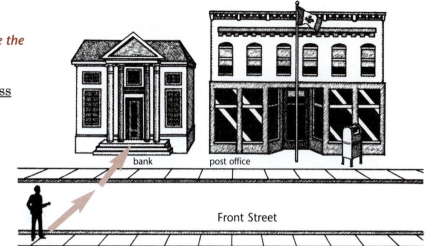

bank   post office

Front Street

Grammar Explanations

Examples

1. Use **prepositions of movement** to talk about **where** someone or something **is going**.

We often use prepositions of movement after verbs like *go, drive, walk, get,* and *run.*

▶ **BE CAREFUL!** Don't use *to* with *home.*

- Bahar is going **to** *the hotel*.
- She's driving **toward** *the bridge*.

- She *goes* **across** the bridge every day.
- She'*s* ***getting*** **out of** her *car*.
- She'*s* ***walking*** **into** her office.

- He's going **home**.
  NOT He's going ~~to home~~.

2. Use ***into*** or ***in*** for <u>movement</u>.

▶ **BE CAREFUL!** Don't use ***into*** for place.

Use ***into*** (or ***in***) and ***out of*** for:
cars, taxis, small boats, small planes

Use ***on*** and ***off*** for:
buses, trains, large boats (ships), large planes, and bikes

- She went **into** the house. OR
- She went **in** the house.

- She's **in** the house now.
  NOT She's ~~into~~ the house now.

- Let's get **into** the car.
- They got **out of** a taxi.

- Did they get **on** the plane?
- She got **off** the plane in Istanbul.

3. Use ***by*** for <u>transportation</u>—to say <u>how</u> someone travels.

A: ***How*** do they get there?
B: Munir usually travels **by** *car*.
C: Haig gets to work **by** *subway*.

Check it out!

Some Common Prepositions ▶▶▶ **APPENDIX 15, page 236.**

1 **MATCH** • *Look at these pictures. Write the correct number next to each sentence.*

1.   2.   3.    4.

<u>5</u> **a.** She walked down the steps.

_____ **b.** She came out of a café.

_____ **c.** She walked past a café.

_____ **d.** She went up the steps.

_____ **e.** Li started from her hotel.

_____ **f.** She went into a café.

 5.    6.

2 **CIRCLE** • *Look at this map and read these directions from a guidebook to Istanbul. Circle the words to complete the directions.*

Explore Istanbul: A walking tour

- Start (from)/ to the beautiful Pera Pallas Hotel.
  1.
- Walk <u>over</u> / <u>along</u> Isktiklal Street <u>to</u> / <u>from</u> Tünel Square.
  2.   **3.**
- Take a short subway ride to Karaköy <u>through</u> / <u>under</u> the streets—
  4.
- just 576 meters <u>from</u> / <u>past</u> start <u>to</u> / <u>off</u> finish!
  5.   **6.**
- Get <u>out</u> / <u>off</u> the subway. Walk <u>up</u> / <u>down</u> the steps to the street.
  7.   **8.**
- Walk <u>past</u> / <u>across</u> the Galata Bridge <u>to</u> / <u>through</u> the New Mosque.
  9.   **10.**
- Walk <u>into</u> / <u>around</u> the mosque. Then go <u>across</u> / <u>along</u> the street.
  11.   **12.**
- Walk <u>past</u> / <u>through</u> the Spice Market. Are you hungry?
  13.
- Go <u>through</u> / <u>into</u> Mehmet Efendi Café. Order coffee and cake.
  14.
- Relax and enjoy!

3 **CHOOSE & COMPLETE** • *Look at the photos. Complete the descriptions with the words from the boxes.*

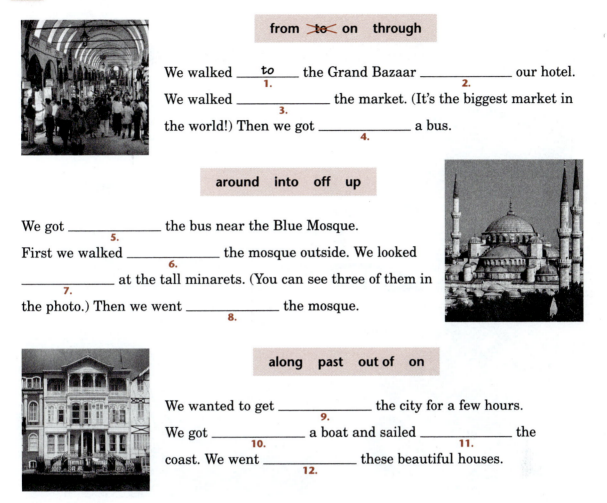

| from | ~~to~~ | on | through |

We walked ___*to*___ the Grand Bazaar _____ our hotel.
1.   2.
We walked _____ the market. (It's the biggest market in
3.
the world!) Then we got _____ a bus.
4.

| around | into | off | up |

We got _____ the bus near the Blue Mosque.
5.
First we walked _____ the mosque outside. We looked
6.
_____ at the tall minarets. (You can see three of them in
7.
the photo.) Then we went _____ the mosque.
8.

| along | past | out of | on |

We wanted to get _____ the city for a few hours.
9.
We got _____ a boat and sailed _____ the
10.   11.
coast. We went _____ these beautiful houses.
12.

4 **EDIT** • *Read this tour schedule. Find and correct six mistakes in the use of prepositions of movement. The first mistake is already corrected.*

\	**Trips from Istanbul ~~at~~ Büyükada Every Day** (with *to* written above)
9:00 A.M.	Guests get up the boat.
9:30–11:00 A.M.	Travel to Büyükada (the largest of the Princes' Islands).
11:00 A.M.	Arrive at Büyükada Island. Passengers get down the boat.
11:30 A.M.–3:00 P.M.	Go to the top of St. George Hill. It's high (almost a mountain!), so we won't walk above the hill. We'll go by horse carriage.
3:00 P.M.	Go under the hill. Tour the town and walk through the beach.
6:00 P.M.	Return to Istanbul.

Two-Word Verbs:
Inseparable

Let's dress up and eat out.

CHECK POINT

Circle T (True) or F (False).

T **F** Lee wants to eat in the park.

T **F** Eva understands Lee's invitation.

CHART CHECK

Check the correct answer.

A two-word verb is a _____.

☐ subject + verb

☐ verb + preposition

INSEPARABLE TWO-WORD VERBS		
SUBJECT	**VERB + PREPOSITION**	
We	**dressed up**.	
	ate out.	
	ran into	Clara.
	got along	very well.

EXPRESS CHECK

Check all the sentences with two-word verbs.

❏ What time do you eat dinner?

❏ We're going to eat out tomorrow night.

❏ Would you like to come along?

❏ We'll probably end up at a movie.

❏ I'll get you a ticket.

❏ You don't have to dress up.

Grammar Explanations	Examples
1. **Two-word verbs** are <u>verbs + prepositions</u> *(up, with, into, out, . . .).* We use them a lot in conversation.	■ Would you like to **eat out** tonight? *(Would you like to eat in a restaurant?)* ■ Lee wants to **go out** with Eva. *(Lee wants to go on a date with Eva.)*
2. **Learn the meaning** of common two-word verbs. It's often hard to guess their meaning.	■ Lee **grew up** in Canada. *(Lee became an adult in Canada.)* ■ They **get along** well. *(They have a good relationship.)* ■ I **ran into** Eva at the movies. *(I met Eva by accident at the movies.)* ■ She likes to **dress up**. *(She likes to put on nice clothes.)* ■ Please don't **hang up**. *(Please don't end this phone call.)* ■ Lee **showed up** with flowers at Eva's home. *(Lee appeared with flowers at Eva's home.)* ■ Please **go on**. I want to hear the whole story. *(Please continue.)*
3. Some two-word verbs are **inseparable**.	■ I **ran into** Eva. Not I ~~ran Eva into~~.
▶ **BE CAREFUL!** You cannot put another word between the verb and the preposition.	■ They **get along** well. Not They ~~get well along~~.
4. Sometimes **another preposition** can follow a two-word verb.	■ I **ran out** *of* ideas. *(I didn't have enough ideas.)* ■ We **signed up** *for* a course. *(We registered for a course.)*

Check it out!

Some Common Two-Word Verbs ➤➤➤ APPENDIX 7, page 231.

Two-Word Verbs: Separable ➤➤➤ UNIT 49, page 216.

1 **FIND** • *Read this article. Underline all the two-word verbs. Go to Appendix 7 on page 231 for help.*

Dating is one way to <u>look for</u> a husband or wife. Did you know . . . ?

♥ In Central and South America, teenagers get together in groups. They often go dancing or hang out at local clubs.

♥ In North America and Europe, teens go out in pairs and in groups. They often go dancing or take in a movie.

♥ In Vietnam, young people grow up with the idea that marriage is a family event. Young men must ask the girl's parents for permission to go out.

MATCH • *Write each two-word verb from the above text next to its definition.*

1. ___go out___ date   **3.** _____ spend time   **5.** _____ meet

2. _____ become an adult   **4.** _____ try to find   **6.** _____ see

2 **CHOOSE** • *Circle the correct words to complete these sentences. Go to Appendix 7 on page 228 for help.*

1. Luis showed <u>out</u> /⟨<u>up</u>⟩ with flowers.

2. I said, "Come <u>in / back</u>. Sit <u>up / down</u>."

3. His car broke <u>down / up</u> on the way to the restaurant.

4. A taxi showed <u>off / up</u>, and we came <u>back / out</u> to my apartment.

5. We didn't eat <u>in / out</u>. We ended <u>down / up</u> ordering pizza.

6. We got <u>along / by</u> really well. I'd like to go <u>back / out</u> with him again!

3 **CHOOSE & COMPLETE** • *Read these sentences. Complete them with the correct two-word verbs from the boxes. Go to Appendix 7 on page 231 for help.*

| eat out   get along   go out   grew up   ~~ran into~~ |

1. Two months ago I ____ran into____ Lola at the library.

2. We started to _____ together—to the movies, a soccer game, dancing.

3. We really _____ well. We have a lot of fun together.

4. Lola and I _____ in the same neighborhood. We know a lot of the same people.

5. Sometimes we _____ at a local restaurant.

| work out   dress up   sign up   go out   comes along |

6. We don't always go alone. Sometimes Lola's sister _____ with us.

7. Lola often wears a nice dress. I sometimes _____ too.

8. We want to _____ for an exercise class.

9. Soon we'll _____ *and* _____ together!

4 **EDIT** • *Read Jason's journal entry. Find and correct six mistakes in the use of inseparable two-word verbs. The first mistake is already corrected.*

>   Many things are different in a foreign country. Dating, for example. Last
>   out
> night I went ~~over~~ with my classmate Tania. We always get very well along in
> class. But I think she was unhappy with our date. I showed at her apartment
> with six yellow flowers. Later I learned that in her country, the number
> six brings bad luck. And yellow flowers mean you want to end the relationship!
>   Tania dressed over for our date in a nice skirt and blouse. I wore jeans.
> Wrong! She asked me to come in. I didn't remove my shoes. Wrong again! Then
> we took the bus to the movies. When we got over the bus, she looked upset.
> Later I learned that in her country men usually "help" women on and off
> buses! Then I didn't pay for her movie ticket. (Back home the girl and guy
> often pay for their own tickets.) Another mistake! I like Tania, and I want
> to go with her again out. I hope she gives me another chance!

Two-Word Verbs:
Separable

Turn off the alarm clock. / Turn it off.

How to Get to Work on Time

7:00 The alarm clock **wakes** you **up**. **Turn** it **off**.

7:05 **Turn on** the shower. Wash and get out.

7:30 **Pick out** a clean shirt. **Put** it **on**.

8:00 **Pick up** your briefcase. Have a nice day!

2   POCKET BOOKS

CHECK *POINT*

Circle the correct answers.

At 7:00 the man will <u>move /</u> <u>stop</u> the alarm clock.

At 7:05 he'll <u>start / end</u> his shower.

At 7:30 he'll <u>get dressed /</u> <u>put his clothes on the chair</u>.

At 8:00 he'll <u>close / lift</u> his briefcase and leave for work.

SEPARABLE TWO-WORD VERBS

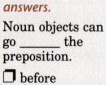

CHART CHECK

Check all the correct answers.

Noun objects can go _____ the preposition.

❏ before

❏ after

Pronoun objects must go _____ the preposition.

❏ before

❏ after

NOT SEPARATED			
SUBJECT	**VERB**	**PREPOSITION**	**NOUN OBJECT**
I	**turned**	**on**	the light.

SEPARATED		
SUBJECT	**VERB**	**NOUN/PRONOUN OBJECT**	**PREPOSITION**
I	**turned**	the light it	**on**.

EXPRESS CHECK

Check the sentences with two-word verbs.

☐ The telephone woke me up at 5:00 A.M.   ☐ Can I put my coat here?   ☐ I dropped my book.

☐ The bus turned left on First Street.   ☐ Harry turned the TV on.   ☐ I picked it up.

Grammar Explanations	Examples
1. Two-word verbs are <u>verbs + prepositions</u> *(up, with, into, out, . . .).* We use them a lot in conversation.	■ I **took** books **back** to the library. *(I returned books to the library.)* ■ He **turned** the TV **on**. *(He started the TV.)*
2. Learn the meaning of common two-word verbs. It's often hard to guess their meaning.	■ Ron **picked out** some new shoes. *(He chose some new shoes.)* ■ He **picked up** his bag. *(He lifted his bag.)* ■ He **took off** his old shoes. *(He removed his old shoes.)* ■ He **put on** his new shoes. *(He put his feet into his new shoes.)* ■ He **put** his shoes **away**. *(He put his shoes in the closet.)* ■ He **threw** the bag **away**. *(He put the bag in the trash.)*
3. Many **two-word verbs** are **separable**. You can put the object: • <u>after the preposition</u> OR • <u>between the verb and the preposition</u>	object ■ Fred **picked up** his book. OR object ■ Fred **picked** his book **up**.
4. BE CAREFUL! Pronoun objects must go <u>between the verb and the preposition</u>.	■ He **picked** it **up**. NOT He ~~picked up it~~. ■ We **turned** it **down**. NOT We ~~turned down it~~.

Check it out!

Some Common Two-Word Verbs ▶▶▶ APPENDIX 7, page 231.
Two-Word Verbs: Inseparable ▶▶▶ UNIT 48, page 212.

1 **FIND** • *Read this self-help article. Underline the separable two-word verbs. Circle their objects. Go to Appendix 7 on page 231 for help.*

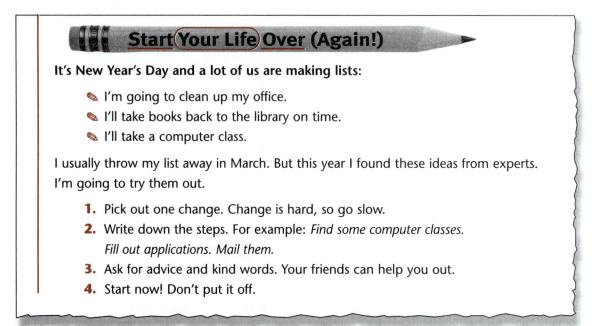

Start (Your Life) Over (Again!)

It's New Year's Day and a lot of us are making lists:

- ✎ I'm going to clean up my office.
- ✎ I'll take books back to the library on time.
- ✎ I'll take a computer class.

I usually throw my list away in March. But this year I found these ideas from experts. I'm going to try them out.

1. Pick out one change. Change is hard, so go slow.
2. Write down the steps. For example: *Find some computer classes.*
   Fill out applications. Mail them.
3. Ask for advice and kind words. Your friends can help you out.
4. Start now! Don't put it off.

2 **DESCRIBE** • *Look at these pictures. Complete the Niles family's New Year's resolutions. Use the words in parentheses.*

1. We'll ___turn the TV off___

   OR **turn off the TV**
   (the TV / turn off)
   at dinnertime.

2. I borrowed money last
   year. This year I'm going

   to _____.
   (it / pay back)

3. I'll _____.
   (this room / clean up)
   I could _____
   (it / turn into)
   an office.

4. I'm going to _____

   _____
   (my books / put away)
   and _____.
   (my clothes / hang up)

5. I'm going to _____

   _____
   (my homework / hand in)
   on time.

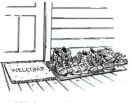

6. We're going to _____

   _____
   (our shoes / take off)
   at the door.

3 | **CHOOSE & COMPLETE** • *Read these conversations. Complete them with the correct form of the two-word verbs from the box and with pronouns. Go to Appendix 7 on page 231 for help.*

> give up   hand in   pick out
> turn down   ~~ask over~~   look over   throw away

1. **MOM:** Why don't you ____ask____ Lyric ____over____ ?

   SHAINA: I ____asked her over____ last week. I think I'll call Tecia.

2. **SHAINA:** I should _____ soda. I drink too much.

   TECIA: Me too. Let's _____ together.

3. **TECIA:** Could you _____ my report? You're a good writer.

   SHAINA: Sure. I'll _____ at school tomorrow.

4. **TECIA:** When are you going to _____ your report _____?

   SHAINA: I'm going _____ tomorrow.

5. **MOM:** Please _____ those running shoes. They're old and dirty.

   GARY: I don't want to _____!

6. **DAD:** Could you _____ the TV _____, please? It's too loud.

   SHAINA: I _____. Is that better?

7. **DAD:** Why don't you _____ some new running shoes?

   GARY: I _____ already. Are these too expensive?

4 | **EDIT** • *Look at these readers' comments on an online bookstore. Find and correct eight mistakes in the use of separable two-word verbs. The first mistake is already corrected.*

>   *It Over*
> **This Is Your Life: Look ~~Over It~~ and Straighten It Out!** by Vera Niles
>
> ★★★★ Niles says we can change our lives. Her advice: Think things over and take small steps. I tried out it. It works.
>
>   ★ My New Year's resolution: Give up books by Vera Niles! This one is awful. I took back it and said, "Give me my money away."
>
> ★★★★ I had too many problems, and I couldn't figure out them. Then I bought Niles's book. Now I'm starting my life under! She's the best!
>
>   ★★★ I followed Niles's plan, and last week I threw back my cigarettes. I gave them out with Niles's help. Her ideas are old, but they're good.

UNIT 50

Sentence Connectors:
and, but, or, so, because

He buys the paper because he likes the cartoons.

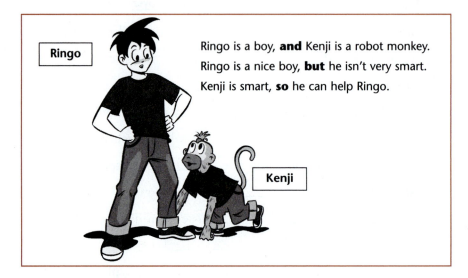

Ringo

Kenji

Ringo is a boy, **and** Kenji is a robot monkey.
Ringo is a nice boy, **but** he isn't very smart.
Kenji is smart, **so** he can help Ringo.

CHECK *POINT*

Check the correct answer.

Why can Kenji help Ringo?

☐ Because Ringo is nice.

☐ Because Kenji is smart.

CHART CHECK →

Circle T (True) or F (False).

T F You can connect two sentences with **and**, **but**, **or**, **so**, or **because**.

SENTENCE 1	CONNECTOR	SENTENCE 2
He buys the paper,	*and*	**he reads** the cartoons.
	but	**he doesn't read** it.
	or	**he buys** a magazine.
He likes the cartoons,	*so*	**he buys** the paper.
He buys the paper	*because*	**he likes** the cartoons.

EXPRESS CHECK

Circle the correct words.

It's raining, <u>so / but</u> Michael is outside.

He's going to buy the puzzle book, <u>and / or</u>

he's going to buy the newspaper.

Grammar Explanations

Examples

1. Use ***and, but, or, so,*** and ***because*** to <u>connect two sentences</u>.	I watched TV. + He read a book. ■ I watched TV, **and** he read a book. The show is popular. + It's not funny. ■ The show is popular, **but** it's not funny. It was late. + I went to bed. ■ It was late, **so** I went to bed.
2. Use ***and*** to <u>add information</u>. Use ***but*** when the information in the second sentence is <u>a surprise</u>. Use ***or*** to show <u>a choice</u>. Use ***so*** to show <u>a result</u>. We usually use a **comma** before ***and, but, or,*** or ***so*** when they connect two complete sentences.	■ I turned on the TV, **and** I watched the show. ■ It was funny, **and** I laughed. ■ I turned on the TV, **but** I didn't watch it. ■ It was funny, **but** I didn't laugh. ■ We can watch TV, **or** we can go out. ■ Will the weather be good, **or** will it rain again? ■ It was a nice day, **so** I went out. ■ I was bored, **so** I watched TV. ■ I like the show, **but** I don't often watch it.
3. Use ***because*** to give <u>a reason</u>. It answers the question ***Why?*** **Don't use a comma** when ***because*** is in the <u>middle of the sentence</u>. ***Because*** can also <u>begin the sentence</u>. The meaning is the same. Use a **comma** when *because* begins the sentence.	**A:** ***Why*** did you go out? **B:** I went out **because** it was a nice day. ■ Most kids love Kenji **because** he's cute. ■ **Because** Kenji is cute, most kids love him.

1 **MATCH** • *Each sentence has two parts. Match the two parts.*

_____d_____ **1.** Ringo was hungry,   **a.** because he loves the game.

_____ **2.** His father was hungry,   **b.** or he could play baseball.

_____ **3.** Because it was cold,   **c.** and his father went to work.

_____ **4.** It was cold,   **d.** but he didn't eat breakfast.

_____ **5.** Ringo went to school,   **e.** Ringo wore his coat.

_____ **6.** After school, he could study,   **f.** so he ate a big breakfast.

_____ **7.** He played baseball   **g.** but his father didn't wear his coat.

2 **COMPLETE** • *Look at this cartoon. Circle the correct words to complete the story.*

1. Toby is walking down the road, but / (and) Pal is / isn't walking with him.

2. Pal is a small dog, but / so he has / doesn't have a big bone.

3. Toby and Pal see a big dog, but / and the big dog sees / doesn't see them.

4. Toby and Pal can / can't run away, so / or they can keep walking.

5. They run away and / because the dog is / isn't very big.

6. Toby falls, but / because Pal doesn't stop / stops.

7. The big dog bites / doesn't bite Toby because / so it's running after Pal.

8. Toby hears the dogs, but / and he can't / can see them.

9. Pal is crying, so / but Toby doesn't run / runs fast.

10. Pal is crying because / so the big dog is / isn't eating his bone.

3

CHOOSE & COMPLETE • *Read these conversations. Complete them with the correct sentences from the box plus* **and, but, or, so,** *and* **because.**

> he practices a lot   I can't buy it for you   do you want to watch TV
> the words are easy   he won the game   we started dinner   I can't read it well
> ~~I don't have any money~~   I'm watching TV   the traffic was bad

1. **ALI:** I want to buy a comic book, <u>but I don't have any money</u>.

    BEA: I just spent all my money, _____. Sorry.

2. **LUC:** Cory played baseball today, _____.

    YVES: He loves baseball, _____.

3. **CARI:** Do you want to go out, _____?

    ZEKI: I don't want to go out _____.

4. **BELA:** We were hungry, _____.

    DITA: That's OK. I'm late _____.

5. **HUNG:** I can speak Japanese, _____.

    THU: Read children's comics. The pictures help, _____.

4

EDIT • *Read this article. Find and correct eight mistakes in the use of* **and, but, or, so,** *and* **because.** *The first mistake is already corrected.*

> **PROFILES** # Hiroshi Fujimoto
>
>
>
>   Hiroshi Fujimoto wanted to write a new comic book, ~~so~~ ^{but} he had no ideas. He couldn't think so there were noisy cats outside. "I need an Idea Machine," he thought. His daughter's toy robot was on the floor, and he stepped on it. Now he had his idea: a robot cat with a lot of magic machines!
>
>   *Doraemon* comic books started coming out in the 1970s, because a TV show came next. Doraemon is the robot cat, so Nobita is a young boy. Nobita isn't very smart, but he has a lot of problems. So he has magic machines, Doraemon can help Nobita. In one story, Nobita wants to have a party, or his house is too small. Doraemon opens his magic door for Nobita's friends, but they walk into a big party room. They are all very happy! Because he makes *real* people happy too, Fujimoto's Doraemon is the most famous cartoon character in Japan.

SelfTest

Circle the letter of the correct answer to complete each sentence.

> **EXAMPLE:**
> Alicia and Paulo _____ students.   A (B) C D
> (A) am   (C) be
> (B) are   (D) is

1. My train arrives _____ 10:05.   A B C D
   (A) at   (C) in
   (B) during   (D) on

2. She takes classes _____ the summer.   A B C D
   (A) at   (C) from
   (B) during   (D) on

3. It's late, _____ I'm not tired.   A B C D
   (A) by   (C) or
   (B) because   (D) but

4. I usually go to work _____ car.   A B C D
   (A) by   (C) on
   (B) in   (D) under

5. Go _____ the steps. Turn right at the bottom.   A B C D
   (A) across   (C) over
   (B) down   (D) up

6. Your glasses are on the floor _____ the table.   A B C D
   (A) between   (C) over
   (B) down   (D) under

7. We got _____ a taxi and went to the museum.   A B C D
   (A) by   (C) on
   (B) into   (D) onto

8. —Are these seats OK? Can you see the movie?   A B C D
   —No. The man _____ me is too tall.
   (A) behind   (C) in front of
   (B) between   (D) to the right of

9. Where did you grow _____?   A B C D
   (A) along   (C) on
   (B) into   (D) up

10. We ran _____ Josh today. He looks great.   A B C D
    (A) along   (C) under
    (B) into   (D) up

224

11. My sister and I get _____ well. We never argue. A B C D
    (A) along   (C) out
    (B) back   (D) over

12. The TV is on. Could you turn _____, please? A B C D
    (A) it off   (C) it under
    (B) off it   (D) under it

13. I put the milk _____. It's in the refrigerator. A B C D
    (A) away   (C) out
    (B) into   (D) over

14. I buy the newspaper every day _____ I like the cartoons. A B C D
    (A) because   (C) or
    (B) but   (D) so

15. I didn't go out. It was raining, _____ I stayed home. A B C D
    (A) because   (C) or
    (B) but   (D) so

SECTION TWO

Each sentence has four underlined parts. The four underlined parts of the sentence are marked A, B, C, and D. Circle the letter of the one underlined part that is NOT CORRECT.

> **EXAMPLE:**
>
> My friends <u>is</u> here, but we <u>are</u> <u>not</u> <u>studying</u>. (A) B C D
>   A   B C   D

16. Our plane left <u>at</u> 11:00 P.M. <u>at</u> Monday, <u>so</u> we slept <u>during</u> the flight. A B C D
               A   B   C   D

17. We got <u>from</u> the subway <u>at</u> River Street, <u>and</u> we walked <u>across</u> the bridge. A B C D
           A   B   C   D

18. It was cold <u>in</u> the house <u>because</u> I <u>put my sweater on</u> and A B C D
                  A   B   C
    <u>turned on the heat</u>.
        D

19. Liv <u>grew up</u> <u>in</u> Stockholm, but she moved <u>at</u> Toronto <u>in</u> 1999. A B C D
        A   B   C   D

20. A noise woke <u>up me</u> <u>at</u> 5:00 A.M., <u>so</u> I <u>got up</u> and went for a run. A B C D
               A B   C   D

21. Do you want to <u>eat out</u>, <u>or</u> do you want to <u>eat</u> <u>in</u> home? A B C D
                 A   B   C D

22. I stayed <u>in</u> Istanbul <u>until</u> three weeks, and then I went <u>to</u> Izmir <u>by</u> bus. A B C D
          A   B   C   D

23. Rita and I met <u>on</u> a concert, <u>but</u> we didn't <u>go out</u> <u>for</u> a few months. A B C D
               A   B   C D

24. I have to be <u>at</u> the office <u>after</u> 9:00 <u>because</u> my <u>meeting</u> starts at 9:00. A B C D
            A   B   C   D

25. The class starts <u>in</u> March, so you should <u>fill out</u> your application and A B C D
                 A   B
    <u>sign for the class up</u> <u>by</u> February 15.
          C   D

Appendices

Glossary

Index

Answer Key

Appendices

1 Irregular Verbs

Base Form	Simple Past	Base Form	Simple Past	Base Form	Simple Past
be	was/were	give	gave	shoot	shot
beat	beat	go	went	shut	shut
become	became	grow	grew	shrink	shrank/shrunk
begin	began	hang	hung	sing	sang
bend	bent	have	had	sink	sank
bet	bet	hear	heard	sit	sat
bite	bit	hide	hid	sleep	slept
bleed	bled	hit	hit	slide	slid
blow	blew	hold	held	speak	spoke
break	broke	hurt	hurt	speed	sped
bring	brought	keep	kept	spend	spent
build	built	kneel	knelt	spill	spilled/spilt
burn	burned/burnt	knit	knit/knitted	spit	spit/spat
buy	bought	know	knew	split	split
catch	caught	lay	laid	spread	spread
choose	chose	lead	led	stand	stood
come	came	leave	left	steal	stole
cost	cost	lend	lent	stick	stuck
cut	cut	let	let	sting	stung
deal	dealt	lie (lie down)	lay	stink	stank/stunk
dig	dug	light	lit/lighted	strike	struck
dive	dived/dove	lose	lost	swear	swore
do	did	make	made	sweep	swept
draw	drew	mean	meant	swim	swam
dream	dreamed/dreamt	meet	met	swing	swung
drink	drank	pay	paid	take	took
drive	drove	put	put	teach	taught
eat	ate	quit	quit	tear	tore
fall	fell	read /rid/	read /rɛd/	tell	told
feed	fed	ride	rode	think	thought
feel	felt	ring	rang	throw	threw
fight	fought	rise	rose	understand	understood
find	found	run	ran	upset	upset
fit	fit	say	said	wake	woke
fly	flew	see	saw	wear	wore
forget	forgot	sell	sold	weep	wept
forgive	forgave	send	sent	win	won
freeze	froze	set	set	wind	wound
get	got	shake	shook	write	wrote

2 Common Non-Action Verbs

FEELINGS	THOUGHTS	SENSES AND APPEARANCE	POSSESSION	VALUE
admire	agree	be	belong	cost
appreciate	believe	feel	have	equal
care	expect	hear	own	weigh
dislike	feel (believe)	look		
doubt	guess	notice		
fear	imagine	see		
hate	know	seem		
like	mean	smell		
love	mind	sound		
need	realize	taste		
prefer	recognize			
regret	remember			
trust	see (understand)			
want	suppose			
wish	think (believe)			
	understand			
	wonder			

3 Common Verbs Followed by the Gerund (Base Form of Verb + *-ing*)

admit	celebrate	dislike	imagine	postpone	report
advise	consider	enjoy	keep (continue)	practice	resist
appreciate	delay	feel like	mention	quit	risk
avoid	deny	finish	mind (object to)	recommend	suggest
can't help	discuss	forgive	miss	regret	understand

4 Common Verbs Followed by the Infinitive (*To* + Base Form of Verb)

afford	can('t) afford	fail	learn	pay	request
agree	can('t) wait	grow	manage	plan	seem
appear	choose	help	mean	prepare	wait
arrange	decide	hope	need	pretend	want
ask	deserve	hurry	neglect	promise	wish
attempt	expect	intend	offer	refuse	would like

5 Common Verbs Followed by the Gerund or the Infinitive

begin	continue	hate	love	remember*	stop*
can't stand	forget*	like	prefer	start	try

*These verbs can be followed by either the gerund or the infinitive but there is a big difference in meaning.

I forgot calling her. (*I called her, but later I didn't remember doing it.*)
I forgot to call her. (*I didn't call her. I forgot to do it.*)

I remembered calling her. (*I called her, and later I remembered doing it.*)
I remembered to call her. (*I called her. I didn't forget to do it.*)

I stopped drinking coffee. (*I drank coffee in the past, but I never drink coffee now.*)
I stopped to drink coffee. (*I stopped doing something else, so I could drink coffee.*)

Some Verbs that Can Have Two Objects

EXAMPLE: I gave **the book to her**. OR I gave **her the book**.

bring	hand	offer	promise	sell	show	teach	throw
give	lend	pass	read	send	take	tell	write

7 Some Common Two-Word Verbs

In this list: • s.o. = someone   s.t. = something
  • **inseparable** two-word verbs have the object after the preposition: **run into** s.o.
  • **separable** two-word verbs have the object between the verb and the preposition: **turn** s.t. **on**

REMEMBER: You can put a **noun object** between the verb and the preposition of **separable** two-word verbs (**call** Jan **up** OR **call up** Jan). You <u>must</u> put a **pronoun object** between the verb and the preposition of separable verbs (**call** her **up** NOT ~~call up her~~).

TWO-WORD VERB	MEANING	TWO-WORD VERB	MEANING
ask s.o. **over**	invite to one's home	**drop out** (**of** s.t.)	quit
blow s.t. **out**	stop burning by blowing	**eat out**	eat in a restaurant
blow s.t. **up**	fill something with air (a balloon)	**empty** (s.t.) **out**	empty completely
blow (s.t.) **up**	(make s.t.) explode	**end up**	reach a final place or condition
break down	stop working (a machine)	**figure** s.o. or s.t. **out**	understand (after thinking about)
break out	happen suddenly	**fill** s.t. **out**	complete (a form, an application)
bring s.t. **about**	make something happen	**fill** (s.t.) **up**	fill completely
bring s.o. or s.t. **back**	return someone or something	**find** (s.t.) **out**	learn information
bring s.t. **out**	introduce (a new product, a book)	**follow** (s.t.) **through**	complete
bring s.o. **up**	raise (children)	**get** s.t. **across**	get people to understand an idea
burn (s.t.) **down**	burn completely	**get ahead**	make progress, succeed
call (s.o.) **back**	return a phone call	**get along**	have a good relationship
call s.t. **off**	cancel	**get back**	return
call s.o. **up**	telephone someone	**get by**	survive
carry on s.t.	continue	**get off** s.t.	leave (a bus, a train)
catch on	become popular	**get on** s.t.	enter (a bus, a train)
cheer (s.o.) **up**	(make someone) feel happier	**get out** (**of** s.t.)	leave (a car, a taxi)
clean (s.o. or s.t.) **up**	clean completely	**get together**	meet
clear (s.t.) **up**	make or become clear	**get up**	rise from bed
come about	happen	**give** s.t. **away**	give without charging money
come along	come with	**give** s.t. **back**	return something
come back	return	**give** s.t. **out**	distribute
come in	enter	**give** (s.t.) **up**	quit
come out	appear	**go along with** s.o.	go with
come up with s.t.	invent	**go back**	return
cross s.t. **out**	draw a line through	**go on**	continue
do s.t. **over**	do again	**go out**	leave
dream s.t. **up**	invent	**go out** (**with** s.o.)	go on a date
dress up	put on special or formal clothes	**go up**	be built
drink s.t. **up**	drink completely	**grow up**	become an adult
drop by/in	visit by surprise	**hand** s.t. **in**	give work to a boss or teacher
drop s.o. or s.t. **off**	take someone/something someplace	**hand** s.t. **out**	distribute

(continued on next page)

Two-Word Verb	Meaning	Two-Word Verb	Meaning
hang out (with s.o.)	*spend time*	stand up	*rise*
hang up	*end a phone conversation*	start (s.t.) over	*start again*
hang s.t. up	*put on a hook or hanger*	stay up	*remain awake*
help (s.o.) out	*assist*	straighten (s.t.)	
hold on	*wait, not hang up the phone*	up/out	*make neat*
keep (s.o. or s.t.)		switch s.t. on	*start a machine or a light*
away	*(cause to) stay at a distance*	take s.t. away/off	*remove*
keep on	*continue*	take s.t. back	*return*
keep up		take s.t. in	*attend (a movie, a concert)*
(with s.o. or s.t.)	*go as fast as*	take off	*depart (a plane)*
leave s.t. on	*not turn off (a light, a radio)*	take s.t. off	*remove a piece of clothing*
leave s.t. out	*not include*	take s.t. out	*borrow from a library*
let s.o. down	*disappoint*	talk s.t. over	*discuss*
lie down	*recline*	tear s.t. up	*tear into small pieces*
look for s.o. or s.t.	*try to find*	think back on	
look out	*be careful*	s.o. or s.t.	*remember*
look s.o. or s.t. over	*examine*	think s.t. over	*consider*
look s.t. up	*try to find in a book or on the Internet*	think s.t. up	*invent*
make s.t. up	*create*	throw s.t. away/out	*put in the trash*
pay s.o. or s.t. back	*repay*	try s.t. on	*put clothing on to see if it fits*
pick s.o. or s.t. out	*choose*	try s.t. out	*find out if something works*
pick s.o. or s.t. up	*lift*	turn s.t. down	*decrease the volume (a radio, a TV)*
point s.o. or s.t. out	*indicate*	turn s.t. in	*give work to a boss or teacher*
put s.t. away	*put something in the correct place*	turn s.o. or s.t. into	*change from one form to another*
put s.t. back	*return something to its original place*	turn s.t. off	*stop a machine or light*
put s.o. or s.t. down	*stop holding*	turn s.t. on	*start a machine or light*
put s.t. off	*delay*	turn out	*have a particular result*
put s.t. on	*cover the body with a piece of clothing or jewelry*	turn up	*appear*
		turn s.t. up	*make louder (a TV, a radio)*
run into s.o.	*meet accidentally*	use s.t. up	*use completely*
run out (of s.t.)	*not have enough of a supply*	wake up	*arise after sleeping*
show up	*appear*	wake (s.o.) up	*awaken*
shut s.t. off	*stop a machine or light*	watch out	*be careful*
sign up (for s.t.)	*register (for an activity)*	work out	*exercise*
sit down	*take a seat*	work s.t. out	*solve*
sit up	*go from a lying to a sitting position*	write s.t. down	*write on a piece of paper*

8   Some Common Nouns with Irregular Plural Forms

A. Nouns with different singular and plural forms

Singular	Plural	Singular	Plural	Singular	Plural
child	**children**	foot	**feet**	mouse	**mice**
man	**men**	tooth	**teeth**	person	**people**
woman	**women**	goose	**geese**		

B. Nouns with the Same Singular and Plural Forms

Singular	Plural
deer	**deer**
fish	**fish**
sheep	**sheep**

C. Nouns that are Always Plural

clothes	jeans	pants	scissors
eyeglasses/glasses	pajamas	shorts	

D. Number Words

The words *dozen, hundred, thousand,* and *million* have the singular form with other numbers.

- Please buy **two dozen** eggs. (NOT: two ~~dozens~~ eggs)
- **Five hundred** people go to this school. (NOT: five ~~hundreds~~ people)

 9 Some Common Non-Count Nouns

REMEMBER: Non-count nouns are singular.
EXAMPLE: The **spaghetti** *is* delicious.

FOOD		LIQUIDS AND GASES	SCHOOL SUBJECTS	IDEAS AND FEELINGS	WEATHER	ACTIVITIES
bread	ice cream	air	art	anger	fog	baseball
butter	lettuce	gasoline	English	beauty	ice	biking
cake	meat	milk	math	fear	rain	football
cheese	pasta	oil	music	friendship	snow	golf
chicken	pizza	oxygen	photography	freedom	wind	hiking
chocolate	salad	water	science	happiness		running
coffee	soup			hate		sailing
cream	spaghetti	**VERY SMALL THINGS**	**MATERIALS**	hope		soccer
fat	tea	dust	cotton	loneliness		swimming
fish	yogurt	flour	glass	love		tennis
		pepper	gold			
		rice	leather			
		salt	paper			
		sand	wood			
		sugar	wool			

NAMES OF CATEGORIES
- equipment   (BUT: computers, phones, TVs…)
- food   (BUT: eggs, vegetables, bananas…)
- furniture   (BUT: beds, chairs, lamps, tables…)
- homework   (BUT: assignments, problems, pages…)
- jewelry   (BUT: bracelets, earrings, necklaces…)
- mail   (BUT: letters, postcards, packages…)
- money   (BUT: euros, yens, dollars…)
- work   (BUT: jobs)

OTHER
(Some non-count nouns don't fit into any of these lists. You must memorize these non-count nouns.)

advice
garbage/trash
information
traffic
news

10 Proper Nouns

REMEMBER: Write proper nouns with a capital letter.

PEOPLE
- first names   Anne, Eduardo, Mehmet, Olga, Shao-fen
- family names   Chen, García, Haddad, Smith
- titles   Doctor, Grandma, Professor
- title + names   Mr. Garcia, Professor Smith, Uncle Steve

PLACES
- continents   Africa, Asia, Australia, Europe, South America
- countries   Argentina, China, Nigeria, Turkey, the United States
- provinces/states   Brittany, Ontario, Szechwan, Texas
- cities   Beijing, Istanbul, Rio de Janeiro, Toronto
- streets   Adalbertstrasse, the Champs-Elysées, Fifth Avenue
- buildings   the Empire State Building, the Petronas Towers
- schools   Midwood High School, Oxford University
- parks   Central Park, the Tivoli Gardens
- mountains   the Andes, the Pyrenees, the Rocky Mountains
- oceans   the Arctic Ocean, the Atlantic, the Indian Ocean, the Pacific
- rivers   the Amazon, the Ganges, the Nile, the Seine
- lakes   Baikal, Tanganyika, Titicaca
- deserts   the Gobi, the Kalahari, the Sahara

LANGUAGES   Arabic, Chinese, Portuguese, Russian, Spanish

NATIONALITIES Brazilian, Japanese, Mexican, Saudi, Turkish

RELIGIONS   Buddhism, Christianity, Hinduism, Islam, Judaism

COURSES   Math 201, Introduction to Computer Sciences

BRANDS   Adidas, Dell, Mercedes, Samsung

TIME
- months   January, March, December
- days   Monday, Wednesday, Saturday
- holidays   Buddha Day, Christmas, Hanukah, New Year's Day, Ramadan

11 Irregular Comparisons of Adjectives and Quantifiers

ADJECTIVE/QUANTIFIER	COMPARATIVE	SUPERLATIVE
bad	worse	the worst
far	farther	the farthest
good	better	the best
a little	less	the least
many/a lot of	more	the most
much/a lot of	more	the most

12   Cardinal and Ordinal Numbers

A. CARDINAL NUMBERS SHOW <u>QUANTITY</u> (*HOW MUCH OR HOW MANY*):

- A week has **seven days**.
- My report is **25 pages** long.
- She is **100 years** old.

0 = zero	10 = ten	20 = twenty	100 = one hundred
1 = one	11 = eleven	21 = twenty-one	101 = one hundred and one
2 = two	12 = twelve	22 = twenty-two	102 = one hundred and two
3 = three	13 = thirteen	30 = thirty	300 = three hundred
4 = four	14 = fourteen	40 = forty	1,000 = one thousand
5 = five	15 = fifteen	50 = fifty	10,000 = ten thousand
6 = six	16 = sixteen	60 = sixty	1,000,000 = one million
7 = seven	17 = seventeen	70 = seventy	10,000,000 = ten million
8 = eight	18 = eighteen	80 = eighty	
9 = nine	19 = nineteeen	90 = ninety	

B. ORDINAL NUMBERS SHOW <u>ORDER</u> (*WHAT GOES FIRST, SECOND, THIRD...*):

- Saturday is the **seventh day** of the week.
- I'm typing the **twenty-fifth page** of my report.
- Today is her **hundredth birthday**.

1st = first	10th = tenth	20th = twentieth	100th = (one) hundredth
2nd = second	11th = eleventh	21st = twenty-first	101st = one hundred and first
3rd = third	12th = twelfth	22nd = twenty-second	102nd = one hundred and second
4th = fourth	13th = thirteenth	30th = thirtieth	300th = three hundredth
5th = fifth	14th = fourteenth	40th = fortieth	1,000th = (one) thousandth
6th = sixth	15th = fifteenth	50th = fiftieth	10,000th = ten thousandth
7th = seventh	16th = sixteenth	60th = sixtieth	1,000,000th = (one) millionth
8th = eighth	17th = seventeenth	70th = seventieth	10,000,000th = ten millionth
9th = ninth	18th = eighteenth	80th = eightieth	
	19th = nineteenth	90th = ninetieth	

13   Some Common Measure Words

CONTAINERS		SERVINGS		SHAPES		MEASUREMENTS	
a bag of	(chips, nuts)	a cup of	(coffee, tea)	a bar of	(candy, soap)	a cup of	(flour, milk)
a bottle of	(soda)	a bowl of	(rice, soup)	a bunch of	(grapes, bananas)	a pint of	(cream)
a box of	(cereal)	a glass of	(milk, water)	a head of	(cabbage, lettuce)	a gallon of	(juice, milk)
a can of	(beans, soup)	a piece of	(cake, paper)	a loaf of	(bread)	a liter of	(milk, water)
a container of	(yogurt, milk)	a scoop of	(ice cream)			a kilo of	(sugar, flour)
a jar of	(honey)	a slice of	(bread, pizza)			a tablespoon of	(oil, salt)
a roll of	(film, paper)					a teaspoon of	(pepper, salt)
a tube of	(toothpaste)					a foot of	(water, snow)
a vase of	(flowers)					a pair of	(glasses, pants)

14 Some Common Abbreviations

AMOUNT			LENGTH			WEIGHT			TEMPERATURE	
teaspoon(s)	**tsp**		inch(es)	**in**		ounce(s)	**oz**		Celsius (Centigrade)	**C**
tablespoon(s)	**tb(s)**		foot/feet	**ft**		pounds(s)	**lb(s)**		Fahrenheit	**F**
pint(s)	**pt**		yard(s)	**yd**		gram(s)	**g**			
quart(s)	**qt**		mile(s)	**mi**		kilogram(s)	**kg**			
gallon(s)	**gal**		meter(s)	**m**						
liter(s)	**l**		kilometers(s)	**km**						

MONTHS OF THE YEAR					DAYS OF THE WEEK	
January	**Jan.**		July	—	Sunday	**Sun.**
February	**Feb.**		August	**Aug.**	Monday	**Mon.**
March	**Mar.**		September	**Sept.**	Tuesday	**Tues.**
April	**Apr.**		October	**Oct.**	Wednesday	**Wed.**
May	—		November	**Nov.**	Thursday	**Thurs.**
June	—		December	**Dec.**	Friday	**Fri.**
					Saturday	**Sat.**

15 Some Common Prepositions

A. PREPOSITIONS OF TIME

PREPOSITION	USE FOR . . .	EXAMPLE
after	• a time • a noun for a length of time	He left **after 9:00**. She saw him **after class**.
at	• an exact point of time • *night*	He came home **at 6:00**. We had lunch **at noon**. It's cold **at night**.
before	• a time • a noun for a length of time	She left **before 9:00**. He saw her **before class**.
by	• the latest possible time	Be at the airport **by 11:00**. (= no later than 11:00)
during	• a noun for a length of time	I took notes **during class**.
for	• a period of time	He studied Russian **for five years**.
from . . . to	• the beginning and end of a period of time	We work **from 9:00 to 5:00**. He lived here **from 2002 to 2005**.
in	• *morning, afternoon,* and *evening* • a month • a season • a year • how long after a specific time	She works **in the morning**. They start school **in September**. We go to the beach **in the summer**. He'll graduate **in 2005**. The bus will leave **in five minutes** (from now) The movie ended **in two hours** (from the start).
on	• a day of the week • a date	It rained **on Monday**. I saw a movie **on the weekend**. Class will start **on February 17**.
until	• the end of a length of time	We'll stay in Tokyo **until Friday**.

236

B. Prepositions of Place

Preposition	Meaning	Example
in		The milk is **in the refrigerator**.
on		I left my keys **on the table**.
under		She keeps her **shoes under the bed**.
over		There's a good light **over my desk**.
in front of		They're sitting **in front of the TV**.
in back of behind		There's a small garden **in back of my house**. It's **behind my house**.
to the right of next to		The café is **to the right of the post office**. It's **next to the post office**.
to the left of next to		Your glasses are **to the left of the computer**. They're **next to the computer**.
across from opposite		The bank is **across from the café**. It's **opposite the café**.
between		In class I sit **between Paulo and Leila**.
near		I live **near the school**.
far (from)		The movie theater is **far from my home**.

C. Prepositions of Movement

Preposition	Meaning	Example
to		I'm going **to the store**.
from		She's coming **from home**.
into		He walked **into a café**.
out of		They came **out of their hotel**.
over		I flew **over the Alps**.
under		Go **under the bridge**.
on		Put the glass **on the table**.
off		The cat jumped **off the bed**.
across		Walk **across the street**.
through		She looked **through the window**.
along		I walked **along the street**.
around		They ran **around the park**.
up		Go **up the stairs**.
down		Go **down the stairs**.
toward		She drove **toward Lisbon**.
past		Don't go **past the hotel**.

16 Contractions with Verb Forms

1. SIMPLE PRESENT, PRESENT PROGRESSIVE, AND IMPERATIVE

Contractions with *Be*

I am	=	**I'm**
you are	=	**you're**
he is	=	**he's**
she is	=	**she's**
it is	=	**it's**
we are	=	**we're**
you are	=	**you're**
they are	=	**they're**

SIMPLE PRESENT	PRESENT PROGRESSIVE
I**'m** a student.	I**'m studying** here.
He**'s** my teacher.	He**'s teaching** verbs.
We**'re** from Canada.	We**'re living** here.

I am not	=	**I'm not**		
you are not	=	**you're not**	or	**you aren't**
he is not	=	**he's not**	or	**he isn't**
she is not	=	**she's not**	or	**she isn't**
it is not	=	**it's not**	or	**it isn't**
we are not	=	**we're not**	or	**we aren't**
you are not	=	**you're not**	or	**you aren't**
they are not	=	**they're not**	or	**they aren't**

SIMPLE PRESENT	PRESENT PROGRESSIVE
She**'s not** sick.	She**'s not reading**.
He **isn't** late.	He **isn't coming**.
We **aren't** late.	We **aren't leaving**.
They**'re not** here.	They**'re not playing**.

Contractions with *Do*

do not	=	**don't**
does not	=	**doesn't**

SIMPLE PRESENT	IMPERATIVE
They **don't live** here.	**Don't run**!
It **doesn't snow** much.	

2. SIMPLE PAST

Contractions with *Be*

was not	=	**wasn't**
were not	=	**weren't**

SIMPLE PAST
He **wasn't** a poet.
They **weren't** late.
We **didn't** see her.

Contractions with *Do*

did not	=	**didn't**

3. FUTURE

Contractions with *Will*

I will	=	**I'll**
you will	=	**you'll**
he will	=	**he'll**
she will	=	**she'll**
it will	=	**it'll**
we will	=	**we'll**
you will	=	**you'll**
they will	=	**they'll**
will not	=	**won't**

FUTURE WITH *WILL*
I**'ll take** the train.
It**'ll be** faster that way.
We**'ll go** together.
He **won't come** with us.
They **won't miss** the train.

Contractions with *Be going to*

I am going to	=	**I'm going to**
you are going to	=	**you're going to**
he is going to	=	**he's going to**
she is going to	=	**she's going to**
it is going to	=	**it's going to**
we are going to	=	**we're going to**
you are going to	=	**you're going to**
they are going to	=	**they're going to**

FUTURE WITH *BE GOING TO*
I**'m going to buy** tickets tomorrow.
She**'s going to call** you.
It**'s going to rain** soon.
We**'re going to drive** to Boston.
They**'re going to crash**!

4. MODALS

cannot or can not	=	**can't**
could not	=	**couldn't**
should not	=	**shouldn't**
would rather	=	**'d rather**

She **can't dance**.
We **shouldn't go**.
I**'d rather take** the bus.

17 Spelling Rules for Base Form of Verb + *-ing* (Present Progressive and Gerund)

1. Add *-ing* to the base form of the verb.

read	read**ing**
stand	stand**ing**

2. Does the verb end in **silent -e**?
   Drop the final **-e** and add *-ing*.

leave	leav**ing**
take	tak**ing**

3. Is the verb **one syllable**? Are the three letters:
   consonant + vowel + consonant (**CVC**)?
   Double the last consonant and add *-ing*.

   C V C
   ↓ ↓ ↓
   s i t   sit**ting**

   C V C
   ↓ ↓ ↓
   r u n   run**ning**

   Do not double the last consonant in verbs that end in
   -w, -x, or **-y**.

sew	sew**ing**
fix	fix**ing**
play	play**ing**

4. Is the word **two or more syllables**? Are the last three
   letters: consonant + vowel + consonant (**CVC**)?
   Double the last consonant only if the last syllable is
   stressed (').

admít	admit**ting**	(The last syllable is stressed, so you double the **-t**.)
whísper	whisper**ing**	(The last syllable is not stressed, so you don't double the **-r**.)

5. Does the verb end in *-ie*?
   Change the *ie* to **y** and add *-ing*.

die	d**ying**

18 Spelling Rules for the Simple Present: Third-Person Singular *(he, she, it)*

1. Add **-s** for most verbs.

work	work**s**
buy	buy**s**
ride	ride**s**
return	return**s**

2. Add **-es** for verbs that end in **-ch, -s, -sh, -x,** or **-z.**

watch	watch**es**
pass	pass**es**
rush	rush**es**
relax	relax**es**
buzz	buzz**es**

3. Does the base form end in **consonant + y?** Change the **y** to **i** and add **-es.**

study	stud**ies**
hurry	hurr**ies**
dry	dr**ies**

4. Does the base form end in **vowel + y?** Add **-s.** (Do not change the *y* to *i*.)

play	play**s**
enjoy	enjoy**s**

5. A few verbs have **irregular forms**.

be	**is**
have	**has**
do	**does**
go	**goes**

19 Spelling Rules for the Simple Past of Regular Verbs

1. Does the the verb end in a **consonant?** Add **-ed.**

return	return**ed**
help	help**ed**

2. Does the verb end in **-e?** Add **-d.**

live	live**d**
create	create**d**
die	die**d**

3. Is the verb **one syllable?** Are the last three letters: consonant + vowel + consonant (**CVC**)? Double the last consonant and add **-ed.**

C V C
↓ ↓ ↓
h o p   hop**ped**

C V C
↓ ↓ ↓
r u b   rub**bed**

Do not double the last consonant in verbs that end in **-w, -x,** or **-y**.

bow	bow**ed**
mix	mix**ed**
play	play**ed**

4. Is the verb **two or more syllables**? Does it end in: consonant + vowel + consonant (**CVC**)? Double the last consonant only if the last syllable is stressed ('́).

prefér	prefer**red**	(The last syllable is stressed, so you double the **-r**.)
vísit	visit**ed**	(The last syllable is not stressed, so you don't double the **t**.)

5. Does the verb end in **consonant + y?** Change the **y** to **i** and add **-ed.**

worry	worr**ied**
carry	carr**ied**

6. Does the verb end in **vowel + y?** Add **-ed.** (Do not change the *y* to *i*.)

play	play**ed**
annoy	annoy**ed**

EXCEPTIONS: pay—**paid**, lay—**laid**, say—**said**

20 Spelling Rules for Regular Plural Nouns

1. Add **-s** to most nouns.

book	book**s**
table	table**s**
cup	cup**s**

2. Does the noun end in **-ch, -s, -sh,** or **-x**? Add **-es**.

watch	watch**es**
bus	bus**es**
dish	dish**es**
box	box**es**

3. Does the noun end in **vowel + y**? Add **-s**.

day	day**s**
key	key**s**

4. Does the noun end in **consonant + y**? Change the **y** to **i** and add **-es**.

baby	bab**ies**
city	cit**ies**
strawberry	strawberr**ies**

5. Does the noun end in **-f**? Change **f** to **v** and add **-es**.

half	hal**ves**	loaf	loa**ves**
leaf	lea**ves**	shelf	shel**ves**

EXCEPTIONS: roof—roof**s**, handkerchief—handkerchief**s**

Does the noun end in **-fe**? Change **f** to **v** and add **-s**.

knife	kni**ves**
life	li**ves**
wife	wi**ves**

6. Does the noun end in **vowel + o**? Add **-s**.

radio	radio**s**
video	video**s**
zoo	zoo**s**

Does the noun end in **consonant + o**? Add **-es**.

potato	potato**es**
tomato	tomato**es**

EXCEPTIONS: kilo—kilo**s**, photo—photo**s**, piano—piano**s**

21 Spelling Rules for the Comparative (-er) and Superlative (-est) of Adjectives

1. Is the adjective **one syllable**? Add **-er** to form the comparative. Add **-est** to form the superlative.

cheap	cheap**er**	cheap**est**
bright	bright**er**	bright**est**

2. Does the adjective end in **-e**? Add **-r** or **-st**.

nice	nice**r**	nice**st**

3. Does the adjective end in **consonant + y**? Change **y** to **i** and add **-er** or **-est**.

pretty	prett**ier**	prett**iest**

EXCEPTION: shy—shy**er**—shy**est**

4. Are the last three letters of the adjective: consonant + vowel + consonant (**CVC**)? Double the consonant and add **-er** or **-est**.

C V C
↓ ↓ ↓
b i g	big**ger**	big**gest**

Do not double the last consonant in words ending in **-w**.

slow	slow**er**	slow**est**

22 Spelling Rules for Adverbs Ending in –ly

1. Add **-ly** to the adjective form.

nice	nice**ly**
quiet	quiet**ly**
beautiful	beautiful**ly**

2. Does the adjective end in **consonant + y**? Change the **y** to **i** and add **-ly**.

easy	eas**ily**

3. Does the adjective end in **-le**? Drop the **e** and add **-y**.

possible	possibl**y**

Do not drop the **e** for other adjectives ending in **-e**.

extreme	extreme**ly**

EXCEPTION: true—tru**ly**

4. Does the adjective end in **-ic**? Add **-ally**.

basic	basic**ally**
fantastic	fantastic**ally**

	USE FOR . . .	EXAMPLE
capital letter	• the pronoun *I* • proper nouns* • the first word of a sentence.	Tomorrow **I** will be here at 2:00. His name is **Karl**. He lives in **Germany**. **When** does the train leave? **At** 2:00.
apostrophe (')	• possessive nouns • contractions**	Is that **Marta's** coat? **That's** not hers. **It's** mine.
comma (,)	• after items in a list • before sentence connectors ***and***, ***but***, ***or***, and ***so*** • after the first part of a sentence that begins with ***because*** • after the first part of a sentence that begins with a preposition	He bought **apples**, **pears**, **oranges**, and **bananas**. They watched TV**, and** she played video games. ***Because*** **it's raining,** we're not walking to work. ***Across from*** **the bank,** there's a good restaurant.
exclamation point (!)	• at the end of a sentence to show surprise or a strong feeling	You're here! That's great! Stop! A car is coming!
period (.)	• at the end of a statement	Today is Wednesday.
question mark (?)	• at the end of a question	What day is today?

* See Appendix 10, page 234 for a list of proper nouns.
** See Appendix 16, pages 238–239 for a list of contractions.

 Pronunciation Table

	VOWELS				CONSONANTS		
SYMBOL	KEY WORD	SYMBOL	KEY WORD	SYMBOL	KEY WORD	SYMBOL	KEY WORD
i	b**ea**t, f**ee**d	ə	ban**a**na, **a**mong	p	**p**ack, ha**pp**y	ʃ	**sh**ip, ma**ch**ine, **st**ation, spe**ci**al, discu**ss**ion
ɪ	b**i**t, d**i**d	ɚ	sh**ir**t, m**ur**der	b	**b**ack, ru**bb**er	ʒ	mea**s**ure, vi**s**ion
eɪ	d**a**te, p**ai**d	aɪ	b**i**te, cr**y**, b**uy**, **eye**	t	**t**ie	h	**h**ot, **wh**o
ɛ	b**e**t, b**e**d			d	**d**ie	m	**m**en
æ	b**a**t, b**a**d	aʊ	**a**b**ou**t, h**ow**	k	**c**ame, **k**ey, **qu**ick	n	su**n**, **kn**ow, **pn**eumonia
ɑ	b**o**x, **o**dd, f**a**ther	ɔɪ	v**oi**ce, b**oy**	g	**g**ame, **g**uest	ŋ	su**ng**, ri**ng**ing
ɔ	b**ou**ght, d**o**g	ɪr	b**eer**	tʃ	**ch**urch, na**t**ure, wa**tch**	w	**w**et, **wh**ite
oʊ	b**oa**t, r**oa**d	ɛr	b**are**	dʒ	**j**udge, **g**eneral, ma**j**or	l	**l**ight, **l**ong
ʊ	b**oo**k, g**oo**d	ɑr	b**ar**	f	**f**an, **ph**otogra**ph**	r	**r**ight, **wr**ong
u	b**oo**t, f**oo**d, st**u**dent	ɔr	d**oor**	v	**v**an	y	**y**es, **u**se, m**u**sic
		ʊr	t**our**	θ	**th**ing, brea**th**	t̬	bu**tt**er, bo**tt**le
ʌ	b**u**t, m**u**d, m**o**ther			ð	**th**en, brea**the**		

STRESS
' shows main stress.

s	**s**ip, **c**ity, **ps**ychology
z	**z**ip, plea**s**e, goe**s**

25 Pronunciation Rules for the Simple Present: Third-Person Singular *(he, she, it)*

1. The third-person singular in the simple present always ends in the letter **-s**. There are three different pronunciations for the final sound of the third-person singular.

/s/	/z/	/ɪz/
talk**s**	love**s**	danc**es**

2. Say **/s/** after these sounds: **/p/, /t/, /k/,** and **/f/**.

top	to**ps**
get	ge**ts**
take	ta**kes**
laugh	lau**ghs**

3. Say **/z/** after these sounds: **/b/, /d/, /g/, /v/, /ð/, /m/, /n/, /ŋ/, /l/,** and **/r/**.

describe	descri**bes**
spend	spen**ds**
hug	hu**gs**
live	li**ves**
bathe	ba**thes**
seem	see**ms**
remain	remai**ns**
sing	si**ngs**
tell	te**lls**
lower	lowe**rs**

4. Say **/z/** after all vowel sounds.

agree	agr**ees**
try	tr**ies**
stay	sta**ys**
know	kn**ows**

5. Say **/ɪz/** after these sounds: **/s/, /z/, /ʃ/, /ʒ/, /tʃ/,** and **/dʒ/**. **/ɪz/** adds a syllable to the verb.

relax	rela**xes**
freeze	free**zes**
rush	ru**shes**
massage	massa**ges**
watch	wa**tches**
judge	ju**dges**

6. ***Do*** and ***say*** have a change in vowel sound.

do	/du/	does	/dʌz/
say	/seɪ/	says	/sɛz/

26 Pronunciation Rules for the Simple Past of Regular Verbs

1. The regular simple past always ends in the letter **-d**. There are three different pronunciations for the final sound of the regular simple past.

/t/	/d/	/ɪd/
race**d**	live**d**	attend**ed**

2. Say **/t/** after these sounds: **/p/, /k/, /f/, /s/, /ʃ/,** and **/tʃ/**.

hop	hop**ped**
work	wor**ked**
laugh	lau**ghed**
address	addre**ssed**
publish	publi**shed**
watch	wa**tched**

3. Say **/d/** after a vowel sound.

agree	agr**eed**
play	pla**yed**
die	di**ed**
enjoy	enj**oyed**
row	r**owed**

4. Say **/d/** after these sounds: **/b/, /g/, /v/, /z/, /ʒ/, /dʒ/, /m/, /n/, /ŋ/, /l/, /r/,** and **/ð/**.

rub	ru**bbed**
hug	hu**gged**
live	li**ved**
surprise	surpri**sed**
massage	massa**ged**
change	chan**ged**
rhyme	rhy**med**
return	retur**ned**
bang	ba**nged**
enroll	enro**lled**
appear	appea**red**
bathe	ba**thed**

5. Say **/ɪd/** after **/t/** and **/d/**. **/ɪd/** adds a syllable to the verb.

start	star**ted**
decide	deci**ded**

1. Regular plural nouns always end in the letter **-s**.
There are three different pronunciations.

/s/	/z/	/ɪz/
book**s**	day**s**	lunch**es**

2. Say /s/ after these sounds: /**p**/, /**t**/, /**k**/, /**f**/, and /**θ**/.

ma**ps**
ha**ts**
bi**kes**
lau**ghs**
brea**ths**

3. Say /z/ after a vowel sound.

d**ays**
k**eys**
sk**ies**
radi**os**
rev**iews**

4. Say /z/ after these sounds: /**b**/, /**d**/, /**g**/, /**v**/, /**m**/, /**n**/, /**ŋ**/, /**l**/, and /**r**/.

la**bs**
be**ds**
ru**gs**
wi**ves**
far**ms**
pe**ns**
ri**ngs**
ba**lls**
ca**rs**

5. Say /ɪz/ after /**s**/, /**z**/, /**ʃ**/, /**ʒ**/, /**tʃ**/, and /**dʒ**/.
/ɪz/ adds a syllable to the noun.

fa**ces**
no**ses**
di**shes**
gara**ges**
wa**tches**
ju**dges**

Glossary

action verb An action verb describes an action.
- Alicia **ran** home.

See also *non-action verb.*

adjective An adjective describes a noun or pronoun.
- That's a **great** idea.
- It's **wonderful**.

adverb An adverb describes a verb.
- She drives **carefully**.
- They **never** work on weekends.

adverb of frequency See *time word.*

affirmative Affirmative means **Yes**.
- He **works**. *(affirmative statement)*
- **Yes**, he **does**. *(affirmative short answer)*

See also *negative.*

apostrophe (') An apostrophe is a punctuation mark. There are apostrophes in contractions and possessives.
- It**'s** the boy**'s** shoe.

See Appendix 23, *Some Capitalization and Punctuation Rules.*

article An article goes before a noun. There are two kinds of articles: indefinite and definite.
The **indefinite** articles are ***a*** and ***an***.
- I ate **a** sandwich and **an** apple.

The **definite** article is ***the***.
- I didn't like **the** sandwich. **The** apple was very good.

auxiliary verb See *helping verb.*

base form of verb The base form of the verb is the simple form without any endings *(-s, -ed, -ing)* or other changes.
- **be**
- **have**
- **go**
- **drive**

capital letter A capital letter is big. The capital letters are: ***A, B, C, D, E, F, G, H, I, J, K, L, M, N, O, P, Q, R, S, T, U, V, W, X, Y, Z.***
- **A**licia lives in the **U**nited **S**tates.

See Appendix 23, *Some Capitalization and Punctuation Rules.* See also *small letter.*

comma (,) A comma is a punctuation mark. It separates the parts of a sentence.
- It's early**,** but I have to leave now.

See Appendix 23, *Some Capitalization and Punctuation Rules.*

common noun A common noun is the word for a person, place, or thing. (But not the name of the person, place, or thing.)
- Jason is a **teacher** at my **school**.

See also *proper noun.*

comparative adjective A comparative adjective describes the difference between two people, places, or things.
- Jason is **taller** than Marta.

See Appendix 11, *Irregular Comparisons of Adjectives.*
See Appendix 21, *Spelling Rules for the Comparative (-er) and Superlative (-est) of Adjectives.*
See also *superlative adjective.*

consonant The consonants are: ***b, c, d, f, g, h, j, k, l, m, n, p, q, r, s, t, v, w, x, y, z.***
See also *vowel.*

contraction A contraction is a short form of a word or words. We write it with an apostrophe (').
- **she's** = she is
- **can't** = cannot

See Appendix 16, *Contractions with Verb Forms.*

count noun A count noun is a noun you can count. It has a singular and a plural form.
- one **book**, two **books**

See also *non-count noun.*

definite article See *article.*

direct object A direct object receives the action of a verb. It is a noun or pronoun.
- Marta kicked **the ball**. I saw **her**.

See also *indirect object.*

exclamation point (!) An exclamation point is a punctuation mark. It shows a strong feeling.
- Stop**!**

See Appendix 23, *Some Capitalization and Punctuation Rules.*

formal/informal We can use formal or informal language. It depends on the people we are talking to. We use **formal** language in business situations or with adults we do not know.

- Good afternoon, Mr. Rivera. Please have a seat.

We use **informal** language with family, friends, and children.

- Hi, Pete. Sit down.

gerund A gerund (**verb + -ing**) is a noun. It can be the subject or object of a sentence.

- **Swimming** is great exercise.
- I enjoy **swimming**.

See Appendix 3, *Common Verbs Followed by the Gerund (Base Form of Verb + -ing.)*

See Appendix 5, *Common Verbs Followed by the Gerund or the Infinitive.*

See Appendix 17, *Spelling Rules for Base Form of Verb + -ing.*

helping verb Some verbs have two parts: a helping verb + main verb. *Be* and *do* are often helping verbs. Modals (*can, should, may . . .*) are also helping verbs.

- I **am** exercising right now.
- **Do** you like to exercise?
- No, I **don't**.
- I **didn't** exercise yesterday.
- I **should** exercise every day.

See also *main verb.*

imperative The imperative form of the verb is the same as the base form. An imperative sentence gives a command or instructions.

- **Hurry**!
- **Don't touch** that!

indefinite article See *article.*

indirect object An indirect object receives something as the result of the action of the verb. It is a noun or pronoun (often a person).

- I told **John** the story.
- He gave **me** some good advice.

See Appendix 6, *Some Verbs that Can Have Two Objects.*
See also *direct object.*

infinitive An infinitive is *to* + **base form** of the verb.

- I want **to leave** now.

See Appendix 4, *Common Verbs Followed by the Infinitive (To + Base Form of Verb).*

See Appendix 5, *Common Verbs Followed by the Gerund or the Infinitive.*

infinitive of purpose An infinitive of purpose (*to* + base form of the verb) gives the reason for an action.

- I go to school **to learn** English.
- I took notes **in order not to forget**.

informal See *formal.*

inseparable two-word verb See *two-word verb.*

irregular See *regular.*

main verb Some verbs have two parts: a helping verb and a main verb. The main verb describes an action or state.

- Jared is **calling**.
- He'll **call** again later.
- Does he **call** every day?

See also *helping verb.*

measure word A measure word tells you how much or how many.

- I bought **a container of** milk and **a pound of** apples.

See Appendix 13, *Some Common Measure Words.*

modal A modal is a type of helping verb. It goes before a main verb and expresses ideas such as ability, advice, obligation, permission, and possibility. *Can, could, will, would, may, might, should,* and *must* are modals.

- **Can** you swim?
- You really **should** learn to swim.

negative Negative means *No*.

- He **doesn't** work. *(negative statement)*
- **No**, he **doesn't**. *(negative short answer)*

See also *affirmative.*

non-action verb A non-action verb does not describe an action. It describes such things as thoughts, feelings, and senses.

- I **remember** that word.
- Chris **loves** ice cream.
- It **tastes** great.

See Appendix 2, *Common Non-Action Verbs.*
See also *action verb.*

non-count noun A non-count noun is a noun that we usually do not count (*air, water, rice, love, . . .*). It has only a singular form.

- The **rice** *is* delicious.

See Appendix 9, *Some Common Non-Count Nouns.*
See also *count noun.*

noun A noun is a word for a person, place, or thing.
- My **sister**, **Anne**, works in an **office**.
- She uses a **computer**.

object An object receives the action of a verb. An object is a noun or a pronoun.
- Layla threw **the ball**.
- She threw **it** to **Tom**.

See Appendix 6, *Some Verbs that Can Have Two Objects.*
See also *subject.*

object pronoun The object pronouns are: *me, you, him, her, it, us, them.*
- I gave **her** a book.
- I gave **it** to **her**.

See also *subject pronoun.*

paragraph A paragraph is a group of sentences. It is usually about one topic.
- Cell phones are very useful, but they are also a big problem. Now we get calls on the train, on the street, and in restaurants. We hear people's conversations with their friends, their parents, and their bosses. There is no "quiet" or "alone" time!

See also *sentence.*

period (.) A period is a punctuation mark. It shows the end of a statement.
- Today is Friday**.**

See Appendix 23, *Some Capitalization and Punctuation Rules.*

phrasal verb See *two-word verb.*

plural Plural means two or more.
- There **are** three **people** in the restaurant.
- **They are** eating dinner.
- **We** saw **them**.

See also *singular.*

possessive Possessive nouns, pronouns, and adjectives show a relationship or show that someone owns something.
- Zach is **Megan's** brother. *(possessive noun)*
- Is that car **his**? *(possessive pronoun)*
- That's **his** car. *(possessive adjective)*

preposition A preposition is a word or group of words that shows time, place, or movement. Prepositions go before nouns and pronouns.
- I went **to** the bank **on** Monday. It's **next to** my office.

See Appendix 15, *Some Common Prepositions.*

pronoun A pronoun is a word used in place of a noun.
- Do you know my brother? Yes, I met **him** last week.

proper noun A proper noun is the name of a person, place, or thing. A proper noun begins with a capital letter.
- **Maria** goes to **Central High School**.
- It's on **High Street**.

See Appendix 10, *Proper Nouns.*
See also *common noun.*

punctuation In writing, punctuation marks (period, comma, . . .) make your meaning clear. For example, a period (.) shows the end of a sentence. It also shows that the sentence is a statement, not a question.
See Appendix 23, *Some Capitalization and Punctuation Rules.*

quantifier A quantifier shows an amount (but not an exact amount).
- Josh bought **a lot of** books last year.
- He doesn't have **much** money.

question A question is a sentence that asks for information. In writing, a question ends with a question mark. There are two types of questions: *yes/no* questions and *wh-* questions.
Yes/No questions are answered by *Yes* or *No.*
- Do you study a lot**?** (Yes, I do OR No, I don't.)

Wh- **questions** ask for information. They start with a question word.
- **Where** is the library**?** (It's on Main Street.)

question mark (?) A question mark is a punctuation mark. It shows the end of a question.
- What time is it**?**

See Appendix 23, *Some Capitalization and Punctuation Rules.*

question word Question words are words such as: *who, what, when, where, which, why, how,* and *how much.* They begin *wh-* questions.
- **Who** is that?
- **What** did you see?
- **When** does the movie usually start?

regular/irregular Most verbs, nouns, and adjectives are regular. They change their form in the same way.
- *Play* is a **regular** verb. Its simple past form (*played*) ends in *-ed.*
- *Go* is an **irregular** verb. Its simple past form (*went*) does not end in *-ed.*

See Appendix 1, *Irregular Verbs.*
See Appendix 8, *Some Nouns with Irregular Plural Forms.*
See Appendix 11, *Irregular Comparisons of Adjectives and Quantifiers.*

sentence A sentence is a group of words that has a subject and a verb. It begins with a capital letter and ends with a period (.), question mark (?), or exclamation point (!).
- **Computers are** very useful.

EXCEPTION: In imperative sentences, the subject is *you*. We do not usually say or write the subject in imperative sentences.
- **Call** her now**!**

sentence connector The words **and, but, so, or,** and **because** are sentence connectors. They connect two sentences to make one sentence.

Paz speaks English. + *He doesn't speak French.*
- Paz speaks English, **but** he doesn't speak French.

separable two-word verb See *two-word verb.*

short answer A short answer answers a *yes/no* question.

A: Did you call me last night?
B: **No, I didn't.** OR **No.**

singular Singular means *one.*
- I **have** one **sister.**
- **She works** in a **hospital.**

See also *plural.*

small letter The small letters are: *a, b, c, d, e, f, g, h, i, j, k, l, m, n, o, p, q, r, s, t, u, v, w, x, y, z.*
See also *capital letter.*

stative verb See *non-action verb.*

subject The subject of a sentence is the person, place, or thing that the sentence is about.
- **Ms. Chen** teaches English.
- **Her class** is interesting.

See also *object.*

subject pronoun The subject pronouns are: **I, you, he, she, it, we, they.**
- **I** read a lot.
- **She** reads a lot too.

See also *object pronoun.*

superlative adjective A superlative adjective compares a person, place, or thing to a group of people, places, or things.
- Cindi is **the fastest** runner on her team.

See Appendix 11, *Irregular Comparisons of Adjectives.*
See Appendix 21, *Spelling Rules for the Comparative* (-er) *and Superlative* (-est) *of Adjectives.*
See also *comparative adjective.*

syllable A syllable is a group of letters with one vowel sound.
- one syllable: **man**
- two syllables: **woman** (*wo-man*)

tense Main verbs have tense. Tense shows the time of the action.
- **simple present:** Fabio *talks* to his friend every day.
- **simple past:** Fabio *talked* to his teacher yesterday.

third-person singular The third-person-singular pronouns are **he, she,** and **it.** In the simple present, the third-person-singular verb ends in **-s.**
- Tomás **works** in an office. (*Tomás — he*)

See Appendix 18, *Spelling Rules for the Simple Present: Third-Person Singular* (he, she, it).
See Appendix 25, *Pronunciation Rules for the Simple Present: Third-Person Singular* (he, she, it).

time word Time words are words such as: **always, usually, sometimes,** and **never.**
- Celia **usually** watches the news at 6:00.

two-word verb A two-word verb has two parts: a verb and a preposition. The meaning of the two-word verb is often different from the separate meanings of the verb and the preposition.
The words in an **inseparable** two-word verb must stay together.
- We **ran into** Tomás at the supermarket.
  (NOT: We ~~ran Tomás into~~ . . .)

The words in a **separable** two-word verb can separate.
- Tom **looked** the word **up** in a dictionary.
- He **looked** it **up.**

See Appendix 7, *Some Common Two-Word Verbs.*

verb A verb describes what the subject of the sentence does, thinks, feels, senses, or owns.
- They **run** two miles every day.
- She **loved** that movie.
- He **has** a new camera.

vowel The vowels are: *a, e, i, o, u.*
See also *consonant.*

wh- question A *wh*-question begins with a question word.
- **Where** are you going?
- **When** did you leave?
- **How** are you?

yes/no question A *yes/no* question begins with a form of **be** or a helping verb. You can answer a *yes/no* question with *yes* or *no.*

A: **Are** you a student?
B: **Yes,** I am. OR **No,** I'm not.

Index

Answer Key

NOTE: In this answer key, where the contracted form is given, the full form is also correct, and where the full form is given, the contracted form is also correct.

UNIT 1 — The Present of *Be:* Statements

CHECK POINT

The man is a prince.
She is a good dancer.

CHART CHECK 1

T, F

CHART CHECK 2

F

EXPRESS CHECK

They're tall.
We're not in the same class.
I'm 20 years old.
He's not a student.

1

MAI: "I'm from Yanquing. It's not far
from Beijing."

SERGEI: "My favorite games are *Shadows*
and *Zones*. I'm not interested in
sports."

LEYLA: "I'm interested in music too. *Mouse
on Mars* is great."

ALVARO: "I love all sports. I'm the captain of
my soccer team."

2
2. We're the same age.
3. I'm from Izmir.
4. It's in Turkey.
5. I'm not a student.
6. My family isn't (OR My family's not) large.
7. My parents are from Istanbul.
8. There are two children.
9. My sister is (OR My sister's) in
high school.
10. She's 16.
11. Her hobby is (OR Her hobby's) music.
12. We're not (OR We aren't) rich.
13. But we're very happy.

3
1. 's
2. 'm, 's, 's not (OR isn't)
3. are, 'm not, 'm
4. 'm, 're not (OR aren't), 're

4

You're
~~You's~~ interested in computer games! I'm
is
interested in them too. My favorite game ~~are~~
'm not
Polar Ice, but I ~~amn't~~ very good at it. My
're not OR *aren't*
other hobby is baseball. You ~~no are~~
interested in sports. Why? Baseball is a
It's
great game. ~~It~~ very popular here. My friends
and I are always in the ballpark after work.
're
They ~~is~~ good hitters. I'm a pretty good
catcher.
're OR *are*
We ~~is~~ both students. Computer class
is
~~are~~ your favorite, right? My favorite class
is history.

Well, it's time for class now. Write soon.

UNIT 2 — The Present of *Be:* Questions

CHECK POINT

now, is afraid of

CHART CHECK 1

T, F

CHART CHECK 2

Why

EXPRESS CHECK

Who's afraid?
Is it a fish?
No, it isn't.

1
2. d   5. b   7. a
3. e   6. g   8. c
4. h

2
2. Is he, No, he's not (OR he isn't).
3. Are you, Yes, I am.
4. Is he, Yes, he is.
5. Are they, No, they're not (OR they aren't).
6. Am I, Yes, you are (OR Yes, I am).

3
2. Are they the same?
3. No, they're not (OR they aren't)
4. What is (OR What's) the difference?
5. Who is (OR Who's) right?
6. Is hypnosis helpful
7. Yes, it is

4

What ~~you are~~ *are you* afraid of? Are you afraid

of long words? *Yes?* Then, you have

hippopotomonstrosesquippedaliophobia!

Phobias have strange names, but they

are very common.

Do you know these phobia facts?

1. What is *triskadekaphobia?*

   a. Fear of the number 13.

   b. Fear of school.

2. ~~Are~~ *Is* *octophobia* the fear of the number 8?

   a. No, it's not. It's the fear of clocks.

   b. Yes, ~~it's~~ *it is*!

3. *Cyberphobia* is a new phobia. What ~~it is~~ *is it*?

   a. It's the fear of motorcycles.

   b. It's the fear of computers.

4. ~~Am~~ *Is* hypnosis helpful for phobias?

   a. Yes. If you don't have *hypnophobia!*

   b. No, ~~they're~~ *it's* not.

UNIT 3 — The Present Progressive: Statements

CHECK POINT

now

CHART CHECK 1

T, F

CHART CHECK 2

F

EXPRESS CHECK

They're calling.
She isn't calling.

1

I'm sitting on the train. All around me

people are using their cell phones.

They're making calls. They're getting calls.

They're speaking to their boyfriends and

girlfriends, their parents, and their bosses!

Phones are ringing everywhere! I'm getting

a headache! Cell phones are very useful, but

they are also a big problem. There is no

"quiet" or "alone" time. Oh, er, . . . excuse

me. I have to go. My phone is ringing.

2
2. 'm going (OR am going)
3. 'm taking (OR am taking)
4. 'm using (OR am using)
5. is looking
6. 'm trying (OR am trying)
7. 're talking (OR are talking)
8. 'm trying (OR am trying)
9. 're listening (OR are listening)

3
2. She's (OR She is) talking on the phone.
3. He's not (OR He isn't OR He is not) eating a sandwich.
4. She's (OR She is) playing a computer game.
5. They're not (OR They aren't OR They are not) sleeping.
6. She's (OR she is) sitting near the window.

4

Hi. I'm ~~write~~ *writing* to you from the train. I ~~are~~ *'m* traveling with my brother Dan. We ~~go~~ *'re going* to Miami to visit our aunt. I can't make calls because Dan ~~sleeps~~ *is sleeping*. He ~~no~~ *'s not* OR *isn't* feeling well. That's why I ~~send~~ *'m sending* this e-mail. There's a problem with this train. ~~It~~ *It's* moving really slowly. Wait a minute—the conductor ~~makes~~ *is making* an announcement. Uh-oh. Now it *isn't* moving. We're ~~have~~ *having* engine problems! Oh, good, Dan ~~wakes~~ *is waking* up. Now I can CALL you!

UNIT 4 The Present Progressive: Questions

CHECK POINT
F

CHART CHECK 1
before

CHART CHECK 2
F

EXPRESS CHECK
Are they sleeping? Yes, they are.

1
2. f	**6.** g	**9.** d
3. e	**7.** c	**10.** a
4. k	**8.** j	**11.** i
5. b		

2
2. What is she wearing?
   She's wearing a mask. (OR A mask.)
3. Is it raining?
   Yes, it is.
4. How many pillows is she using?
   She's using four pillows. (OR Four.)
5. Is she listening to music?
   No, she's not (OR she isn't).
6. Are the cats sleeping?
   Yes, they are.
7. What is the cat dreaming about?
   The cat is (OR The cat's OR It's) dreaming about a mouse. (OR A mouse.)

3
4. are . . . calling
5. Are . . . sitting
6. No, I'm not
7. are . . . calling
8. Are . . . calling
9. Yes, I am
10. are . . . coming
11. Are . . . listening
12. Yes, I am

4
Right now, are you ~~think~~ *thinking*: Why ~~I am~~ *am I* feeling so tired? Millions of people have a sleep problem. Maybe you have one too.

Take this short quiz at bedtime:

	I am Yes, ~~I'm.~~	No, I'm not.
1. Are you ~~try~~ *trying* to sleep?	☐	☐
2. ~~Is~~ *Are* you worrying about it?	☐	☐
3. ~~Do~~ *Are* you taking this quiz now (but you really want to be asleep)?	☐	☐

If you answered "yes," we can help you!

Call Sam's Sleep Center for help. 555-7777.

Open 24 hours.

SelfTest

(Total = 100 points. Each item = 4 points.)

SECTION ONE
1. D	**5.** C	**8.** B	**11.** D
2. B	**6.** A	**9.** D	**12.** B
3. A	**7.** D	**10.** B	**13.** D
4. A			

SECTION TWO

(Correct answers are in parentheses.)

14. **B** (is)
15. **C** (talking)
16. **B** (are cats)
17. **C** (studying)
18. **D** (not)
19. **A** (are)

20. **A** (am not)
21. **D** (?)
22. **B** (are)
23. **A** (They're)
24. **A** (There are)
25. **B** (talking)

UNIT 5 The Simple Present:
Statements

CHECK POINT

F

CHART CHECK 1

The verb for *he, she,* or *it* ends in *-s.*

CHART CHECK 2

F

EXPRESS CHECK

drinks, doesn't

1
2. F
3. F
4. F
5. T

6. F
7. T
8. F
9. T

2
3. work
4. grows
5. don't (OR do not) drink
6. drink
7. have
8. has
9. gets
10. don't (OR do not) take
11. add

3
3. His workday doesn't begin at 9:00.
4. He leaves the office at 7:15.
5. He has a half hour for lunch.
6. He doesn't take breaks.
7. He always has a meeting in the morning.
8. He doesn't have meetings in the afternoon.

4
I'm so tired. I work too much. I ~~take never a~~ *never take* break. My boss always ~~want~~ *wants* me to stay late. HE doesn't ~~stays~~ *stay* late! I ~~gets~~ *get* up every day at 6:00, and I ~~no~~ *don't OR do not* stop work until 7:00. I rarely ~~having~~ *have* time to see my friends. I also drink too much coffee! I usually have more than five cups a day. Some people say that coffee ~~relax~~ *relaxes* them, but not me! It ~~help~~ *helps* me stay awake at the office, but the caffeine ^*usually* makes me ~~usually~~ nervous. Then, I can't sleep at night. Like now! Maybe I should try tea.

UNIT 6 The Simple Present:
Questions

CHECK POINT

T

CHART CHECK 1

F, F

CHART CHECK 2

before

EXPRESS CHECK

Do you laugh a lot?
When do you laugh?

1
2. c
3. a
4. f

5. b
6. d

2
2. How often do you meet?
3. Do you have a leader?
4. Yes, we do
5. Does she have a degree in laughing?
6. No, she doesn't
7. How much does your club cost?

3
2. do . . . do
3. do . . . wear
4. Do . . . wear

5. do . . . meet
6. Does . . . mean

4 I am very interested in your laughing clubs.

They sound wonderful! I'd like to become a

trainer. I have just a few questions:

1. Where ~~train you~~ people?
   do you train

2. When ~~the training begins~~?
   does the training begin

3. How long does it ~~takes~~ to become a trainer?
   take

4. How much ~~costs the training~~?
   does the training cost

5. Do trainers make a good salary?

6. Do you ~~gets~~ part of the money?
   get

Sincerely yours,

Hee Hee Jones

P.S. ~~Has you~~ an e-mail address?
   Do you have

UNIT 7 **Non-Action Verbs**

CHECK **POINT**

now

CHART CHECK

F

EXPRESS CHECK

I see the stars.
My sister has a rabbit.

1

What <u>do</u> you <u>see</u>?

It<u>'s</u> a beautiful night. Todd, Kim, and Omar
are looking up at the sky.

TODD: <u>Do</u> you <u>see</u> the man in the moon?

KIM: What <u>do</u> you <u>mean</u>? It <u>looks</u> like a
rabbit to me.

OMAR: I <u>don't understand</u> you guys!
I <u>think</u> it<u>'s</u> a woman. And she's
reading a book!

Three people are looking at the same
moon, but they <u>see</u> three different things.
What about *you?* Look at the moon. What
<u>do</u> *you* <u>see</u>?

2
2. want
3. are
4. showing
5. don't know
6. sounds
7. Do
8. need
9. remember
10. doesn't have
11. looks
12. does
13. mean
14. does
15. look
16. see

3
2. need
3. Does . . . have
4. don't know
5. are . . . going
6. smell
7. 'm (OR I am) following
8. tastes
9. don't (OR do not) like
10. 're not (OR aren't) drinking
11. smells
12. think
13. like
14. want
15. Do . . . have

4 I ~~sit~~ in the cafeteria of the Space Museum
   'm sitting
with my friend Alicia. ~~Are you remembering~~
   Do you remember

our visit here last year? This place is
awesome. ~~Are you seeing~~ the photo on this
   Do you see

card? It's a new picture of Mars. Do you
~~wanting~~ to get a poster of it? I have one
   want

for my room. It ~~looking~~ great. Well,
   looks
~~we're needing~~ to go. They ~~close~~ the cafeteria
   we need   *'re closing OR are closing*

now. Take care.

UNIT 8 **Present Progressive
and Simple Present**

CHECK **POINT**

now

CHART CHECK

present progressive
simple present

EXPRESS CHECK

	Now	Every day
We're watching TV.	✓	☐
Do you watch the news?	☐	✓
She isn't reporting the news.	✓	☐
What does she do?	☐	✓
The TV isn't working.	✓	☐

1 It's 11:00 P.M. and Daljit Dhaliwal is reporting the news. All around the world people are watching her. Who is she? Why do millions of people watch her every weekday night? Dhaliwal is a newscaster. Her family comes from India, but Dhaliwal was born in London. Now she is living in the United States. She works for CNN International, the 24-hour international news channel. Dhaliwal is very serious about the news. "News is serious business," she often says. And when Dhaliwal reports the news, people listen.

2
2. reports, is watching
3. wears
4. is wearing
5. is drinking
6. drinks
7. thinks
8. loves, is enjoying

3
2. run
3. watch
4. 'm (OR am) talking
5. 'm (OR am) getting
6. run
7. love
8. see
9. 're (OR are) wearing
10. wear
11. get
12. die
13. is starting

4 I **'m sitting** ~~sit~~ in my new home in Atlanta, Georgia, and I'm looking out my living room window. **It looks** ~~It's looking~~ very different from my street in London. The sun ~~shines~~ **is shining**! In London, it rains a lot. Also, only one person ~~walks~~ **is walking** on the street right now. In London, people usually walk everywhere. I REALLY need a driver's license! My friend Rina ~~is driving~~ **drives** me to work every day. My schedule is different too. ~~I'm reporting~~ **I report** the news at 5:00 every afternoon, not 11:00 at night. It's time to go now. Rina ~~drives~~ **is driving** into my driveway.

UNIT 9 The Imperative

CHECK POINT
telling the man to do things

CHART CHECK
F, T

EXPRESS CHECK
Open the door.
Don't open the door.

1
2. f   5. g
3. d   6. e
4. a   7. b

2
2. Dry   9. Be
3. Use   10. Don't burn
4. Put   11. Cut
5. Don't use   12. Don't cut
6. Cook   13. Serve
7. Don't cook   14. Enjoy
8. Take

3
2. sit   6. come
3. be   7. Don't forget
4. Don't touch   8. Don't park
5. Eat

4 Your Mom is home this evening. Please ~~calls~~ *call*

her at 6:00. There are some samosas from

the Indian restaurant in the refrigerator.

~~You try~~ *Try* them. They're delicious. ~~Heats~~ *Heat* them

for one minute in the microwave. But ~~no~~ *don't* use

HIGH. Joan and Ana are coming tonight.

~~Buy please~~ *Please buy* some more soda. ~~You not~~ *Don't* forget,

OK? I don't have time to go to the store.

SelfTest

(Total = 100 points. Each item = 4 points.)

SECTION ONE

1. **D**	5. **C**	9. **A**	13. **C**
2. **A**	6. **C**	10. **C**	14. **B**
3. **A**	7. **D**	11. **A**	15. **C**
4. **C**	8. **D**	12. **B**	

SECTION TWO

(Correct answers are in parentheses.)

16. **D** (is drinking)	21. **D** (tell)
17. **D** (usually speaks)	22. **D** (has)
18. **B** (*delete* you)	23. **D** (*delete* being)
19. **A** (is ringing)	24. **C** (don't)
20. **B** (reading)	25. **C** (doesn't)

UNIT 10 The Past of *Be*

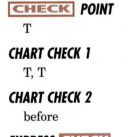

CHECK POINT

T

CHART CHECK 1

T, T

CHART CHECK 2

before

EXPRESS CHECK

was, were

1
- They <u>were</u> on Earth for about 160 million years.
- They <u>were</u> everywhere on Earth.
- There <u>were</u> many different kinds.
- Tyrannosaurus rex <u>was</u> 20 feet (6 meters) tall.
- Compsognathus <u>wasn't</u> big. It <u>was</u> only 3.3 feet (1 meter) long.
- Some of the big dinosaurs <u>weren't</u> meat-eaters.

2

1. was	4. weren't, were
2. was	5. wasn't, was
3. was	6. was, were

3

3. were	9. were
4. was	10. Was
5. Were	11. Yes, it was
6. was	12. was
7. was	13. were
8. weren't	14. were

4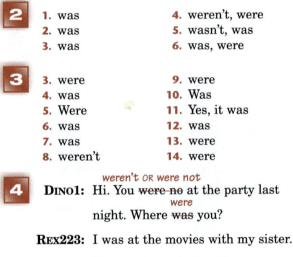

DINO1: Hi. You ~~were no~~ *weren't* OR *were not* at the party last
night. Where ~~was~~ *were* you?

REX223: I was at the movies with my sister.
We saw Jurassic Park 4.

DINO1: How ~~it was~~ *was it*?

REX223: Great! The dinosaurs ~~was~~ *were*
fantastic.

DINO1: Was the movie scary?

REX223: No, it ~~was~~ *wasn't*. I ~~no was~~ *wasn't* OR *was not* scared, but
my sister was a little scared.
How ~~the party was~~ *was the party*?

DINO1: OK. There ~~was~~ *were* a lot of people.
But I was disappointed that you
~~wasn't~~ *weren't* there.

The Simple Past of Regular Verbs:
Statements

CHECK POINT

T

CHART CHECK 1

-ed

CHART CHECK 2

T

EXPRESS CHECK

He painted a picture of his father.
His father moved.
His father didn't like the painting.

1
2. F	**5.** T
3. F	**6.** T
4. F	**7.** T

2
2. He didn't travel to Russia in 1907.
   He traveled to Spain.
3. He didn't live in Paris for twenty years.
   He lived in Paris for nine years.
4. He didn't return to Spain in 1921.
   He returned to Mexico in 1921.
5. He didn't marry Frida Kahlo in 1939.
   He married Frida Kahlo (OR her) in 1929.
6. He didn't die at age eighty.
   He died at age seventy-one.

3
2. worked
3. returned
4. didn't (OR did not) want
5. wanted
6. started
7. didn't (OR did not) copy
8. studied
9. watched
10. filled
11. didn't (OR did not) like
12. changed

4
At fifteen, I ~~starting~~ **started** art classes. After that,

I hated school. I did not do homework.

I ~~carryed~~ **carried** art books with me all the time.

In math class, I ~~look~~ **looked** at pictures. In English

class, I copied them. In history class, I

colored them. I ~~save~~ **saved** all my money for paints

and brushes. Then my report card arrived.

My mother looked at it, and she said,

"You ~~not~~ **didn't OR did not** learn a thing!" "I learned a lot

about art," I said. The next week we visited

the High School for the Arts. I ~~did walk~~ **walked**

in the door, and I smelled paint. I liked

school again.

The Simple Past of Irregular Verbs:
Statements

CHECK POINT

Many people died.

CHART CHECK 1

F, T

CHART CHECK 2

The base form of the verb goes after *didn't*.

EXPRESS CHECK

I saw the movie last night.
It had a sad ending.

1
Jack (was) very happy, but he (had) no money.
He (met) Rose on the *Titanic*. Rose (had) pretty
clothes and rich friends, but she (was) very
unhappy. She wanted to end her life. Jack
stopped her, and the two (fell) in love. They
(were) happy together, but Rose's mother
didn't like Jack. She wanted a rich husband
for Rose. At the end, Rose (found) Jack on the
sinking ship. They (held) hands and jumped
into the water. Rose lived. She (lost) Jack, but
she never (forgot) him.

2. fell	**6.** held
3. found	**7.** lost
4. forgot	**8.** met
5. had	

2
2. didn't (OR did not) hear
3. saw
4. was
5. hit
6. didn't (OR did not) see
7. began
8. didn't (OR did not) have
9. got
10. went
11. came
12. had

3
2. left
3. hit
4. sank (OR went down)
5. went
6. saw
7. came
8. lost
9. found

4
Molly Brown ~~comes~~ *came* from a poor family. She
didn't ~~went~~ *go* to high school. She left home
and ~~gots~~ *got* married. In 1894, her husband
~~finded~~ *found* gold and they became rich. Soon
after, her husband left her, but Molly didn't
feel sad. She ~~maked~~ *made* friends with rich and
famous people in New York and Europe. She
~~were~~ *was* with many of them on the *Titanic*. On
that terrible day in 1912, Molly was a hero.
She helped save many other passengers.
Because of this, she ~~become~~ *became* famous as
"The Unsinkable Molly Brown."

UNIT 13 The Simple Past: Questions

CHECK POINT
finished

CHART CHECK 1
start with *did*

CHART CHECK 2
F, T

CHART CHECK 3
What, How

EXPRESS CHECK
Did they go? Yes, they did.

1
2. f
3. e
4. a
5. b
6. d

2
2. did . . . do
3. Did . . . send
4. Yes, I did
5. Did . . . use
6. No, I didn't
7. was

3
2. Who did she go with? (OR with who(m) did she go?)
(She went with) Ann Bancroft.
3. Did they arrive at the North Pole?
No, they didn't.
4. Where did they arrive?
(They arrived) at the South Pole.
5. How did they carry food?
(They carried food) on sleds.
6. Did they eat chocolate?
Yes, they did.
7. Did they wear warm clothes?
Yes, they did.
8. Did they have a computer?
Yes, they did.

4
I am writing a report about your trip, and
I have some questions. How did you ~~went~~ *go* to
Antarctica?
~~Does~~ *Did* you leave from South America?
How many miles ~~you traveled~~ *did you travel* every day?
Did it ~~snows~~ *snow*?
What did you ~~ate~~ *eat*?
What *was* your favorite food on the trip?
Where did you ~~sleeping~~ *sleep* at night?
Why did you stop your trip for two weeks?

SelfTest

(Total = 100 points. Each item = 4 points.)

SECTION ONE

1. D	5. D	9. D	13. A
2. B	6. B	10. C	14. B
3. D	7. B	11. B	15. D
4. A	8. C	12. B	

SECTION TWO

(Correct answers are in parentheses.)

16. D (arrive)	21. D (wrote)
17. B (did you)	22. A (lived)
18. A (was)	23. B (go)
19. D (went)	24. D (buy)
20. A (was he)	25. D (was)

UNIT 14 — The Future with *Be going to*

CHECK POINT

F

CHART CHECK 1

F

CHART CHECK 2

We use *am, is,* or *are* in short answers.

CHART CHECK 3

T

EXPRESS CHECK

We're going to buy a new computer.
Computers are going to change.

1
2. F   5. T
3. T   6. T
4. F

2
2. 'm (OR am) not going to eat
3. 'm (OR am) not going to take
4. are going to come
5. is (OR 's) going to be
6. 's (OR is) going to rain

3
3. 're (OR are) going to have
4. Are . . . going to drive
5. Yes, we are
6. 're (OR are) going to love
7. Are . . . going to take
8. Yes, we are
9. Am . . . going to park
10. Yes, you are
11. 'm (OR am) going to get
12. Is . . . going to rain
13. Yes, it is

4
Computers are a big part of our lives now.
That's ~~no~~ *not* going to change. We're going to use
computers even more in the future. How *is*ᵥ
your computer going to look? How are you
going ᵥ*to* use it? Here are some ideas:
- Computers ᵥ*are* not going to look like boxes.
- They're going to be much smaller.
- Cameras and telephones ~~is~~ *are* going to be
  part of many computers.
- Your car ~~are~~ *is* going to talk to you.
- Your refrigerator is going ᵥ*to* buy your
  groceries on the Internet.
- You're ~~no~~ *not* going to carry your computer.
  You're going to wear it. Computers are
  ~~go~~ *going* to become part of your clothing.

UNIT 15 — The Future with *Will*

CHECK POINT

future

CHART CHECK 1

T, F

CHART CHECK 2

before

EXPRESS CHECK

When will he arrive?

1 I <u>won't have</u> time to wash the dishes before dinner.

I'<u>ll be</u> at Madame Y's. I <u>won't be</u> home before 6:00. Sorry!

I'<u>ll call</u> you from the car phone on the way home.

I'<u>ll bring</u> pizza.

2. T   **3.** F   **4.** T   **5.** T

2
2. won't (OR will not) have only one baby.
3. 'll (OR will) live in a big house.
4. won't (OR will not) own a small car.
5. won't (OR will not) be a teacher.
6. 'll (OR will) get married.

3
3. Where will I live?
4. Will my parents live with me?
5. No, they won't
6. Will Jennifer and I get married?
7. Yes, you will
8. When will we get married?
9. Will we have children?
10. Yes, you will

4 Will I ~~am~~ ^{be} rich?

Will my business ~~is~~ ^{be} successful?

Will I find true love?

What ~~my future will~~ ^{will my future} be?

Madame Y will ~~answers~~ ^{answer} these questions

and more.

She'll ~~will~~ ^{'ll OR will} tell you your future!

Call Madame Y. 555-NEXT. You ~~willn't~~ ^{won't OR will not}

be sorry!

SelfTest

(Total = 100 points. Each item = 4 points.)

SECTION ONE

1. D	**5.** D	**9.** C	**13.** D
2. B	**6.** C	**10.** A	**14.** A
3. B	**7.** C	**11.** B	**15.** D
4. B	**8.** C	**12.** B	

SECTION TWO

(Correct answers are in parentheses.)

16. A (Are)	**21. B** (is going to)
17. D (leave)	**22. D** (call)
18. A (is)	**23. D** (tomorrow night)
19. C (are you)	**24. A** (are you)
20. B (will you)	**25. B** (to take)

UNIT 16 Word Order: Statements

CHECK POINT

Children and adults

CHART CHECK 1

F

CHART CHECK 2

There are two ways to write a statement with two objects.

EXPRESS CHECK

We sent a book to our friend.
They sent Phil a letter.

1
2. They gave him a bed in a closet.
3. He wore old clothes.
4. Then Hogwarts School sent a letter to Harry.
5. The letter changed his life.
6. Hogwarts teaches magic to young wizards.
7. Harry made friends at Hogwarts.
8. His friends gave him gifts at Christmas.
9. He rode a broomstick.
10. He found a magic stone.

2
2. Olivia gave Eliza a rabbit.
3. Liam showed cards to Eliza.
4. Eliza showed Liam her new broom.
5. Liam gave a scarf to Eliza.
6. Hector handed Liam a book.

3
2. . . . she wrote stories all the time.
3. She read the stories to her friends.
4. Rowling studied French in college.
5. She taught English in Europe.
6. Rowling wrote her first book in a café.
7. She finished her book in Scotland in 1994.
8. The book won many prizes in England in 1997.

4
Christmas was great. I gave your gifts
~~in the morning to Harry~~. He loved the
to Harry in the morning
liked the chocolate
sweater. He ~~the chocolate liked~~ too.

He was surprised. Harry's aunt and

uncle never send gifts to Harry. We ate
Christmas dinner at noon
~~at noon Christmas dinner~~. I had a lot

of turkey, ham, potatoes, and pie. We got
gifts after dinner
~~after dinner gifts~~. I got three mice. Then we
threw snowballs outside
~~outside threw snowballs~~ for hours. We went

to sleep early—we were so tired!
another letter to you OR you another letter
I'll write ~~to you another letter~~ soon.

Hogwarts is great, but I miss home.

UNIT 17 — Word Order:
Wh- Questions

CHECK POINT
ask

CHART CHECK
F, F

EXPRESS CHECK
Who asked you?
What happened next?

1
2. e   4. f   6. d
3. a   5. c

2
2. had the idea
3. did Griffin ask
4. watch
5. hosts
6. play
7. did the #1 winner win
8. do I get

3
3. When did Gustave Eiffel complete the Eiffel Tower?
4. What did John Logie Baird invent?
5. How many floors does the Jin Mao building in China have?
6. How many people live in Mexico City?
7. When did Einstein win the Nobel Prize?
8. Who invented the microwave oven?

4
I would like to be on your show. How
do I get
~~I get~~ on it? I hear there's a test. How many
does the test have
questions ~~the test has~~? When do I take the
gives
test? Who ~~does give~~ the test? Where do I

take the test? How do I prepare for the test?
happens
After I take the test, what ~~does happen~~
do people get
next? When ~~people get~~ the results?

SelfTest

(Total = 100 points. Each item = 4 points.)

SECTION ONE

1. **B**	4. **B**	7. **B**	10. **B**
2. **D**	5. **C**	8. **C**	11. **B**
3. **B**	6. **B**	9. **A**	12. **D**

SECTION TWO

(Correct answers are in parentheses.)
13. **D** (a letter last week)
14. **B** (teaches math)
15. **C** (a movie last night)
16. **B** (took)
17. **C** (book to me)
18. **C** (every year *goes after* in Europe)
19. **B** (saw you OR did you see)
20. **A** (after class *goes after* the teacher)
21. **B** (made dinner)
22. **B** (did she)
23. **C** (Miguel)
24. **B** (*delete* did)
25. **B** (saw you OR did you see)

UNIT 18 — Nouns: Common/Proper, Singular/Plural

CHECK POINT

name
address
business hours
Website address

CHART CHECK

small
Plural

EXPRESS CHECK

watch, T-shirts, pens

1
- 4000 <u>people</u> work there.
- They come from more than 50 <u>countries</u>.
- You can buy a (pet) there.
- You can buy <u>clothes</u> for your (pet)
- You can listen to free <u>concerts</u>.
- You can buy a real (car) for your <u>children</u>!

2
3.	pan	8.	vase
4.	glasses	9.	pair of glasses
5.	loaves	10.	pair of jeans
6.	strawberries	11.	knives
7.	watches	12.	pairs of pants

3
2.	address is	7.	restaurants sell
3.	Tourists . . . go	8.	desserts taste
4.	People love	9.	store has
5.	store sells	10.	shorts . . . are not
6.	Jeans are		

4
Hi! I love England, and ~~london~~ ^{London} is great. On ~~monday~~ ^{Monday} we went to Harrods. There were so many ~~persons~~ ^{people} there! I bought a lot of ~~thing~~ ^{things}. My ~~jean was~~ ^{jeans were} really old, so I got two new pairs. They have great things for ~~childs~~ ^{children} too. I bought two ~~watch~~ ^{watches}—one for my little ~~Brother~~ ^{brother} and one for Jennie. One strange ~~things~~ ^{thing}: The store ~~have~~ ^{has} a dress code! You can't come in if your clothes ~~is~~ ^{are} dirty. And

you can't wear bicycle shorts in the store. (But you can buy ~~it~~ ^{them} there, of course!!) See you in a few ~~Weeks~~ ^{weeks}.

UNIT 19 — Nouns: Count/Non-Count

CHECK POINT

calories

CHART CHECK

T, F

EXPRESS CHECK

Apples are cheap today.
There's only one egg in the refrigerator.

1
Good News: Some "bad <u>food</u>"^N is really good for you. (But remember to eat small portions.)
- <u>Nuts</u>^C are healthy. They have a lot of <u>fat</u>^N, but it's a healthy type.
- <u>Chocolate</u>^N is good! It's good for your teeth and for your heart. It makes you feel good too.
- <u>Coffee</u>^N isn't bad. It helps you work or study.

Bad News: Junk <u>food</u>^N *is* really bad for you.
- <u>Hamburgers</u>^C from fast-food restaurants are high in <u>fat</u>, and it's not a healthy type. They also have a lot of <u>salt</u>^N.
- <u>Soda</u>^N is high in <u>sugar</u>^N. Nothing in it is good for you.

Remember, the rules for a good diet are still the same: Eat lots of <u>vegetables</u>^C, <u>fruit</u>^N, <u>beans</u>^C, <u>fish</u>^N, and <u>chicken</u>^N.

2

1. a (OR one) can of soda
   a (OR one) banana
2. a (OR one) piece of cheese
   an (OR one) apple
   a (OR one) glass of milk
3. a (OR one) bowl of noodles
   a (OR one) cup of tea
4. a (OR one) bag of nuts
   a (OR one) container of yogurt

3

3. cup	12. burns
4. sugar	13. eggs
5. cup	14. flour
6. butter	15. is
7. butter	16. chocolate
8. is	17. smells
9. bars	18. nuts
10. chocolate	19. Nuts
11. chocolate	20. taste

4

Was your mother right about chicken ~~soups~~ *soup* for a cold? Write T (True) or F (False) for each statement.

___ 1. Don't drink ~~milks~~ *milk* when you have
   a cold.
___ 2. A teaspoon of brown ~~sugars~~ *sugar* is
   healthier than a teaspoon ^*of*^ white sugar.
___ 3. Carrots ~~is~~ *are* good for your eyes.
___ 4. Chocolate ~~are~~ *is* bad for your teeth.
___ 5. ~~Nut is~~ *Nuts are* unhealthy.

UNIT 20 **Articles:** *A/An* and *The*

CHECK POINT

T, F, F

CHART CHECK

Bob's house is small.

EXPRESS CHECK

a
the

1

2. Have an apple.
3. It's on the shelf.
4. Turn off a light.
5. I'll walk the dog.
6. Take the bag.

2

1. b. a	2. a. a	3. a. a
c. a	b. a	b. an
d. the	c. the	c. The
e. the	d. The	
f. The		

3

1. b. the	3. a. the
c. a	b. a
d. a	c. a
2. a. the	4. a. a
b. a	b. the
c. a	c. the
d. an	

4

The
~~A~~ refrigerator is not working.
I saw ~~the~~ *a* mouse in ~~a~~ *the* kitchen last night!
The
~~An~~ ceiling in the living room is leaking.
I need ~~a~~ *an* umbrella when I sit on the sofa!
There was a lot of water on ~~a~~ *the* living room
floor this morning.

UNIT 21 **No Article: (Ø)** or *The*

CHECK POINT

F

CHART CHECK

You can use no article (Ø) with non-count nouns.

EXPRESS CHECK

the CD
the music

1

2. F
3. F
4. F
5. F

2
2. awards
3. the leader
4. the music
5. the musicians
6. Rock music
7. concerts . . . the world
8. The concerts
9. The King
10. action movies
11. Rock stars . . . bad actors
12. the movie
13. the bad guy . . . the movie

3
1. b. *no article (Ø)*
   c. *no article (Ø)*
2. a. the
   b. *no article (Ø)*
   c. *no article (Ø)*
   d. the
3. a. the
   b. *no article (Ø)*
   c. the
   d. *no article (Ø)*

4. a. the
   b. the
   c. *no article (Ø)*
   d. the
   e. the
   f. *no article (Ø)*
   g. *no article (Ø)*

4
~~The rock~~ ^{Rock} music has a great new band.
The group, Far Mountain, just released its
first CD. *Walking along the River* is a good
beginning. The leader, Grace Lee, has a
beautiful voice, _{the} songs are very interesting, and
the musicians are great. Lee wrote several
songs for _{the} CD. Her songs are about loneliness,
~~the~~ hope, and friendship. ~~The friends~~ ^{Friends} are
important to Lee. One of her best songs,
"Where Are They?" is about her schoolmates
in Taiwan. You can hear _{the} song on the group's
Website, www.farmountain.com. Jorge Santos
is the guitar player, and _{the} drummer is
Zhang Teng-hui.

Quantifiers:
Some and *Any*

CHECK POINT

more than one gray sweater

CHART CHECK

questions, negative statements

EXPRESS CHECK

some, any

1
You can find flea markets all over the world:
in city streets, parking lots, and fields. Read
what <u>some people</u> at a local market found
this weekend. Then find a flea market in
your neighborhood. Maybe you won't find
<u>any treasures</u>, but you'll certainly have
<u>some fun</u>!

- I wanted <u>some old dishes</u>. I didn't find (any),
  but I got <u>some cups</u>.
- They have <u>some great vintage clothes</u>.
  (*Vintage* means at least twenty years old.)
  I bought <u>some sweaters</u>. I also bought
  <u>some jewelry</u> from around 1920.
- I don't see <u>any paintings</u> here, but I found
  <u>some photographs</u> and <u>CD's</u>.
- I got <u>some comic books</u>. They were cheap!
  I wanted <u>some toys</u> too, but there aren't
  (any) today.

cups	photographs
vintage clothes	CD's
sweaters	comic books
jewelry	

2
1. b. some
   c. any
   d. some
2. a. any
   b. any
   c. some
   d. some
   e. some
3. a. some
   b. any
   c. Some

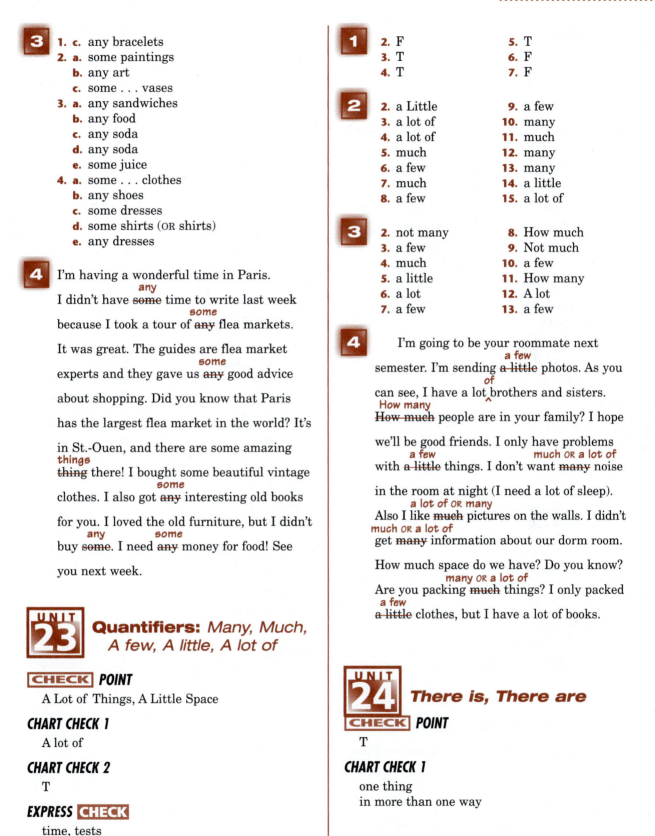

3 1. **c.** any bracelets
2. **a.** some paintings
   b. any art
   c. some . . . vases
3. **a.** any sandwiches
   b. any food
   c. any soda
   d. any soda
   e. some juice
4. **a.** some . . . clothes
   b. any shoes
   c. some dresses
   d. some shirts (OR shirts)
   e. any dresses

4 I'm having a wonderful time in Paris.
            any
I didn't have ~~some~~ time to write last week
            some
because I took a tour of ~~any~~ flea markets.

It was great. The guides are flea market
           some
experts and they gave us ~~any~~ good advice

about shopping. Did you know that Paris

has the largest flea market in the world? It's

in St.-Ouen, and there are some amazing
things
~~thing~~ there! I bought some beautiful vintage
           some
clothes. I also got ~~any~~ interesting old books

for you. I loved the old furniture, but I didn't
      any   *some*
buy ~~some~~. I need ~~any~~ money for food! See

you next week.

UNIT 23 **Quantifiers:** *Many, Much, A few, A little, A lot of*

CHECK POINT
A Lot of Things, A Little Space

CHART CHECK 1
A lot of

CHART CHECK 2
T

EXPRESS CHECK
time, tests

1 2. F   5. T
3. T   6. F
4. T   7. F

2 2. a Little   9. a few
3. a lot of   10. many
4. a lot of   11. much
5. much   12. many
6. a few   13. many
7. much   14. a little
8. a few   15. a lot of

3 2. not many   8. How much
3. a few   9. Not much
4. much   10. a few
5. a little   11. How many
6. a lot   12. A lot
7. a few   13. a few

4 I'm going to be your roommate next
            a few
semester. I'm sending ~~a little~~ photos. As you
            of
can see, I have a lot ^ brothers and sisters.
How many
~~How much~~ people are in your family? I hope

we'll be good friends. I only have problems
      a few   *much* OR *a lot of*
with ~~a little~~ things. I don't want ~~many~~ noise

in the room at night (I need a lot of sleep).
       a lot of OR *many*
Also I like ~~much~~ pictures on the walls. I didn't
much OR *a lot of*
get ~~many~~ information about our dorm room.

How much space do we have? Do you know?
         many OR *a lot of*
Are you packing ~~much~~ things? I only packed
a few
~~a little~~ clothes, but I have a lot of books.

UNIT 24 **There is, There are**

CHECK POINT
T

CHART CHECK 1
one thing
in more than one way

CHART CHECK 2

F, F

EXPRESS CHECK

Is, there is

1 There's a new restaurant in town! It's called Jason's. I ate there last night, and there were many people there. In fact, there were no empty tables. There's a good reason for that. The food is great! The menu is small, but there are always many "Specials." Last night there was grilled mushroom pizza, and it was delicious. Try Jason's, and bring the whole family. There is no special children's menu at Jason's, but there is something for everyone.

a lot of customers
great food
"Specials"

2
2. There isn't
3. There are
4. There are
5. There aren't
6. There's

3
1. c. There are
   d. Is there
   e. No, there isn't
   f. There's
2. a. Are there
   b. Yes, there is
   c. are there
   d. There are
3. a. There's
   b. are there
   c. No, there aren't
   d. Is there
   e. Yes, there is

4
        were
There ~~are~~ a lot of customers last night, so
        there are
this morning ~~there're~~ some problems. First,
      any   *are*
the food. There aren't ~~no~~ tomatoes. There ~~is~~
      there
potatoes, but ~~they~~ aren't any onions. And I
      were
can't find any eggs. How many ~~was~~ there

      aren't
last night? We need these things for today's
menu! Second, there ~~isn't~~ any clean pots this
      Was there
morning. ~~There was~~ a problem with the hot

water last night?

SelfTest

(Total = 100 points. Each item = 4 points.)

SECTION ONE

1. B	5. B	8. C	11. C
2. C	6. C	9. B	12. A
3. A	7. B	10. D	13. B
4. C			

SECTION TWO

(Correct answers are in parentheses.)

14. C (Lisbon)	20. D (the)
15. B (is)	21. B (a/her friend)
16. A (some)	22. D (the music)
17. D (a few)	23. D (tastes)
18. D (water)	24. A (glass of milk)
19. D (an)	25. D (women)

UNIT 25
Pronouns:
Subject and Object

CHECK POINT

the son
the mother

CHART CHECK

T

EXPRESS CHECK

She gave him a gift.

1 All over the world, people give gifts. But they give different things in different ways.

- In Japan, people often give gifts. But they never open them in front of the giver.
- In the United States and Canada, a man often gives his girlfriend flowers on Valentine's Day (February 14). He sometimes gives her chocolate too.
- In Korea, older people give new money to children on New Year's Day. They give it to them for good luck.
- In Peru, a man gives flowers to his girlfriend. But he doesn't give her yellow flowers. They mean: The relationship is finished.

2
2. They . . . them
3. He . . . it . . . her
4. She . . . him . . . them
5. I . . . it . . . you
6. He . . . me

3
1. b. He
   c. me
   d. it
   e. It
2. a. I
   b. him
   c. He
   d. it
   e. me

3. a. I
   b. They
   c. us
   d. we
4. a. I
   b. He
   c. it
   d. me
   e. him
   f. we

4 Thank ~~yous~~ _you_ so much for the green sweater. ~~He~~ _It_ looks really good on me. My girlfriend ~~she~~ likes the color a lot. Do you remember my girlfriend Lisa? ~~He~~ _She_ wanted to wear it! (I told ~~she~~ _her_, maybe next week.) Mom and Dad gave ~~I~~ _me_ a great party. I invited ten of my friends. ~~They~~ _We_ all went to the water park. We

stayed there all afternoon. Then Mom and Dad ~~they~~ took us to the movies.

I hope you're both fine. When are you going to visit ~~we~~ _us_ again? We miss you a lot.

Possessives

CHECK POINT
Do you own this?

CHART CHECK 1
-'s or -s'

CHART CHECK 2
F, T, T

EXPRESS CHECK

SUBJECT PRONOUN	POSSESSIVE ADJECTIVE	POSSESSIVE PRONOUN
I	my	mine
she	her	hers
we	our	ours
they	their	theirs

1 Can't find your wallet? Don't panic! "People lose their things every day," says Ron Findler, head of the College Lost and Found office. "Our job is to help them find them again."

Jan Peterson is one happy example. "When I lost my keys, I was very worried. My teacher sent me to the Lost and Found office. Mine weren't the only lost keys! Other people's keys were there too. I was lucky I got them back."

So, if you lose your stuff, run (don't walk!) to the College Lost and Found office. Their hours are Monday to Friday, 9:00–5:00. Closed on weekends.

2

1. **b.** Jenkin's
   c. yours
   d. mine
   e. roommate's
2. **a.** her
   b. your
   c. sister's
   d. her
   e. hers
3. **a.** our
   b. your
   c. Mine
   d. my
   e. her
   f. hers

4. **a.** Whose
   b. mine
5. **a.** your
   b. Mine
   c. my
   d. children's
   e. theirs

3

2. umbrella . . . mine
3. helmet . . . yours (OR his)
4. shoes . . . theirs
5. crutches . . . his
6. rings . . . ours

4

Lost!   Nokia cell phone. Please call ~~mine~~ *my*
           Her
           sister. ~~Their~~ number is 555-3457.
           man's
Found! A ~~mans~~ brown wallet with money
           yours
           inside. Describe it and it's ~~your~~!
           555-3298
           Their
Lost!   Help us find our cats. ~~They~~ names
           are Candy and Cane. 555-2338.
Found! I found a pair of purple sunglasses
           Monday night. Give me a call if you
           yours
           think they are ~~ours~~! 555-3849
           her
Found! Woman with green coat left ~~hers~~
           briefcase on the M15 bus.
           Call 555-3457.

UNIT 27 *This, That, These, Those*

CHECK POINT
   F

CHART CHECK 1
   this, these

CHART CHECK 2
   F

EXPRESS CHECK
   These, that, it

1

2. a   4. f   6. b
3. d   5. c

2

1. **B:** That
2. **A:** these
   B: they, that
3. **A:** this
   B: This

4. **A:** those
   B: Those
5. **A:** This
   B: This

3

2. **a.** These are
   b. That's
3. **a.** These are
   b. Those are

4. **a.** This is
   b. Those are

4
                  This
Hi! ~~These~~ is a picture of the Leaning Tower
of Pisa. I'm drinking a cup of cappuccino at
                                  This is
a café across from it right now! ~~That's~~ the
best cappuccino (and the best view) in the
                                  Those
world! Last week we were in Venice. ~~That~~
gondolas on the Grand Canal are beautiful!
We took lots of pictures. Italy is really
beautiful. There are flowers everywhere.
This
~~That~~ café, for example, has flowers on every
                                  those
table. Speaking of flowers—how are ~~these~~
flowers in your garden?
This is
~~This's~~ a great trip! See you soon. Carla

UNIT 28 One, Ones

CHECK POINT

shoes

CHART CHECK

two or more things, *this*

EXPRESS CHECK

ones

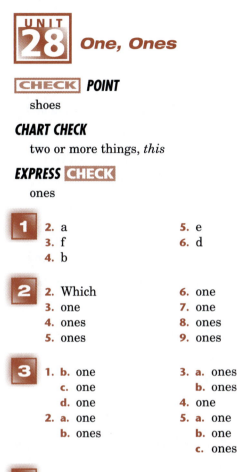

1
2. a
3. f
4. b
5. e
6. d

2
2. Which
3. one
4. ones
5. ones
6. one
7. one
8. ones
9. ones

3
1. b. one
   c. one
   d. one
2. a. one
   b. ones
3. a. ones
   b. ones
4. one
5. a. one
   b. one
   c. ones

4
That was a great party last night! Your best
one
~~ones~~ of all! We really had a good time. The

food was delicious—especially the cookies.
ones
I loved the ~~one~~ with the chocolate on top.
The ones
I think I ate more than ten of them! ~~Ones~~

with the nuts were good too.

    I enjoyed meeting your friends and

the people you work with. I'm sorry that
Which
I didn't meet your boss. ~~What~~ one was she?

    The only problem was my shoes. I really
ones
must buy more comfortable ~~one~~.

    Have a Happy New Year! And a healthy
one
~~ones~~ too.

SelfTest VII

(Total = 100 points. Each item = 4 points.)

SECTION ONE

1. B
2. A
3. C
4. B
5. D
6. A
7. B
8. B
9. A
10. D
11. A
12. C
13. D
14. C

SECTION TWO

(Correct answers are in parentheses.)
15. B (*delete* she)
16. A (Delgado's)
17. C (those)
18. C (those)
19. D (one)
20. D (mine)
21. A (Their)
22. A (that)
23. C (these)
24. D (it)
25. D (our)

UNIT 29 Adjectives

CHECK POINT

F

CHART CHECK

T, F

EXPRESS CHECK

He's a great pet.

1
Pets are (popular) around the world. Here are
some (interesting) facts about pets:

• In China people think cats are (lucky.)

• In (Arab) countries people think dogs are (dirty.)

• Italians don't like dogs very much, but
they think cats are (wonderful) pets.

• Pets are (common) in England. Fifty percent
of homes have one.

• In Africa pets are (uncommon.)

• Dogs are very (popular) in the United
States, but people also keep fish, hamsters,
and guinea pigs.

2
2. small bed
3. black bowl
4. friendly pet
5. big cage
6. afraid

3
2. these important questions
3. a big dog
4. a small apartment
5. Cats are independent
6. dogs are dependent
7. A goldfish is cheap
8. pets are expensive
9. are wonderful friends
10. a big responsibility

4
Guess what! I got a ~~kitten new~~ ^{new kitten} yesterday!
(Well, she's not new. I adopted her after
I saw ~~an ad cute~~ ^{a cute ad} in the newspaper.) She's
black and gray with ~~whites~~ ^{white} paws. (We call
her "Socks.") She's beautiful, and she _{'s OR is} smart.
She's friendly with people, but she doesn't
like other cats—especially ~~bigs~~ ^{big} cats! All my
friends say, "She ~~adorable is~~ ^{'s OR is adorable}." You're going to
love her!

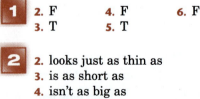

UNIT 30 **Comparisons:** *As . . . as*

CHECK POINT
the same

CHART CHECK
T

EXPRESS CHECK
Aki isn't as tall as Ukon.

1
2. F
3. T
4. F
5. T
6. F

2
2. looks just as thin as
3. is as short as
4. isn't as big as
5. isn't as thin as
6. is as tall as
7. isn't as long as

3
2. n't (OR not) as tall as
3. as expensive as
4. as far
5. as good

4
I'm spending the summer in Yokohama. It's
a very big city, but not as big ~~than~~ ^{as} Tokyo.
But, it <u>is</u> as international <del>as</del>. It's a very
modern city—~~as just~~ ^{just as} modern as Vancouver.
I'm living with a Japanese family—the
Watanabes. They're great. Their daughter
Ryoko is my age. We are very similar, and
we're now almost ^{as}∧close as sisters. Her little
sister is as funny ~~like~~ ^{as} Emmy.
I'm studying Japanese! It isn't as ~~easier~~ ^{easy}
as French, but I'm learning a little every day.
Please write.

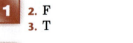 **Comparative Adjectives**

CHECK POINT
different

CHART CHECK
F, F

EXPRESS CHECK
He's older than me.
My sister is younger.
She's more athletic than us.

1
2. F
3. T
4. F
5. T

2
2. dirtier
3. more expensive than
4. higher
5. worse than
6. happier than

3 2. better
3. slower
4. more popular
5. more expensive

6. larger than
7. heavier
8. shorter

4 Sibling rivalry is competition between brothers and sisters. Which brother is
smarter
~~more smart~~? Which sister is ~~popularer~~?
more popular
better
Who gets ~~good~~ grades than the other?

Sibling rivalry is not unusual in families.

It is _more_ unusual on the tennis court.

The Williams sisters, Venus and Serena, are star tennis players. They often compete.
more difficult
Is it ~~difficulter~~ or ~~more~~ easier to play against your own sister? The sisters say the _game_ is important—not the other player.

Does their relationship make their game
interesting
more ~~interestinger~~? Some people think the game is not as exciting when sisters play.

I don't agree. I think their games are more
exciting
~~excitinger~~. Venus and Serena are both
than
better ~~as~~ most other players in the world—sisters or not.

UNIT 32 Superlative Adjectives

CHECK POINT
shorter

CHART CHECK
T, F

EXPRESS CHECK
Sorge's is the best restaurant in town.
It's not the most expensive restaurant.
It's on the busiest street.

1 2. e
3. b
4. f

5. a
6. d

2 2. highest
3. biggest
4. heaviest

5. most expensive
6. oldest

3 2. the hottest
3. The heaviest
4. the fastest
5. the highest
6. the most intelligent
7. the driest

4
Most Amazing
The ~~Amazingest~~ Facts on Earth

Who is the oldest person in the world?
most
Who bought the ^ expensive shoes? What is
smallest   _worst_
the ~~smaller~~ TV? Where is the ~~baddest~~ air on earth? You will find all these facts and many more in _The Guinness Book of World_
most popular
Records—the ~~popularest~~ book of modern times. Kids call it the greatest birthday gift of all. Parents love it too. For you, maybe
most
the facts about movie stars will be the ^
best
interesting. But for me, the ~~goodest~~ chapter is "Amazing Nature." _Please_ ask me, "What's
longest
the ~~long~~ river in the world?"

UNIT 33 Adjectives with _Very, Too,_ and _Enough_

CHECK POINT
T

CHART CHECK
too, very

EXPRESS CHECK
1. Sparkles
2. Bozo
3. Zombo

1
Last week we looked at a MINI Cooper. First I said, "This car is <u>too small</u> for us." The MINI Cooper is for four people, but we are four <u>very large</u> people! Then we got in. Surprise! The front seat was <u>big enough</u> for my tall husband. The back seat was <u>wide enough</u> for two teenagers with backpacks. The MINI Cooper is only 14.6 feet long, and I parked it in a <u>very small</u> space ("Too <u>small</u>," said my daughter. She was wrong.) Most important, it's a <u>very safe</u> car. And we're lucky: It isn't <u>too expensive</u> for us.

2. T   **4.** F   **6.** T
3. T   **5.** T

2
2. too loud   **5.** old enough
3. big enough   **6.** very light
4. very tired

3
2. is (OR 's) too dangerous
3. isn't (OR 's not OR is not) too expensive
4. is (OR 's) big enough
5. isn't (OR 's not OR is not) comfortable enough
6. is (OR 's) quiet enough
7. isn't (OR 's not OR is not) cheap enough
8. isn't (OR 's not OR is not) too small

4
good enough
Is your car "almost ~~enough good?~~"

• Is it big enough for your family, but too ~~much~~ big for city parking?
very safe OR safe enough
• Do you feel ~~too safe~~, but not very comfortable on long trips?

Test-drive a new Beep today. It's ~~very big~~ for
big enough
big families. It's ~~enough safe~~ for your teenage
safe enough
driver. Drive it to the mall or across the
comfortable enough
country—it's ~~too comfortable~~ for every trip.

Nothing can stop the Beep—the worst road isn't too bad for this car. The smallest
too small
parking spot isn't ~~small enough~~. But don't
very
wait—the new Beep is a ~~too~~ popular car, and

not too
it's selling fast. For you, "~~too not~~ bad" really isn't good enough. Buy a Beep. Today.

CHECK POINT
1 and 4

CHART CHECK
T, F

EXPRESS CHECK
The music is slow.
They skate slowly.

1
ID: Why did you start skating?

TM: As a kid, I played ball (badly), but I skated (well). It was a (good) sport for me.

ID: Were you always a (serious) skater?

TM: No. I didn't want to work (hard), and prizes weren't (important) to me.

ID: You skate (seriously) now.

TM: I watched the Olympics a few years ago. My feelings changed (fast) after that.

ID: Well, you looked (great) today on the ice. Maybe I'll see you at the Olympics.

TM: Sure! Maybe I'll be (lucky)!

2
2. terrible   **5.** well
3. friendly   **6.** perfect
4. terribly

3
2. beautifully   **9.** well
3. beautiful   **10.** easily
4. good   **11.** important
5. fast   **12.** dark
6. cold   **13.** late
7. warmly   **14.** big
8. funny   **15.** hard

4 Skating fans, listen up! *The Cutting Edge* is
a romantic movie with ~~greatly~~ *great* skaters. The
stars are practicing for the Winter Olympics.
Kate Mosely looks ~~beautifully~~ *beautiful* on the ice, but
she isn't a ~~nicely~~ *nice* person. All her partners
leave quickly. Then her coach introduces her
to Doug Dorsey. Doug was a hockey star, so
he skates ~~good~~ *well*. At first, they argue. To Kate,
Doug is the wrong choice (he's not a dancer).
To Doug, ice dancing isn't a ~~seriously~~ *serious* sport.
But Doug learns ~~fastly~~ *fast*, and they are ~~well~~ *good*
partners. Do they get to the Olympics? Rent
the movie and see. The conversation is
~~funnily~~ *funny*, and the story moves quickly.

SelfTest  VIII

(Total = 100 points. Each item = 4 points.)

SECTION ONE

1. A	5. B	9. A	13. A
2. B	6. B	10. D	14. C
3. A	7. B	11. B	15. A
4. D	8. D	12. C	

SECTION TWO

(Correct answers are in parentheses.)

16. A (new car)	21. C (just as)
17. D (good as)	22. D (interesting)
18. B (than)	23. A (best)
19. A (the youngest)	24. B (worst)
20. A (cute)	25. A (very)

UNIT 35 Ability: *Can, Could*

CHECK POINT
flies

CHART CHECK 1
T, F

CHART CHECK 2
can or *could*

EXPRESS CHECK
couldn't, can

1 Eduardo Martín Sturla is a professional
triathlete from Argentina. He <u>can swim</u>,
he <u>can ride</u> a bike, and he <u>can run</u>. Many
people <u>can do</u> these things too. But most
people <u>can't do</u> them as fast (or for as long)
as triathletes. In a triathlon, athletes
compete in all three sports without a break.

In his first triathlon, Sturla <u>couldn't bike</u>
or <u>run</u> fast enough. He finished almost last,
but he didn't quit. In 2001 he wanted to
compete in Brazil, but he <u>couldn't pay</u> for a
plane ticket. Then his girlfriend returned his
ring. No girlfriend and no money—it was a
very hard time for Eduardo! A friend gave
him an airplane ticket so he <u>could fly</u> to
Brazil. He finished first! He <u>couldn't win</u>
his girlfriend's heart, but he <u>could win</u>
a triathlon!

2
2. can ride	5. can't run
3. can skate	6. could run
4. could skate	

3
2. A: Could she ride a bike
B: Yes, she could
A: Can she ride a bike
B: Yes, she can

3. A: Can she run
B: No, she can't
A: Could she run
B: Yes, she could

4. A: Can she jump
B: No, she can't
A: Could she jump
B: No, she couldn't

4 I'm so tired! I'm surprised I can ~~to~~ write!!

I just finished my first triathlon! (Sara was

in the race too, but she couldn't ~~finishes~~.) [finish]

This morning I got up at 5:30. (I'm glad I

could ~~slept~~!) I took a quick shower and put [sleep]

on my swim suit. The race started at 7:30.

I can still feel the cold water! It was very

green, and I could ~~no~~ see very well. But [n't OR not]

I finished the first part of the race. I got

out of the water and ran to my bike. I can

usually ~~biking~~ very fast. This time I had [bike]

trouble. But, again, I finished. After the bike

race, I went for the run. The big question

was this: ~~I could~~ continue to run fast? Well, [Could I]

I didn't win the triathlon, but I finished.

And I learned an important lesson. A year

ago I thought: Me in a triathlon? Never!

Now I know I can ~~to~~ do it!

UNIT 36 Suggestions: *Why don't,*
Let's, How about

CHECK POINT
has a good idea

CHART CHECK 1
T

CHART CHECK 2
Suggestions with *Let's* can be affirmative or
negative.

CHART CHECK 3
F

EXPRESS CHECK
Let's go to the cafeteria.
How about getting some coffee?
Why don't we get some dessert?
Let's not stay here.

1 KARL: I'm hungry.
  EVA: Me too. <u>How about getting something
    to eat?</u>
  KARL: OK. But <u>let's not go to the school
    cafeteria.</u> I hate that place.
  EVA: Why do you hate the school cafeteria?
  KARL: The food is terrible. <u>Why don't we go
    to Joe's for pizza?</u>
  EVA: Good idea. But <u>how about leaving
    now?</u> I have a 1:00 class.
  KARL: Fine. <u>Let's go.</u>

  2. F   4. F
  3. T   5. T

2 2. doesn't   7. don't
  3. get   8. Why don't
  4. having   9. Let's not
  5. .   10. Let's
  6. make

3 2. getting some dessert?
  3. get tickets.
  4. see a serious film.
  5. going to the library?
  6. make that suggestion?

4 1. How about ~~get~~ new copying machines? [getting]

    The old ones don't work well.

  2. A lot of students want to study on the
    weekend. Why ~~don't~~ the library have [doesn't]

    longer hours on Sunday~~X~~ [?]

  3. Why ~~you don't~~ get coffee machines? [don't you]

  4. Let's ~~having~~ a special room for cell phone [have]

    users. The library needs to be quiet!

  5. The study rooms are too dark. Why don't
    you ~~getting~~ more lights? [get]

  6. How about ~~put~~ the library phone number [putting]

    on this Web page? I can't find it!

UNIT 37 Requests:
Will, Would, Can, Could

CHECK POINT
Brenda wants Tina to help her.

CHART CHECK
T, F

EXPRESS CHECK
Could you give me a ride?
Can you help me?
Will you please explain this?
Would you call me tomorrow?

1
2. help
3. please buy
4. Sorry, I can't
5. Sure
6. No problem

2
2. you please close the window?
3. you please wash the dishes?
4. you please buy more soda?
5. you please answer the phone?
6. you please check the oven?

3
3. Will (OR Would OR Can OR Could) you (please) make
4. Of course OR Certainly OR Sure OR No problem
5. will (OR would OR can OR could) you (please) clean
6. Of course OR Certainly OR Sure OR No problem
7. Will (OR Would OR Can OR Could) you (please) wash
8. Of course OR Certainly OR Sure OR No problem
9. will (OR would OR can OR could) you (please) ask
10. I'm sorry (OR Sorry), I can't.

4
Emma,

I bought the soda, but I forgot the chips.

Could you ~~got~~ ^{get} them?

Thanks.

Brian

Tyler,

Would you ~~choosing~~ ^{choose} some CD's for the party

tonight?

Sara

Sara,

We still need more chairs!

Will you ~~ask please~~ ^{please ask} José to bring some?

Emma

Brian,

I made some brownies for dessert.

Could you get some ice cream_✗ [?]

S.

Of course OR Certainly OR Sure OR No problem
~~Yes, I could~~.

Vanilla or chocolate?

B.

UNIT 38 Permission:
May, Can, Could

CHECK POINT
F

CHART CHECK 1
may, can, or *could*

CHART CHECK 2
could

EXPRESS CHECK
May I use the computer now?
Can we start the test?
Could I come in?

1
2. a
3. f
4. e
5. c
6. b

2

2. **A:** I use
   B: Sorry, not now.
3. **A:** I (OR we) walk
   B: Sure, go ahead.
4. **A:** I (OR we) smoke
   B: Sorry, you can't.
5. **A:** I (OR we) swim
   B: No, it isn't safe.
6. **A:** I (OR we) take
   B: Go ahead. They love it.

3

3. Can I (OR we) build
4. Yes, you can OR Certainly OR Of course
   OR Sure
5. May I bring
6. No, you can't
7. Can she use
8. Yes, she can OR Certainly OR Of course
   OR Sure
9. Could we stay
10. No, you can't
11. Can I ride
12. Yes, you can OR Certainly OR Of course
    OR Sure

4

This place has a million rules! We can't
~~listening~~ *listen* to music after 9 P.M. We ~~can no~~ *can't*

swim alone. We can't do anything! Could I

~~to~~ come home, please?

Tommy

Hi Tommy—
No, you ~~couldn't~~ *can't*. You just got there! You'll

have fun soon—we're sure of it!

Dear Mr. and Mrs. Jones—
May Tommy ~~goes~~ *go* on a boat trip? Please mail

permission.

Hi Mom and Dad—
The boat trip was really fun! Can I ~~came~~ *come*

here again next year?

SelfTest

(Total = 100 points. Each item = 4 points.)

SECTION ONE

1. **C**	5. **B**	9. **C**	12. **A**
2. **A**	6. **B**	10. **B**	13. **A**
3. **A**	7. **A**	11. **B**	
4. **C**	8. **C**		

SECTION TWO

(Correct answers are in parentheses.)

14. **D** (tomorrow)	20. **D** (.)
15. **C** (walk)	21. **D** (open)
16. **D** (park)	22. **C** (you please)
17. **B** (park)	23. **B** (understand)
18. **D** (send)	24. **C** (can't)
19. **B** (may not)	25. **B** (riding)

 UNIT 39 **Desires:**
Would like, Would rather

CHECK POINT
"Do you want fruit?"

CHART CHECK 1
a noun, an infinitive

CHART CHECK 2
T, F

EXPRESS CHECK
to have, have

1

2. T	5. F	7. T
3. T	6. F	8. F
4. T		

2

1. not wait
2. to move
   like, to move
3. Do
   I don't
4. Would, like
   not

3

2. would . . . rather eat
3. 'd (OR would) rather have
4. 'd (OR would) like
5. Would . . . like to have
6. would
7. 'd rather not OR wouldn't
8. Would . . . like to see
9. Would . . . rather have
10. 'd (OR would) rather see
11. 'd (OR would) like to have
12. would . . . like
13. 'd (OR would) like
14. 'd (OR would) rather eat

4

We received 150 surveys. Only one person
~~woulds~~ like soup! All other passengers
would

would rather ~~to~~ have salad. About half
to
(78 people) would like have pasta, and the
^

rest would rather not. Only a few people

want more vegetables. More than 100 would
to have more choices OR *more choices*
like ~~to more choices~~. For the dessert choices,
rather not
75% would ~~not rather~~ have fruit for dessert.
like
It seems most people would ~~liking~~ ice cream.

UNIT 40 **Possibility:**
May, Might, Could

CHECK POINT

F

CHART CHECK 1

the future

CHART CHECK 2

F

EXPRESS CHECK

It could snow next week.
We might not have class tomorrow.

1

"Hi, it's Jill. There's going to be a big
storm. There <u>could be</u> several tornadoes."
Jill Lee and Cy Davis are weather
scientists. Today they are going to follow a
storm and study it.

"We <u>may find</u> tornadoes to the north,"
says Jill. She's looking at a computer in the
car. Suddenly, they see a dark cloud to the
east—a tornado! Jill calls the weather
station. Her report <u>might save</u> lives.

"Hurry, Cy! It <u>could get</u> here in
minutes," Jill says. "We <u>may not get</u> away
in time."

2. Maybe   **5.** Maybe
3. Yes   **6.** Maybe
4. Maybe

2

2. might   **9.** could
3. may   **10.** may
4. may   **11.** might
5. may not   **12.** 's not going to
6. 's going to **13.** might
7. could   **14.** may not
8. could

3

2. might invite
may not OR might not
3. might order
might be OR may be OR could be
4. may take
might OR may OR could
5. may go
6. may not (be) OR might not (be),
might follow

4

Are you ready for weather emergencies?
be
Many people might not. They think,
^

"It won't happen here." Wrong. It *could*
happen
~~happened~~ here. Get ready now!

• You might ~~to~~ lose electricity. Have plenty

of batteries—you will need them for your

radio and flashlights.
may not
• There ~~mayn't~~ be clean water for some

time. Buy bottled water.
close
• Your supermarket may ~~closes~~. You should

have plenty of canned food.

• Stay calm. Remember—your first idea
~~not might~~ might not be the best idea. Think before

you act.

A storm or tornado could hit tomorrow!
You never know! Will you OR Are you going to ~~Might you~~ be ready?

UNIT 41   Advice: *Should, Ought to*

CHECK POINT
T

CHART CHECK 1
T, F

CHART CHECK 2
F

EXPRESS CHECK
A: should, Should
B: shouldn't

1   "When in Rome do as the Romans do."
This means travelers <u>should learn</u> the
customs of the place they are visiting. Well,
what if you really *are* going to Rome? What
<u>should</u> you <u>do</u>? What <u>shouldn't</u> you <u>do</u>?
• You <u>should shake</u> hands when you meet
someone for the first time.
• You <u>should say</u> hello and goodbye to
people in restaurants and stores.
• You <u>shouldn't chew</u> gum in public (for
example: stores and restaurants).
• And finally, you <u>ought to learn</u> a little
Italian. *Buon viaggio!* "Have a nice trip!"

2. Say hello to people in a store.
4. Speak Italian with Italians.

2
2. should look
3. should say
4. shouldn't give
5. shouldn't point
6. should arrive

3
3. you ought to be
4. Should she study
5. Yes, she should
6. She should learn
7. What should I bring
8. You should bring
9. You should give
10. should I bow
11. No, you shouldn't
12. You should shake

4   What should you ~~you should~~ do in these situations?

1. You're in the U.S. talking to your teacher.
How far should you ~~you should~~ stand from her?

  a. 1.5 ft (45.72 cm)

  b. 3 ft (91.44 cm)

  c. 5 ft (152.4cm)

2. Todd is in Saudi Arabia. He meets a
Saudi businessman. He should _____.
  a. shake hands   **b.** ~~bows~~ bow   **c.** kiss

3. You're sitting in a restaurant in Turkey.
You should not ~~no~~ show _____.

  a. the inside of your wallet

  b. your gloves

  c. the bottom of your shoes

4. You're in Taiwan. You shouldn't ~~be~~ touch

the _____ of another person's child.

  a. arm   **b.** head   **c.** hand

UNIT 42   Necessity: *Have to, Must, Don't have to, Must not*

CHECK POINT
A white shirt and a tie are necessary.

CHART CHECK 1
F, T

CHART CHECK 2
T

EXPRESS CHECK

has, wear

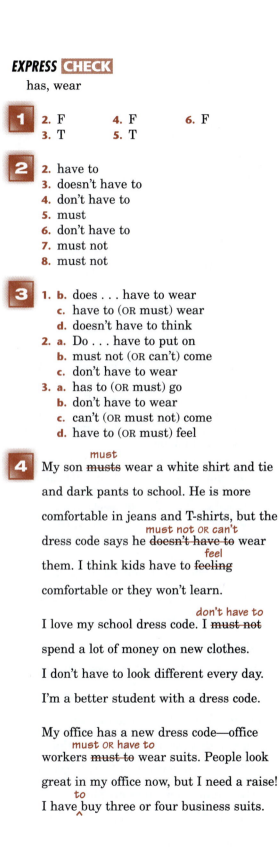

1
2. F   4. F   6. F
3. T   5. T

2
2. have to
3. doesn't have to
4. don't have to
5. must
6. don't have to
7. must not
8. must not

3
1. b. does . . . have to wear
   c. have to (OR must) wear
   d. doesn't have to think
2. a. Do . . . have to put on
   b. must not (OR can't) come
   c. don't have to wear
3. a. has to (OR must) go
   b. don't have to wear
   c. can't (OR must not) come
   d. have to (OR must) feel

4
        must
My son ~~musts~~ wear a white shirt and tie
and dark pants to school. He is more
comfortable in jeans and T-shirts, but the
       must not OR can't
dress code says he ~~doesn't have to~~ wear
           feel
them. I think kids have to ~~feeling~~
comfortable or they won't learn.

             don't have to
I love my school dress code. I ~~must not~~
spend a lot of money on new clothes.
I don't have to look different every day.
I'm a better student with a dress code.

My office has a new dress code—office
      must OR have to
workers ~~must to~~ wear suits. People look
great in my office now, but I need a raise!
      to
I have buy three or four business suits.

SelfTest

(Total = 100 points. Each item = 4 points.)

SECTION ONE

1. **D**	5. **D**	9. **C**	12. **B**
2. **D**	6. **C**	10. **C**	13. **B**
3. **B**	7. **A**	11. **D**	14. **C**
4. **D**	8. **D**		

SECTION TWO

(Correct answers are in parentheses.)

15. **A** (can't/must not) 21. **A** (Should)
16. **D** (rather not) 22. **C** (rather have
17. **C** (would)   OR like)
18. **B** (shouldn't) 23. **A** (*delete* to)
19. **C** (will)   24. **D** (bring)
20. **A** (don't have to) 25. **C** (do we have)

UNIT 43 Gerunds and Infinitives

CHECK POINT

F

CHART CHECK 1

Gerunds, Infinitives

CHART CHECK 2

before

EXPRESS CHECK

visiting, to tell

1
Parker Yia-Som McKenzie
McKenzie (enjoys talking) about the history
of his people. He's writing a dictionary of
Kiowa, his Native American language. He
started it in 1911, and he <u>hopes to finish</u> soon.
Rose Freedman
Freedman (enjoys learning) languages. She
already speaks five, and she's studying
Spanish. She didn't (quit working) until
her 80's. Now she paints and watches a lot
of basketball.

Daisy Nakada

Nakada taught English in Japan and traveled to schools all over the world for her work. She (keeps trying) new things and she hopes to stay active many more years.

Leo Ornstein

Ornstein became a famous pianist as a teenager. In his 20's he decided to start a music school. He (quit performing), but he continued to write music. Ornstein died at the age of 109.

2

2. smoking	7. not to be
3. not eating	8. spending
4. having	9. not to have
5. exercising	10. to stay
6. to see	

3

2. to take	6. to watch
3. to lose	7. not being
4. eating	8. having
5. listening	

4

100 Years Young

Jack Delano's family wanted ~~giving~~ *to give* him a big birthday party, but they didn't expect ˄ *to* see all sixty-seven relatives. "People kept ~~to come~~ *coming*," Jack's granddaughter Myra said. "It was amazing."

Jack was born in 1895 in Salerno, Italy. He went to Canada in 1920, but he didn't plan to stay. Then in 1921, he met Celia in his night school class. That same night, Jack decided not ~~going~~ *to go* back to Salerno. "Two months later, I visited Celia's family and I asked to marry their daughter," he said.

Jack sold his business a few years ago. He enjoys ~~no~~ *not* working, but he stays active. He recommends ~~to~~ keeping close to family and friends.

UNIT 44 Infinitives of Purpose

CHECK POINT

Why

CHART CHECK

F, T

EXPRESS CHECK

Roberto left early in order not to miss the train.
I can use my computer to watch movies.
She sent an Instant Message to say *hi*.

1

2. a	4. c	6. e
3. f	5. b	

2

2. came to read	7. sent . . . to show
3. stayed to play	8. needed. . . . in order not to worry
4. 'm (OR am) . . . to study	9. spent . . . to use
5. send . . . in order not to spend	10. meet . . . to talk
6. used . . . to make	11. to drink OR drink

3

2. to send	7. to call OR call
3. to play	8. to use
4. to help	9. to clean up
5. to carry	10. to practice
6. to check	

4

Angkor Wat is so beautiful—you have to see it to ~~believing~~ *believe* it! I used my new camera to ~~takes~~ *take* photos. Right now, I'm in the Playstation Café in Phnom Penh. It's midnight, and I'm drinking coffee ~~for~~ *to* stay awake. I waited an hour ˄ *to* get a computer! You have to come early ˄ *in* order not to wait.

A lot of people use this café to go online.

I'll say goodnight now. I have to get up early in order ~~don't~~ *not to* miss my plane tomorrow. Please e-mail me soon to ~~told~~ *tell* me your news (or just to say *hi*).

SelfTest

(Total = 100 points. Each item = 4 points.)

SECTION ONE

1. **B**	5. **C**	9. **D**	12. **D**
2. **D**	6. **A**	10. **B**	13. **D**
3. **C**	7. **C**	11. **D**	
4. **C**	8. **A**		

SECTION TWO

(Correct answers are in parentheses.)

14. **A** (writing)	20. **A** (to)
15. **C** (take)	21. **B** (being)
16. **B** (to study)	22. **C** (in order not)
17. **D** (sending)	23. **B** (exercising)
18. **B** (hiking)	24. **D** (playing)
19. **D** (to take)	25. **B** (improve)

 **Prepositions** of Time

CHECK POINT

T, F, ?

CHART CHECK 1

2:15 P.M.

CHART CHECK 2

three weeks

EXPRESS CHECK

Their plane is going to leave at 5:15.
They'll arrive on Monday morning.

1
- England and France began the Concorde project <u>in 1962</u>.
- The first test flight was <u>on April 9,1969</u>.
- <u>In 1976</u> flights began between London and Bahrain and between Paris and Rio.
- <u>By 2000</u> most flights traveled between New York City and Paris or London.

- The Concorde crossed the Atlantic <u>in 3 hours and 50 minutes</u>.
- A flight left Paris <u>on Wednesday</u> <u>at 10:30 A.M.</u> Paris time. It arrived in New York <u>on Wednesday</u> *before* 10:30 A.M. New York time!
- The last flight was <u>in 2003</u>.

2
1. **b.** at
   c. by
2. **a.** on
   b. in
   c. at
3. **a.** in
   b. for
   c. from . . . to

3
1. **b.** by
   c. at
2. **a.** during
   b. in
   c. until
3. **a.** for
   b. in
   c. on
   d. on
   e. until

4
Here I am—18,000 meters (about 49,000 feet) above the ground. My first Concorde flight! We boarded the plane ~~in~~ _at_ 10:00 A.M.—a half hour ~~after~~ _before_ takeoff. In a few seconds we were high in the sky. There's no movie ~~at~~ _during_ the flight. It's too short! But I listened to music during our wonderful lunch. We're going to land ~~on~~ _in_ twenty minutes. That's at 8:24 A.M. New York time—~~in~~ _on_ the same day we left Paris! Because of the time difference, we're going to arrive BEFORE our departure time! It's great to arrive early ~~on~~ _in_ the morning. We're going to see a play ~~on~~ _in_ the evening. I'll call you ~~at~~ _on_ Monday, and I'll see you ~~in~~ _on_ Thursday!

UNIT 46 Prepositions of Place

CHECK POINT

glasses

CHART CHECK

Where?

EXPRESS CHECK

on, next to, in

1

It's Not Always in the Bank!

Do you keep your money in the bank? Some people don't. Some people keep their money at home. But where is it safe? On a table? I don't think so! Under a pillow? Not really! Experts say: The best place for your money *is* in the bank. But if you really want to keep it near you all the time, hide it in an unusual place. And write it down, so you don't forget where! One day you'll want to find it again!

2
2. under
3. between
4. behind
5. near
6. on
7. in
8. under
9. between

3
2. in
3. in
4. between
5. across from
6. on
7. across from
8. at
9. to the left
10. to the right
11. across from
12. next to
13. in

4

Last week I received a big check for my birthday. I hid it ~~in~~ ^at^ home, but then I couldn't remember where! I looked everywhere. It wasn't ~~on~~ ^in^ my desk drawer (I often keep money there). Maybe it was in the

dictionary. I have a large dictionary ~~over~~ ^on^ a book shelf next ^to^ my desk. I sometimes keep money ~~in~~ ^between^ ^ two pages. But it wasn't there!

Maybe it fell between the two cushions on my couch. But I looked, and it wasn't between ~~they~~ ^them^. I looked ~~in~~ ^on^ the floor ~~over~~ ^under^ the couch. Not there. Then I remembered! The check was ~~on~~ ^in^ the bank ~~at~~ ^on^ Main Street!!

UNIT 47 Prepositions of Movement

CHECK POINT

F

CHART CHECK

going from one place to another place

EXPRESS CHECK

across, into

1
b. 2 d. 6 f. 3
c. 4 e. 1

2
2. along
3. to
4. under
5. from
6. to
7. off
8. up
9. across
10. to
11. around
12. across
13. through
14. into

3
2. from
3. through
4. on
5. off
6. around
7. up
8. into
9. out of
10. on
11. along
12. past

4   **Trips from Istanbul ~~into~~** *to*

        Büyükada Every Day

                 on

9:00 A.M.   Guests get ~~up~~ the boat.

9:30–11:00 A.M.

           Travel to Büyükada (the largest of the Princes' Islands).

11:00 A.M.   Arrive at Büyükada Island.

              off

           Passengers get ~~down~~ the boat.

11:30 A.M.–3:00 P.M.

           Go to the top of St. George Hill.

           It's high (almost a mountain!), so

                   up

           we won't walk ~~above~~ the hill.

           We'll go by horse carriage.

              down

3:00 P.M.   Go ~~under~~ the hill. Tour the town

                along OR *on*

           and walk ~~through~~ the beach.

6:00 P.M.   Return to Istanbul.

UNIT 48   **Two-Word Verbs:**
                   Inseparable

CHECK POINT

F, F

CHART CHECK

verb + preposition

EXPRESS CHECK

We're going to eat out tomorrow night.
Would you like to come along?
We'll probably end up at a movie.
You don't have to dress up.

1   Dating is one way to <u>look for</u> a husband or wife. Did you know . . . ?

- In Central and South America, teenagers <u>get together</u> in groups. They often go dancing or <u>hang out</u> at local clubs.
- In North America and Europe, teens <u>go out</u> in pairs and in groups. They often go dancing or <u>take in</u> a movie.

- In Vietnam, young people <u>grow up</u> with the idea that marriage is a family event. Young men must ask the girl's parents permission to <u>go out</u>.

1. go out	**4.** look for
2. grow up	**5.** get together
3. hang out	**6.** take in

2

2. in, down	**5.** out, up
3. down	**6.** along, out
4. up, back	

3

2. go out	**6.** comes along
3. get along	**7.** dress up
4. grew up	**8.** sign up
5. eat out	**9.** go out, work out

4   Many things are different in a foreign country. Dating, for example. Last night I

        out

went ~~over~~ with my classmate Tania. We

      get along very well

always ~~get very well along~~ in class. But I think she was unhappy with our date. I

         up

showed ~~^~~ at her apartment with six yellow flowers. Later I learned that in her country the number six brings bad luck. And yellow flowers mean you want to end the relationship!

                  up

    Tania dressed ~~over~~ for our date in a nice skirt and blouse. I wore jeans. Wrong! She asked me to come in. I didn't remove my shoes. Wrong again! Then we took the bus

                 on OR *off*

to the movies. When we got ~~over~~ the bus, she looked upset. Later I learned that in her country men usually "help" women on and off buses! Then I didn't pay for her movie ticket. (Back home the girl and guy often pay for their own tickets.) Another mistake! I like

         out with her again

Tania, and I want to go ~~with her again out~~. I hope she gives me another chance!

UNIT 49 Two-Word Verbs:
Separable

CHECK POINT

stop
start
get dressed
lift

CHART CHECK

before, after
before

EXPRESS CHECK

The telephone woke me up at 5:00 A.M.
Harry turned the TV on.
I picked it up.

1 Start Your Life Over (Again!)

It's New Year's Day and a lot of us are
making lists:

• I'm going to clean up my office.
• I'll take books back to the library on time.
• I'll take a computer class.

I usually throw my list away in March. But
this year I found these ideas from experts.
I'm going to try them out.

1. Pick out one change. Change is hard, so
go slow.
2. Write down the steps. For example:
Find some computer classes.
Fill out applications. Mail them.
3. Ask for advice and kind words. Your
friends can help you out.
4. Start now! Don't put it off.

2 **2.** pay it back
3. clean up this room OR clean this room up,
turn it into
4. put away my books OR put my books away,
hang up my clothes OR hang my clothes up
5. hand in my homework OR hand my
homework in
6. take off our shoes OR take our shoes off

3 **2.** give up
give it up
3. look over
look it over
4. hand . . . in
hand it in
5. throw away
throw them away
6. turn . . . down
turned it down
7. pick out
picked them out

4 This is Your Life: Look ~~Over it~~ and
   it Over
Straighten it Out! by Vera Niles

★★★★ Niles says we can change our lives.
Her advice: Think things over and take
        it out
small steps. I tried ~~out it~~. It works.

★ My New Year's resolution: Give up books
                              it back
by Vera Niles! This one is awful. I took ~~back it~~
         back
and said, "Give me my money ~~away~~."

★★★★ I had too many problems, and I
           them out
couldn't figure ~~out them~~. Then I bought
                              over
Niles' book. Now I'm starting my life ~~under~~!
She's the best!

★★★ I followed Niles's plan, and last week
     away   *up*
I threw ~~back~~ my cigarettes. I gave them ~~out~~
with Niles's help. Her ideas are old, but
they're good.

UNIT 50 Sentence Connectors:
and, but, or, so, because

CHECK POINT
Because Kenji is smart.

CHART CHECK
T

EXPRESS CHECK
but, or

1
2. f   5. c
3. e   6. b
4. g   7. a

2
1. is
2. but . . . has
3. and . . . sees
4. can . . . or
5. because . . . is
6. but . . . doesn't stop
7. doesn't bite . . . because
8. but . . . can't
9. so . . . runs
10. because . . . is

3
1. **BEA:** so I can't buy it for you
2. **LUC:** and he won the game
   YVES: so (OR and) he practices a lot
3. **CARI:** or do you want to watch TV?
   ZEKI: because I'm watching TV
4. **BELA:** so (OR and) we started dinner
   DITA: because the traffic was bad
5. **HUNG:** but I can't read it well
   THU: and the words are easy

4
　　Hiroshi Fujimoto wanted to write a new
comic book, ~~so~~ *but* he had no ideas. He couldn't
think ~~so~~ *because* there were noisy cats outside.

"I need an Idea Machine," he thought. His
daughter's toy robot was on the floor, and he
stepped on it. Now he had his idea: a robot
cat with a lot of magic machines!

　　Doraemon comic books started coming
out in the 1970's, ~~because~~ *and* a TV show came
next. Doraemon is the robot cat, ~~so~~ *and* Nobita is

a young boy. Nobita isn't very smart, ~~but~~ *so OR and* he
has a lot of problems. ~~So~~ *Because* he has magic
machines, Doraemon can help Nobita. In one
story, Nobita wants to have a party, ~~or~~ *but* his
house is too small. Doraemon opens his
magic door for Nobita's friends, ~~but~~ *and* they
walk into a big party room. They are all very
happy! Because he makes *real* people happy
too, Fujimoto's Doraemon is the most famous
cartoon character in Japan.

SelfTest

(Total = 100 points. Each item = 4 points.)

SECTION ONE

1. **A**	5. **B**	9. **D**	13. **A**
2. **B**	6. **D**	10. **B**	14. **A**
3. **D**	7. **B**	11. **A**	15. **D**
4. **A**	8. **C**	12. **A**	

SECTION TWO

(Correct answers are in parentheses.)

16. **B** (on)
17. **A** (off OR out of)
18. **B** (so)
19. **C** (to)
20. **A** (me up)
21. **D** (at)
22. **B** (for)
23. **A** (at)
24. **B** (before OR by)
25. **C** (sign up for the class)